# WE SHALL OVERCOME

## SACRED SONG ON THE DEVIL'S TONGUE
### (THIRD EDITION)

Isaias Gamboa

Edited by JoAnne F. Henry, Ph.D., and Audrey Owen

Isaias Gamboa

We Shall Overcome: Sacred Song on the Devil's Tongue

Copyright © 2011, 2012, 2016, 2026
TXu001771986
ISBN: 978-0615475288
Amapola Publishers
Beverly Hills, California
All Rights Reserved, including the right of reproduction
in whole or in part in any form.
4-CD Audio-Book narrated by the author and including Negro Spirituals, Slave Narratives, and much more is now available on Amazon.com and iTunes.com
Join us at: www.WeShallOvercomeFoundation.org
Cover design by Isaias Gamboa

## Dedication

    This book is written in humility and in the service of my Lord and Redeemer, Jesus Christ. I dedicate my efforts herein to the countless unsung heroines of the African-American Church, the African-American Civil Rights Movement, and the vanishing African-American nuclear family. As you read Louise Shropshire's remarkable life story, may you also be moved to recognize and acknowledge someone like her in your own church, community, or family.

vi

# Contents

**Preface** ........................................................................................................ xi
**Acknowledgements** ................................................................................... xv

## Part One: The Quest for Truth and the Struggle for Equality and Atonement

**Chapter 1  A Gathering Storm** ....................................................................... 1
**Chapter 2  A Time to Speak** ........................................................................... 5
    White, Black, Other .......................................................................................... 6
    The One Drop Rule ........................................................................................ 13
    The Saints ..................................................................................................... 20
    A Call to Service ........................................................................................... 25
**Chapter 3  A Time to Search** ....................................................................... 33
**Chapter 4  A Time to Mend** ......................................................................... 36
    No Direction Home ....................................................................................... 38
    The Hallmark Moment .................................................................................. 39
    Action Item #1 / Reparations U.S.A.A.R.A. .................................................. 42
**Chapter 5  Circling the Drain** ..................................................................... 46
    The Wash ...................................................................................................... 49
    Far From Home ............................................................................................. 54
**Chapter 6  A Great Awakening** ................................................................... 57
**Chapter 7  Woman's Work / Harriet Tubman** ............................................ 62
    And Still She Rose ........................................................................................ 64
    The Negro is Free ......................................................................................... 67

## Part Two: The Life of Louise Shropshire and the Untold Story of We Shall Overcome

**Chapter 8  Strange Fruit** .............................................................................. 71
**Chapter 9  Amazing Grace** .......................................................................... 79
    The End of the Beginning ............................................................................. 87
    Powerful Friends ........................................................................................... 91
    George Remus .............................................................................................. 93
**Chapter 10 A Time for War** ......................................................................... 95
**Chapter 11 Georgia Tom** ........................................................................... 101
**Chapter 12 New Prospects** ....................................................................... 107
**Chapter 13 The Battlefield General** ......................................................... 121
    The Bus Boycotts ....................................................................................... 125
    "Bombingham", Alabama ............................................................................ 127
    Helping Hands ............................................................................................ 128
    Revelations ................................................................................................. 131
    A New Home .............................................................................................. 134

| | |
|---|---|
| The Birmingham Campaign | 136 |
| **Chapter 14 Song of the South** | 139 |
| The House that Jefferson Built | 142 |
| Action Item#2 / Founding Fathers | 147 |

## Part Three: The Misappropriation of We Shall Overcome

| | |
|---|---|
| **Chapter 15 Great White Hunters** | 151 |
| The Recording Expeditions | 152 |
| The First Kill | 158 |
| **Chapter 16 Sacred Songs** | 164 |
| **Chapter 17 The Folk Process** | 168 |
| The Myth | 171 |
| The Facts | 172 |
| The Douglass Easterling Report | 173 |
| The Stephen Goukas Report | 175 |
| **Chapter 18 Sweet Chariots** | 177 |
| Martin and Malcolm | 187 |
| **Chapter 19 The Way to the Cross** | 196 |
| **Chapter 20 We Believe** | 222 |
| **Chapter 21 Unarmed Truth** | 226 |
| The Folk Mafia | 228 |
| The Pete Seeger Interviews | 230 |
| The Guy Carawan Interview | 232 |
| **Chapter 22 The Great Song Robbery** | 234 |
| Crime and Punishment | 235 |
| Action Item #3 / Copyright Reform | 238 |
| **Chapter 23 Un-caged** | 240 |
| **Chapter 24 A Love Supreme** | 246 |

| | |
|---|---|
| **Copyright Status Update (2026)** | 249 |
| **About the Author** | 250 |
| **Bibliography** | 253 |
| **Index** | 260 |

# Preface

There is a time for everything. Throughout history, there have been a number of massive, rare, and, excluding biblical prophecy, unforeseeable events. These extraordinary occurrences of exceptional magnitude and global consequence have often been set off by equally extraordinary, and all too often, horrifying human beings. –Human beings who have, for better or for worse, stunned, transformed, and enlightened the world.

In his 2004 book, *Fooled by Randomness,* author Nassim Nicholas Taleb refers to such exceptional events and the people behind them as "Black Swans." Such occurrences can manifest in destructive or productive forms… good or evil. Some notable historical examples are: Moses and the Biblical Exodus, the birth, crucifixion, and resurrection of Jesus Christ, Johann Gutenberg's printing press, Martin Luther's 95 Theses, Christopher Columbus, Charles Darwin's *Origin of Species*, Sir Alexander Fleming (inventor of penicillin), Adolf Hitler, the bombing of Hiroshima, Albert Einstein, Dr. Martin Luther King Jr., the personal computer, the Internet, the September 11 disaster, and the election of US President Barack Obama.

Given the tremendous social and political influence, worldwide recognition, and massive global footprint of the freedom song We Shall Overcome, I believe that once the revelations in this book are widely disseminated, the seeds of such a historic event will take root.

**The Rev. Dr. Martin Luther King Jr.** called We Shall Overcome **"the Battle-Cry of the Civil Rights Movement."** Indeed, it was. The US Library of Congress has also affirmed the song's historical importance, stating:

*"We Shall Overcome has circled the globe and has been embraced by Civil Rights and pro-democracy movements in dozens of nations worldwide. From Northern Ireland to Eastern Europe, from Berlin to Beijing, and from South Africa to South America, its message of solidarity and hope has been sung in dozens of languages, in presidential palaces and in dark prisons, and it continues to lend its strength to all people struggling to be free."* [1]

On June 17, 2015, a white man opened fire during a prayer meeting at Emanuel African American Episcopal Church in Charleston, South Carolina. Nine people, including the church's pastor, were killed in cold blood. The shooter, a white supremacist, declared his mission was "to kill black people." Days later, mourners of many races held a vigil and closed with a rendition of "We Shall Overcome." Grief-stricken African American President Barack Obama delivered the eulogy for the historic church's slain pastor, Rev. Clementa C. Pinckney.

As influential as We Shall Overcome has proven since the raging 1960s, the mere mention of its name still invokes bitter feelings in the minds and hearts of African

---

[1] Source: US Library of Congress; We Shall Overcome Historical Period: Postwar United States, 1945-1968

Americans, who, nearly 400 years after being abducted from their African homelands, continue to suffer murder, abuse, degradation, humiliation, and indignity in America. To these proud people — the descendants of kings, queens, philosophers, and warriors — memories of We Shall Overcome and the Civil Rights Movement cue a montage of hatred and cruelty, painfully reminding them of America's unrecognized and unpaid debt to African Americans for the kidnapping, murder, torture, abuse, and exploitation inflicted upon their bodies, minds, and futures. To Black Americans, We Shall Overcome still represents a prayer for freedom, dignity, and equality, not yet answered... a battle not *yet* won.

For more than fifty years, this powerful anthem has spoken to people of all races and colors across the globe, an enlightened cry for peace and love in the face of hatred, injustice, and cruelty. For American Blacks, however, such high-minded ideas have been largely relegated to an ethnically marginalized place, condescendingly referred to as "Black-History Month"—the back of America's ideological bus. More than 150 years after being *physically* emancipated from slavery, Black Americans are still fighting to be recognized and treated as true equals in the eyes of their White American brothers.

Here and all over the world, the true message of We Shall Overcome has always been about this promise, and for that reason, the song's global, social, cultural, and historical significance has remained unequaled. Just as they have for world leaders and events of great importance, countless journalists, authors, filmmakers, historians, and educators worldwide have produced books, lectures, dissertations, articles, films, newscasts, and blogs related to We Shall Overcome. Many, in an earnest attempt to chronicle the origins and impact of this extraordinary cultural production, tried, however, and all got it wrong.

As unbelievable as it may seem, before the publication of this book, almost everything printed about the origins of We Shall Overcome, which the US Library of Congress has called "The most powerful song of the 20th century," is wrong. This book seeks to correct this troubling historical blunder by providing, in great detail, the untold story of "We Shall Overcome" and its original author, Louise Shropshire. As a product of this effort, in the name of truth, honor, justice, and decency, I hope to "encourage" those individuals and organizations who currently claim illegitimate rights to We Shall Overcome to clean their hands and do the right thing by returning this song to its rightful place in the public domain.

Because of the previously undiscovered and unpublished facts contained within these pages, much of this book is, in effect, "new" American history. It can transport its readers to places they have never been, to learn things they've never imagined, and to encounter people they'd never heard of. The possibility of achieving these objectives fueled my determination to research and document these facts. At the same time, this remarkable story filled me with a profound sense of duty and responsibility to leave no stone unturned in the pursuit of the truth. In the interest of transparency and editorial accuracy, it has been my highest aim to present the information in this book using well-sourced, well-documented empirical facts supported by strong, explicit, and verifiable evidence.

Over the course of five years, I've interviewed and consulted numerous sources, including many of Louise Shropshire's closest living family members, former members of her church choirs, and former church members. I also unearthed forgotten newspaper articles, church records, and scores of extraordinary newly discovered documents and photographs. In the vast majority of cases, I have found multiple sources to validate and authenticate the astonishing historical information contained herein. I sincerely hope that, as a result of this book, additional evidence, testimony, and documentation chronicling the details of Louise Shropshire's extraordinary life and works will surface.

## Organization

To provide contextual support for my research, observations, and conclusions, this book covers substantial historical ground. Its main topics are:

- The true origin of, *We Shall Overcome.*
- A brief history of Louise Shropshire's personal, spiritual, and family life.
- A contextual history of Black exploitation in America.

- The struggle of Black Americans to gain equality.

- Evidence of the misappropriation of, *We Shall Overcome.*

- Evidence of Louise Shropshire's original authorship of, We Shall Overcome.

- What is owed to Louise Shropshire

- What mainstream America owes to African-Americans

Chapters 17 and 21 contain most of the information and evidence directly related to the misappropriation of Louise Shropshire's sacred hymn, If My Jesus Wills, more commonly known as "I'll Overcome," which was adapted into We Shall Overcome. However, reading the entire text reveals much more to this story. Due in no small part to American slavery and the repressive post-slavery laws that made it illegal for African Americans to become educated, the principal subject of this book was poorly educated. This disadvantage led to the theft and exploitation of her valuable intellectual property, as well as that of countless others like her. That said, for those of you who may not recognize or understand any word in this book, please borrow or buy a dictionary or go to www.merriam-webster.com. Learn it, own it, *then* read on. Knowledge is power

This book is written for nonprofit educational purposes to promote social and cultural discourse, commentary, criticism, and research. A substantial portion of the proceeds from the book will directly benefit the poor, uneducated, and needy through the **We Shall Overcome Foundation**, an IRS-recognized 501(c)(3) nonprofit organization. www.WeShallOvercomeFoundation.org (not affiliated with the We Shall Overcome Fund)

*Please note:*

At times, this book will use the following terms interchangeably: "Black Church" with "African American Church"; "Black" with "Negro," "Colored," or "African American"; and "white" with "Caucasian." Additionally, the terms "African American Church" or "Black Church" are used to refer primarily to independent, historically Black congregations of established Christian-Protestant denominations, including but not limited to: the National Baptist Convention, U.S.A., Incorporated (NBC); the National Baptist Convention of America, Unincorporated (NBC); the Progressive National Baptist Convention (PNBC); the African Methodist Episcopal (A.M.E.) Church; the African Methodist Episcopal Zion (A.M.E.Z.) Church; the Christian Methodist Episcopal (C.M.E.) Church; the Church of God in Christ; the Holiness Church; and the Pentecostal Church. Some events in this book may appear out of precise chronology.

Last but not least, it is essential to note that this book is written from a Judeo-Christian worldview, as were the Declaration of Independence and the U.S. Constitution. It also reflects the cognitive orientation of four of this book's principal subjects, Rev. Mother Louise Shropshire, Rev. Dr. Martin Luther King Jr., Rev. Fred Shuttlesworth, and Rev. Thomas A. Dorsey.

# Acknowledgments

I wish to express my appreciation to the grandson of Louise Shropshire, Robert Anthony Goins Shropshire, for his patience with hundreds of phone calls, interviews, correspondence, and appeals, so that his grandmother's remarkable story could be shared with the world. Robert, I believe you have truly fulfilled your grandmother's dying wish.

In addition, I would like to offer a very special thank you to Dr. P. Eric Abercrumbie, Executive Director of Diversity and Community Relations at the University of Cincinnati, for his tremendous faith, support, passion, and dedication to this project. I would also like to thank the University of Cincinnati President, Santa J. Ono, PhD, and the University of Cincinnati for their extraordinary commitment to preserving Louise Shropshire's historic sheet music, photographs, artifacts, and documents, and for making "The Louise Shropshire Family Papers" collection available to the world.

A special thank you is also due to Mr. Phillip Bennie, Ms. Diana McClure Crosley, and Dr. Shelley J. Hamler for their support and confidence in this project.

The interviews and support from those listed below were also vital to telling this extraordinary story. To these people, I am deeply grateful.

Rev. Otis Moss Jr., Patricia Shuttlesworth, Fred Shuttlesworth Jr., Ruby Bester-Shuttlesworth, Otis Williams, Dr. Rabbi Gary P. Zola, Pat Boone, Richard Perry, Jane Fonda, Bill Dern, Mel Carter, Mrs. Bobby Grevious, Rueben Grevious, Derek Grevious, Mrs. Joycella Harris, Mrs. Betty Daniels Rosemond, Rev. Harold Bester of the Greater New Light Baptist Church, Cincinnati, Ohio; Rev. Dr. Cecil "Chip" Murray, Prof. Jetro Da Silva PhD., the Berklee College of Music, Darnise Martin, PhD., Yakub Hazzard, Esq.; Roman Silberfeld, Esq.; Camille Moore-Hunley Esq., Edgar and Toni Smith, Mrs. Viola E. King-Smith, Annette Richardson-King, Antoinette Sutton-King, Patricia Jones, Izora B. Hood-King, Brian Ennix, Mrs. Betty Shropshire, Connie D. Blackwell, Barbara Brown, Phillip Drucker, Esq.; Shawnese Lewis, Dan Morgan, Roshon Morgan, Mrs. Alice McCloud, Kelly Crabb, Jackie Shropshire, Jacquala Shropshire, Terry Dillard, Simone Sheffield, Michael R. Shapiro, Esq.; Barrett Laroda, Gregory Loomis, Esq.; Harrison Dillard, Rev. Damon Lynch Jr., Karen Floyd, Dick Weiland, Sarah Weiss and Hyung J. Park.

I also thank my beloved parents, Danilo Julian de la Trinidad Gamboa y Mora, and Carmen Gamboa-Beckles Howard, for their resolute love and support. May they rest in peace. I am grateful to my three sons, Daniel, Gabriel, and Noah, for reminding me to walk a path that leads them to Christ, and to the strong, loving, and intelligent women in my family, including my wife, Janaína; my three sisters, Ruth, Noemi, and Maria Del-Carmen; and my two extraordinary daughters, Noraniece and Alexandria. Without these influential people in my life, this book would not have been possible.

# Chapter 1

# A Gathering Storm

*"I refuse to accept the view that mankind is so tragically bound to the starless midnight of racism and war, that the bright daybreak of peace and brotherhood can never become a reality... I believe that unarmed truth and unconditional love will have the final word."*
-**Rev. Dr. Martin Luther King, Jr.**[2]

I suspect that, like me, most people have taken for granted over the years that the author of "We Shall Overcome"—the song that served as the sanctified soundtrack for the American Civil Rights Movement and helped spread awareness of hatred, racism, discrimination, and oppression against African Americans—was African American. Well, as it turns out, she was. Disturbingly, however, as of the writing of this book, the song's true original author has not been recognized as such. Meanwhile, four folk singers, including Pete Seeger and his powerful music publisher, The Richmond Organization, have, for more than fifty years, unconscionably and unlawfully claimed legal and commercial rights to this iconic song, despite asserting that it was of "unknown" origins.

The U.S. Library of Congress has named, We Shall Overcome: *The Most Powerful Song of the Twentieth Century"*, adding, *"Word for word, the short, simple lyrics of 'We Shall Overcome' might be some of the most influential words in the English Language"*[3]. But who, in fact, *did* author these influential words? To whom does, We Shall Overcome truly belong?

This book will answer these critical questions honestly, factually, and without prejudice. In doing so, it will support the claim that the *We Shall Overcome* we've all sung and revered for more than half a century was *not* authored by those who currently claim copyright ownership of the song but by Rev. Mother **Louise Shropshire**, an extraordinary African-American woman, devoted servant of the African American Church, and close friend of Rev. Dr. Martin Luther King Jr. This book will also demonstrate that Shropshire's sacred

---

[2] King Jr., Martin Luther and John Bellm; I Have a Dream; Harper Collins; 1985; p. 110 / Excerpt from Nobel Prize Speech
[3] LibraryofCongress.org 2009 "We Shall Overcome"
"Historical Period: Postwar United States, 1945-1968"

hymn, ***If My Jesus Wills*** (more commonly known in its day as ***I'll Overcome***), is the true antecedent of We Shall Overcome.

These pages will show how America's well-entrenched system of social, political, economic, and educational inequality for Black people enabled those who have illegally profited from the exploitation of We Shall Overcome to evade accountability for their unconscionable acts of misappropriation and cultural desecration.

## Peddle and Spin

I committed myself to the first mile of this expedition, driven not only by a strong desire to know the truth and ease my exasperations but also by the need to share the tremendous gratification I felt while excavating the jeweled story of this remarkable yet unrecognized African-American woman – a woman I soon recognized as of great spiritual, cultural, and historical significance. Before long, however, my journey had taken me past the point of no return, as I found myself deeply immersed in a larger-than-life narrative of profound depth and magnitude.

I realized this story was so much more than a historical postscript. It was an epic saga of good versus evil; of sacred faith versus blind ambition; of slave and master, milk and honey, sin and pastor, God and money. It was a battle rooted in a war that had been waged since the beginning of man's fall from grace. Disguised as friends and sympathizers, these men had stolen a priceless, sacred artifact of the African-American people. There were thieves in the temple.

It weighed on me that although this universally revered freedom song had been called upon to comfort and inspire the downtrodden and to transform corrupt governments all over the world, the world knew relatively little about the song's true author, sacred origins, and historical context…let alone its unlawful misappropriation and exploitation. And whatever so-called "information" *was* available—information that scholars and journalists had relied on for more than half a century—was, I found, laced with deliberate embellishments, half-truths, omissions, and outright lies. Though such characteristics have long been considered hallmarks of many popular folk songs, to African Americans, We Shall Overcome was no folk song. It was an anthem of faith and hope—a sacred promise made to them by their creator. To Blacks in America, We Shall Overcome was and is sacrosanct. To those men, however, who, like slave-masters and overseers before them, sought to profit from the unpaid exploitation of African-American human endeavor, not so much.

At the very least, I found the deceitfully contrived information about the true origins of We Shall Overcome disturbingly offensive and manifestly unacceptable. –Unacceptable for an anthem of hope wailed by tear-drenched mourners on the rainy streets of Atlanta as they marched behind Martin Luther King Jr.'s casket, pulled by two mules on a wooden farm wagon. –Unacceptable for an anthem of courage scrawled on the bloody shirts of unarmed Chinese protesters during the Tiananmen Square Massacre. –Unacceptable for an anthem of determination chanted in the streets of Germany by 30,000 protesters as the Berlin Wall came tumbling down. –And unacceptable for a song on the quivering lips of

Frederick John Harris in 1965 as he walked to the gallows in Johannesburg, South Africa, who, according to his hangman, "sang the anthem even as he dropped". [4]

Perhaps the historical fabrications woven together by the claimants of We Shall Overcome were motivated by more than just money. Did fame and power also drive their ambitions? During one of his celebrated discourses, Sir Winston Churchill declared: "History will be kind to me, for I intend to write it." And so he did in his memoir, "The Gathering Storm," in which he favorably characterizes his role in the events leading up to World War II.

Perhaps, like Churchill, Pete Seeger and his associates felt obliged to craft their own historical narrative about "We Shall Overcome" and, in doing so, circumvent U.S. Copyright laws. Perhaps they realized the need to protect their golden goose by carefully constructing a Potemkin village of half-truths, misinformation, and outright lies.

Capitalizing on his association with We Shall Overcome, Pete Seeger—with his trademark blue-collar short sleeves rolled up to his Harvard-educated elbows—went on to peddle the Civil Rights anthem for a fortune across television, film, million-selling record albums, and sold-out crowds worldwide—splitting the ill-gotten gains with his purported co-authors, Guy Carawan, Frank Hamilton, Zilphia Horton, and his music publisher, The Richmond Organization. Seeger would spin a colorful, fictional tale of the song's origins to feed the hungry, unsuspecting masses. As a result, We Shall Overcome became the most popular and profitable song Pete Seeger ever performed. [5]

Seeger's rise to fame was buoyed by the mainstream American media, which sipped from Seeger's intoxicating, socially conscious elixir and venerated him as a champion of freedom and an icon of international folk music. Perhaps relying on preexisting American social and psychological biases, for more than half a century, no recognized journalist or scholar deemed it necessary to fact-check Seeger's well-crafted We Shall Overcome story; thereby abandoning well-established standards of ethics, accuracy, and factual reporting. As a direct result, three generations of Americans and freedom lovers across the globe would grow to maturity believing a lie—that We Shall Overcome was written *and owned* by four Caucasian folk singers and their music publisher. Legendary journalist Edward R. Murrow must be turning over in his grave.

My tolerance, however, for Pete Seeger's We Shall Overcome dog-and-pony show reached its limit when I learned of an ambitious campaign to nominate him for a Nobel Prize. A Nobel Prize? The same prize awarded to Mother Theresa, Albert Einstein, and Dr. Martin Luther King Jr.? Well, that was more than I could stomach. I knew it was time to exercise the faith and determination that God had given me. I knew it was time to act.

---

[4] Terry Bell with Dumisa Buhle Ntsebeza; Unfinished Business: South Africa, Apartheid and Truth; Verso / 2003; p. 46.
[5] Pete Seeger; Live interview with Tim Robbins for Pacifica Radio; Published by We Shall Overcome Foundation on April 1, 2012. https://www.youtube.com/watch?v=A3q-_4kE8RI / 4:15.

Isaias Gamboa

# Chapter 2

# A Time to Speak

*"No Lie Can Live Forever"*
**-Thomas Carlisle**

When first approached in 1992 by former *Double Action Theatre* bandmate Robert A. Goins, my ears perked up like sails to the wind upon hearing that he believed his grandmother, Louise Shropshire—a lifelong member of the African-American Baptist Church—was the original, yet unattributed author of We Shall Overcome. Given the song's well-documented global footprint and the rarely celebrated role of women in the African-American Civil Rights movement, I could not have been more eager to hear more. My buoyant enthusiasm, however, soon gave way to disillusionment as Robert explained that, aside from his grandmother's oral statements, he had no actual evidence or documentation to support his beliefs. Alas, denied my voyage of discovery, I went from Christopher Columbus to Robinson Crusoe in about five minutes flat. High and dry, I understood just how difficult it would be to affirm such an extraordinary and unprecedented claim without irrefutable, rock-solid evidence. I also recognized that I had barely met Robert a few weeks earlier and that what little I *had* learned about him during that time did little for his credibility. Oh well, at the time I was a single father of three and could scarcely have afforded the resources required to launch such an expedition anyway. With nothing else to go on, I presumed Robert's story to be a fish tale…just another one of those larger-than-life family legends we've all heard.

After our conversation, Robert and I agreed to revisit the subject at a later date. Little did either of us know how long that would be. Soon after the release of our debut (and only) CD, our musical group disbanded. Hardly more than a year after our first meeting, Robert and I went our separate ways. Shortly thereafter, his grandmother, Louise Shropshire, passed away. I wouldn't hear from him again for about 17 years, but this time would be different. This time there would be much more than tenuous oral history to fill my sails and guide my voyage. This time, unimpeachable evidence, supported by extensive research, first-hand testimony, compelling interviews, historical documents, artifacts, and astonishing photographic evidence, would help me chart a steady course across the formidable oceans of time. –A course that would lead me to a treasure of immeasurable cultural worth. –A treasure, I would later realize, many Americans would rather I had left buried.

The timing of my next conversation with Robert would coincide with another important chapter in American history and in my life, and it would prove pivotal in my decision to pursue this undertaking with determination, conviction, and faith.

## White – Black – Other

It was November 2009, and **Barack Obama**—a café-latte-complexioned biracial man—had just been elected the 44th president of the United States of America in a decisive victory over Arizona Senator John McCain. The world was still in shock, as was I—and loving it! For the sake of people of color all over the globe, I could not have been more thrilled to know that Americans—like it or not—now had their first "Black president"—or did they?

President Barack Obama - Pete Souza, Photographer

It had been widely reported before the 2008 U.S. presidential election that then-Senator Barack Obama's father, Barack Obama Sr., was a Black Kenyan, and his mother, Stanley Ann Dunham, was a White woman from Kansas. Aside from President Obama's desire to help disadvantaged and marginalized Americans, one of the many reasons I felt I could identify with him was that, like me, he was also of "mixed race"—another "*other*," if you will. In my mind, this commonality gave me a particular understanding of his past and present life, a glimpse into his family photo albums, and a relatable appreciation of what President Obama had likely experienced and endured as a youth—experiences that, being a mere two years his junior, I understood helped shape the man President Obama was now.

Although I was born in beautiful San Jose, Costa Rica, my family and I immigrated to Los Angeles, California, in August 1965—the month of the infamous Watts Riots. Ignited by a police traffic stop gone wrong, the Watts Riots were a violent 6-day revolt against racial injustice and police abuse in the economically disadvantaged Los Angeles community of Watts. Watts contained the city's three largest subsidized housing projects, Nickerson Gardens, Jordan Downs, and Imperial Courts. The "Projects," as they are known by residents, were highly concentrated areas of urban poverty and blight. By the early 1960s, these three housing developments comprised 2,408 units occupied by nearly 100% Black citizens. These citizens, due in large part to the city's discriminatory housing, employment, educational, and political policies, were among the poorest in Los Angeles. The Watts Riots quickly escalated into an uprising of 30,000 residents, resulting in 34 deaths, 1,000 injuries, and 40 million dollars in property damage over the six days and nights of unrest. For Watts, Los Angeles, and America, the flag of the African-American Civil Rights Movement was at full mast.

Moving to the U.S. from Costa Rica was an ambitious endeavor for my family, but not without precedent. My mother, Carmen Gamboa Beckles Howard, was a registered nurse who had earned her bachelor's degree in nursing on a full scholarship from the University of Colorado at Boulder. After returning to Costa Rica to work as a nurse for a couple of years, she was offered a position at the Los Angeles County USC Hospital. Being fluent in English *and* Spanish, she was in high demand in a big city like L.A. Given her dream of one day leading a staff as a hospital director, the lack of opportunity at the time for educated women of color in Costa Rica made it clear this was an offer she could not refuse. Executing such a plan, however, might require some divine intervention. My mother, a Baptist since childhood, and my father—a devout Catholic—prayed each night for help in finding a practical way to move our then-family of five to America. My father, Danilo Julian de la Trinidad Gamboa y Mora, had worked many years in Costa Rica and the Panama Canal Zone as an operations manager for the United Fruit Company. However, unlike my mother, he spoke no English whatsoever. This hindrance substantially limited his employment prospects in the U.S. Their prayers were answered, and help arrived in the form of my grand-uncle, **H.A. Howard.**

H. (Herbert) A. Howard, or "Uncle Howard" as I called him, was a prominent Black Los Angeles real estate broker and banker who, in 1919, emigrated from Jamaica to the Jim Crow US to make his fortune. He was a modest, gentle man, but in my eyes, he was Superman. Well before the song "We Shall Overcome" was ever intoned, men and women like my grand-uncle were working with their minds, bodies, hearts, and fortunes to achieve liberty, civil rights, dignity, and equality for Black Americans.

In 1928, Uncle Howard brokered the sale of the Hotel Somerville in Los Angeles—later renamed the Dunbar Hotel. Dubbed "The Colored Ritz" during the 1930s and 1940s, this posh, four-story, 100-room structure was the undisputed epicenter of African-American culture in Los Angeles. Built 100 percent by African-American laborers, craftsmen, and contractors, the luxury hotel was also financed entirely by African-American community leaders. The Somerville/Dunbar was one of only a few quality hotels in America that accepted non-Whites at the time. In June 1928, the same month it opened, the Hotel Somerville hosted the first West Coast national convention of the NAACP, where W.E.B. Du Bois was a featured speaker. [6]

The Hotel Somerville's original owner was **John Alexander Somerville,** H.A. Howard's Jamaican-born friend and associate. In 1907, Somerville became the first African American to graduate from the University of Southern California and later from the USC School of Dentistry, graduating at the top of his class. His wife, Vada Watson-Somerville, was the second. Somerville also passed the state dental board exams with the highest score on record.

In 1946, H.A. Howard co-founded Los Angeles's first independent Black-owned bank, the Broadway Savings and Loan Association (later renamed Broadway Federal Bank), which began operations in a three-room storefront office in South Los Angeles with an initial capitalization of $150,000. The institution was founded to provide residential and small-business loans to the local African-American community, which, like in most other Black communities in America, was being systematically denied these fundamental wealth-building entitlements by the city's white-owned lending institutions. In 2021, Broadway Federal Bank merged with the Washington, D.C.-based City First Bank. As of 2026, it is the largest Black-led financial institution in the U.S. Uncle Howard was the bank's first president and manager. His love and support for my family and me had a profound influence on my life.

With my grand-uncle's uncle's considerable assistance, my family moved to Los Angeles and settled in the historic West Adams district. A then-predominantly African-American community, West Adams was only a few blocks from the culturally significant neighborhood known as Sugar Hill. Formerly a sought-after community for well-heeled White Angelinos, Sugar Hill became home in the 1940s to an elite group of Black business leaders, entrepreneurs, and entertainers, including Hattie McDaniel, Joe Lewis, John and Vada Somerville, Lena Horne, Norman Houston, Pearl Bailey, and Ray Charles. But not before initiating a legal challenge against restrictive real estate covenants created to prevent Black residents from buying homes in the area. Prominent African-American NAACP attorney Loren Miller—the son of a slave—successfully represented Oscar®-winning actress Hattie McDaniel in her fight to own property on Sugar Hill. Dubbed The Sugar Hill Case, Miller later established legal precedent by deftly arguing before the Supreme Court, "It is

---

[6] Douglass Flamming. *Bound For Freedom: Black Los Angeles in Jim Crow America,* University of California Press / 2005, p. 291

time that members of the Negro race are accorded, without reservations or evasions, the full rights guaranteed them under the 14th Amendment to the Federal Constitution."

Life in L.A. as a first-generation Afro-Costa Rican immigrant of "mixed-race" would prove quite educational for me, even at five years old. Except for a few years at the mostly Hispanic Saint Agnes Parish School, throughout my youth, I attended the predominantly African-American public schools in the community where I lived. I can still vividly recall my first day of first grade.

In 1968, Twenty Fourth Street School was a predominantly Black elementary school in the West Adams district of Los Angeles. Before class each day, I recall a disorderly scene of kids running and squealing in all directions and in all octaves across the black asphalt playground. I also remember it seemed as though everyone had someone to play with, except me…and dark skin, except me…and afros, except me. And oddly, no one seemed to be carrying a notebook, pencil, or paper, except me. That first day, I felt very much like a pebble tossed into Niagara Falls—hoping there might be others like me at the bottom of it all. Then the school bell rang, and I was quickly shepherded into a single-file line of fidgety first graders, waiting to be led into class by our first-grade teacher, Mrs. Tishler.

I remember Mrs. Tishler as a tall, slightly tanned, thirty-something Caucasian woman with big blonde hair and blue eyes. She reminded me of the models in the Sears catalog. After corralling us into her classroom, she led us in reciting the Pledge of Allegiance, then instructed us to sit down. After introducing herself to a *seemingly* all-African-American group of kids, she quickly explained the roll-call procedure, then dropped her head and began calling names:

*"Anthony Adams?"* -*"Here"*
*"Michael Adams?"* -*"Here"*
*"Carla Brown?"* -*"Here"*
*"Lisa Brown?"* -*"Here"*

Before long, I found myself spellbound as Mrs. Tishler, never looking up, made her way down the list of names like a well-oiled locomotive—as if she had done this a thousand times.

*"Ronald Davis?"* -*"Here"*
*"Terri Dillard?"* -*"Here"*.

Fascinated by her steady, almost melodic cadence, in stark contrast to my classmates' notably dull responses, it suddenly occurred to me that she was chugging along in alphabetical order. -*Yikes!* Even at five years old, I knew this wasn't good. I could hear the train a-comin', and I was tied to the tracks. I was petrified. This was kindergarten all over again.

*"Andrew Edwards?"* -*"Here"*
*"Beverly Edwards?"* -*"Here"*

Then, all of a sudden, came a pause. The train had shrieked to a grinding halt. There were no "F's" on the roll-call sheet. My chest sank as I realized Mrs. Tishler's train was stalled on a G-name… MY G-name. In America, I learned, *Isaías Gamboa* doesn't roll off the tongue very well. Upon seeing my name, Mrs. Tishler's awkward, seemingly endless silence would be followed by her sincerely mystified plea:

"Eye... Eye... Isis? (sigh...) Could you help me with this, sweetie?" she begged.

Now, perhaps it was my irresistibly wavy locks—parted to one side like Napoleon Dynamite (thanks, Mom)—or my dashing, horizontally striped turtleneck (in September? Thanks again, Mom), but somehow the entire class of five- and six-year-olds had ingeniously discerned that by 'sweetie,' Mrs. Tishler was referring to ME. Then, all at once, as if choreographed, my highly amused classmates rotated in their seats and, with all eyes on me, waited ever so patiently for me to offer Mrs. Tishler my expert linguistic tutelage. Mortified, I knew I had to do *something,* and I summoned the courage to recite an audacious yet incredibly soft "*here.*" Apparently dissatisfied with my stoic response and *clearly* not grasping the social repercussions at stake, Mrs. Tishler would accept nothing less from me than the Full Monty.

*"How do you pronounce that, sweetie?"* she asked.

-Again with '*sweetie'?* Well, I did a quick peripheral scan of the room and confirmed that, yes, all eyes were *still* on me. Well, as if it were my last, I took a deep breath and replied, *"Eye-zay-us,"* which, of course, Mrs. Tishler kindly asked me to repeat for phonetic clarification. Perhaps encouraged by my class participation, my new teacher then felt the need to make matters much worse by adding:

*"That's such a pretty name. Where are you from?"*

I could feel the two dozen or so kids in the room boring holes through me with their eyes, wondering how much lunch money I was carrying. Well, suffice to say, ten minutes into the first day of *first* grade, my five-year-old social life was over—well before it had begun. I now had a spitball target on my back—one that seemed to remain affixed for the next 11 years or so. Thank *you*, Mrs. Tishler. It just so happened that the very next name called was that of the class bully.

-"Andre Harris?" (staring at me)    ..."Here."
- To borrow a Stephen Sondheim lyric from the Broadway musical *West Side Story*:
**"Life can be bright in America—if you can fight in America."**

Well, wouldn't you know, dear old Mrs. Tishler was not *quite* finished with me. That same morning after roll call, she tried, unsuccessfully, to convince me—a five-year-old—that my *birth* name, "Isaías," was actually "Isaiah," misspelled. Suddenly, my quiet disposition left the room. Had I known the word, I would likely have been expelled. However, to the best of my ability, I explained to my dear schoolmarm that *Isaías* was the *Spanish* spelling of the Old Testament prophet Isaiah, which in *English* is spelled Isaiah. What Mrs. Tishler did not know was that my brilliant mother, Carmen Gamboa Beckles-Howard, had filled my five-year-old head and heart with knowledge of the Bible, pride in my biblical name, and a basic understanding of my culture and heritage. (thanks, mom)

Perhaps in an attempt to further bewilder the horde of open-mouthed kids in the room, but much more likely because of my refusal to acquiesce to her suggestion, Mrs. Tishler decided that a little "Black-history" lesson was in order. Well, believe it or not, my

Caucasian first-grade teacher, on our *first* day of class, to a room full of afro-ed and corn-rowed six-year-olds, declared the following:

*"You know, all of your ancestors came to the United States as slaves."*

Wow! FIRST GRADE? Are you kidding me? Well, guess whose little livid hand shot up? Try as I did to keep my lips together, I informed Mrs. Tishler that *my* ancestors had *not* come to America as slaves but had, according to my mother, lived free in Jamaica after escaping from the English (true story). I elected to omit the fact that my father was of Spanish descent, with white skin and blue eyes like hers. I figured I had enough trouble. The rest of first grade is a blur.

After that day and throughout most of my youth, few weeks passed without someone asking me, *"What are you?"* I've never understood why, all my life, people have tried so hard to categorize me into one group or another. –Black, Latino, Hispanic, African-American, Costa Rican, Afro-Caribbean, Mulatto… Sometimes I wonder what kind of world we would live in if we were all blind? What kinds of people would we marry? What kinds of friends would we have? What kinds of homes would we live in, or what clothes would we wear?

It is the *words* of a book that hold its value, not the color of ink or paper. If we are to survive as a species, humans must view one another through the prism of love, respect, and compassion…not pigment. Genetic diversity may one day save the world. Well, as I said, I now felt something I had in common with our new president. Funny, the things you remember.

My Family / Circa 1965 (That's me in the vest)

# The One-Drop Rule

Slave children from New Orleans /Courtesy U.S. Library of Congress

An understanding of America's fixation on racialism is necessary to understand the misappropriation of Louise Shropshire's hymn, If My Jesus Wills. Few examples illustrate this problem better than America's obsession with the race of President Barack Obama.

America's 44th President, Barack Hussein Obama, is a man. He is a husband and the father of two daughters. He is a man who graduated from Columbia University and Harvard Law School, where he was elected president of the Harvard Law Review. He is a man who, after graduating from Harvard, practiced civil rights law and taught constitutional law at the University of Chicago Law School. He was elected to the Illinois State Senate, where he served three terms before becoming the 44th President of the United States of America.

Instead of citing President Obama's outstanding credentials and qualifications, had I been listing the performance specifications of a high-performance or luxury vehicle, an intelligent buyer would have considered color options relatively minor. However, in the United States of America, skin color still matters and can not only determine where you live, work, and die but also tragically whether you live, work, or die.

Although it shouldn't matter, in America, because President Obama's mother was white and his father Black, he is considered "mixed race"—neither white nor Black but both. Like a cappuccino or a hot fudge sundae, one would think such a genetic synthesis would blur the lines of racial distinction and discrimination. However, in America, such enlightened mindsets seem incompatible with its history of hierarchical values and a deeply entrenched ethnocentric system of power, reinforced by asserting political, educational, cultural, and economic advantages over those of the perceived subordinate class or caste. A mere 150 years ago, these same values justified and sanctioned the enslavement and exploitation of human beings for profit.

Though it disregards the laws of reason, in America—the land of the *"Venti-half-caf-no-foam-non-fat-vanilla-soy-double-shot-extra-hot-latte"*—President Barack Obama's race is still classified as "Black." In America, our president's well-documented genetic and cultural fusion cannot be, or perhaps *will not* be, processed by its either-white-or-Black racial classification mainframe. Given the rape of hundreds of thousands of Black female slaves by their White American slave owners and overseers, doing so would oblige many, if not most, Caucasian Americans to also fall into this "Black" category. I suspect that if all Americans were to submit to DNA genealogy testing, the overwhelming majority of us would be found to have much more than one drop of African blood running through our veins. - Imagine all the colorful family reunions and Thanksgiving celebrations when all the Black and White families are united as one! What a wonderful world this would be. Well, guess who's *not* coming to dinner?

In the United States, there is a long-practiced and well-entrenched racialist code commonly referred to as **the "One-Drop Rule."** This term refers to the racial and social classification of people with even *one drop* of sub-Saharan (i.e., African) blood as Black. Although the origins of this practice may date back to slavery, in practical terms it is a twentieth-century American invention. This custom, codified by law, allowed American Whites to continue the legal subjugation, isolation, discrimination, and segregation of

Blacks long after their *physical* enslavement was legally abolished. Let's be honest. Well before importing the first kidnapped African slaves to North America, Europeans regarded themselves as superior in one way or another to people of African descent with darker skin. Southern American Whites even waged war to continue to physically and ideologically imprison African Americans in a subordinate cultural, social, political, and economic class.

The One-drop Rule is an example of the long-held practice of **hypodescent** by far too many White Americans, who still fundamentally regard the Black race as inferior in one way or another to themselves.[7] Fortunately, there *are* ever-growing numbers of Americans, White and otherwise, who do not incubate such loathsome ignorance in their hearts and minds. Many of these white Americans have fought and died in their efforts to abolish slavery, racism, and inequality in America. Sadly, for now, these enlightened human beings appear to be in the minority.

## Race and the Misappropriation of We Shall Overcome

My research into the origins of "We Shall Overcome" inevitably led me to consider the possible relevance of race and **cultural appropriation** in this matter. Although the subject of race has always been a very painful and uncomfortable one for many Americans—especially those who consider the election of President Barack Obama evidence of a "post-racial" America—I could not ignore the elephant in the room. The question was whether the stereotypes many American whites held—that Blacks were intellectually inferior—played a role in the misappropriation of Louise Shropshire's hymn, and if so, to what extent? After all, Louise Shropshire composed her hymn during her teens—sometime between 1932 and 1942, when educational discrimination and segregation were the law of the land. Not surprisingly, it didn't take long for some folks to accuse me of playing the so-called **"race card"** by suggesting that legendary folk singer Pete Seeger's role in claiming We Shall Overcome as his own may have had racial undertones. Well, those people had obviously never read Seeger's 2008 interview with Joshua Klein for the online magazine Pitchfork.com:

**"The good and bad are all tangled up together. American popular music is loved around the world because of its African rhythm. But that wouldn't have happened if it wasn't for slavery." –Pete Seeger** [8]

White men institutionalized racism in America to devalue the very existence and humanity of Black people. This allowed them to justify the kidnapping, ownership, murder, rape, and torture of Black people in their unholy quest to accumulate wealth and compete for scarce resources. Today, white people in America continue to benefit from a perceived elevated social, intellectual, and cultural status, as well as the overt and passive economic and educational advantages of this institutionalized system. This phenomenon has been referred to as **"White Privilege"**.

---

[7] Leon Bankston, Carl Leon; Racial and Ethnic Relations in America: Ethnic entrepreneurship; Salem Press; 2000; p. 498.

[8] AK Press; 2004; Klein, Joshua / Pitchfork.com / 2008 / "Interviews / Pete Seeger" http://pitchfork.com/features/interviews/7543-pete-seeger

In 1968, educator, anti-racist activist, and diversity trainer **Jane Elliot**, a white woman, became known for her "Blue Eyes/Brown Eyes Exercise." In this novel social experiment, Elliot divided third-graders with blue and brown eyes into "inferior" and "superior" groups, respectively. She then asked the "brown-eyed kids" to treat the "blue-eyed students" as inferiors. Elliot has conducted this experiment with children and adults for almost 50 years and has appeared on **The Tonight Show Starring Johnny Carson, The Oprah Winfrey Show, and The Ellen DeGeneres Show**. In a 2003 online interview for PBS / Frontline, Jane Elliot concluded the following:

*"…we are still conditioning people in this country and, indeed, all over the globe to the myth of white superiority. We are constantly being told that we don't have racism in this country anymore, but most of the people who are saying that are white. White people think it isn't happening because it isn't happening to them."* [9]

Racism takes many forms. Pete Seeger's rationalizations about how American slavery produced good American music reveal a dangerously covert form of racial bias and discrimination against Black people, one that mainstream American society has accepted. My own experiences as a "man of color" living in a *very* racially polarized America were more than enough to sustain my trepidation. However, I found Seeger's statements particularly disturbing because they seemed to passively endorse the notion that in America, when it comes to increasing the wealth and improving the lives of white people, the ends justify the means. Racial bias or predisposition, even in passive or subconscious forms, *is* still a form of racism.

**Dr. Chester Middlebrook Pierce** is the former president of the American Board of Psychiatry and Neurology and currently serves as Professor Emeritus of Education and Psychology at Harvard Medical School. In his book, **Offensive Mechanisms**, Dr. Pierce writes:

*"Racism in the United States is a public health and mental health illness. It is a mental disease because it is delusional"…"There are still other dimensions of racism. It is a contagious disease. There may not exist a white or black man in this country who has never had to operate from one side or the other of a line drawn against a black man. For the black man to violate this line, often legally drawn, is to invite the most sinister and ultimate catastrophe. While the white man, even the most indefatigable, non-conforming liberal, is liable to have to take advantage of racial prerogative to the detrimental exploitation of some hapless—if unseen—black."* [10]

Dr. Pierce is not alone in these observations. In 1946, Nobel Prize-winning physicist, **Dr. Albert Einstein,** gave a speech in which he referred to racism as *"a disease of white people"*.[11] Earlier that year, he published an article for Pageant magazine entitled "The Negro Question," in which he asserted the following:

---

[9] PBS / Frontline, Jan. 1, 2003; *A CLASS DIVIDED / An Unfinished Crusade: An Interview with Jane Elliott /* http://www.pbs.org/wgbh/frontline/article/an-unfinished-crusade-an-interview-with-jane-elliott/
[10] Pierce, Chester (1970). "Offensive Mechanisms". In Barbour, Floyd. *The Black Seventies*. Boston, Massachusetts: Porter Sargent Publisher.
[11] Jerome, Fred and Taylor, Rodger; Einstein on Race And Racism; Rutgers University Press; Jul 25, 2006; p. 88.

*"There is, however, a somber point in the social outlook of Americans. Their sense of equality and human dignity is mainly limited to men of white skin. Even among these, there are prejudices of which I, as a Jew, am clearly conscious; but they are unimportant in comparison with the attitude of the "Whites" toward their fellow-citizens of darker complexion, particularly toward Negroes. The more I feel an American, the more this situation pains me. I can escape the feeling of complicity in it only by speaking out.*

*"Many a sincere person will answer: 'Our attitude towards Negroes is the result of unfavorable experiences which we have had by living side by side with Negroes in this country. They are not our equals in intelligence, sense of responsibility, or reliability.'*

*"I am firmly convinced that whoever believes this suffers from a fatal misconception. Your ancestors dragged these black people from their homes by force; and in the white man's quest for wealth and an easy life, they have been ruthlessly suppressed and exploited, degraded into slavery."*[12]

I pondered whether Drs. Einstein and Pierce's observation that many American whites believe Black people are less intelligent than themselves rang true in relation to the misappropriation of "We Shall Overcome." Once again, I soon found that even suggesting such an idea offended many whites, who sincerely believe no serious racial issues still exist in the US and that a noble person like Pete Seeger was incapable of being racist. So, in the interest of enlightenment, I asked some of these skeptics, independently, to help me conduct my own little experiment. I proposed that they ask the next few white people they encountered which race they believed President Barack Obama to be. If their subjects answered "Black," I instructed them to ask how they arrived at that conclusion. Because President Obama's mother was White, why wouldn't these subjects consider the President to be White instead of Black? It didn't take long for my skeptics to realize they, in fact, *were* the subjects. I finished my experiment by asking them if they knew in what month Black History Month was observed in America. After a bit of silence, each correctly answered, "February?" I then asked the question, "When is *White* History Month?" A much longer pause was followed by a change of expression and then their answers, "Every other month." The responses to these questions underscore the persistence of the One Drop Rule in America and also validate Drs. Pierce and Einstein's theory on racism in America. I was convinced that this clandestine strain of racism was very much responsible for the attitudes that motivated Pete Seeger and his associates to take what did not belong to them from those they perceived as intellectually inferior.

### The Stereotype Threat

Racism and racial biases, conscious or otherwise, are noxious and can cause immeasurable damage to others. Studies show that the humiliating stereotypes imposed for centuries by Whites in America upon Blacks have had devastating and debilitating psychological effects on the ability of Blacks to perform academically at their best. During the 1990s, psychologists **Joshua Aronson, PhD; Steven Spencer, PhD; and Claude Steele, PhD**, identified a phenomenon known as "**Stereotype Threat**." Their research, and that of many experts after them, found that African-American students enrolled in college as members of a minority group stereotyped as academically inferior scored much lower on

---

[12] Einstein, Albert; The Einstein Reader; Citadel Press, Jun 1, 2006; The Negro Question; p. 120.

examinations when reminded of their race beforehand. The research found that African-American students scored equally with white students when informed that their test was a "laboratory problem-solving task." However, when given the same test but told it was intended to measure their intellectual abilities, Black students scored significantly lower. According to the research, it was clear that the prospect of social evaluation suppressed the intellectual performance of the Black students. In 2006, the American Psychological Association affirmed, *"Stereotype Threat Widens Achievement Gap."* [13]

Not surprisingly, this phenomenon is not restricted to minorities. The same study found that white male college students majoring in math and engineering, who had also achieved high scores on the math portion of the SAT, underperformed considerably when told the test was to measure "why Asians appear to outperform other students on tests of math ability." These findings were published in The Journal of Personality and Social Psychology. [14]

Race should never be considered when determining the beauty, intelligence, worth, content, or character of a human being. Doing so wrongly apportions value to this superficial trait and will ultimately lead to the annihilation of our species. Should you find yourself describing someone in terms of their race, e.g., "this Black guy at work" or "this Asian girl in my class," consider why it was necessary to mention the color of their skin, and know that you—yes, YOU—are part of the problem. For centuries, attitudes such as these have justified the devaluation of Black Americans and the shameless pilfering of their physical, intellectual, and cultural inventions, production, resources, and possessions—assets such as Louise Shropshire's sacred hymn, *If My Jesus Wills*. The objective here is to educate…not offend—to prescribe a treatment for the malignant spread of racism in America by first recognizing its seemingly benign presence on the surface of our society.

Although President Obama self-identifies as African American, his need to do so can be traced to necessary cultural and political objectives and solidarities.[15] He is simply offering the simplest response to the insistent question, "What are you?" If America's habitual practice of compartmentalizing human beings by race were merely a benign idiosyncrasy of its ideology, it would hardly be worth mentioning. However, there are far more serious—ill-omened implications.

A biopsy, if you will, of its diseased tissue reveals that a manifestation of America's racial-classification system has spread to the very heart of American capitalism—Wall Street. As of March 2025, only 27 African American executives have *ever* been appointed CEO of a Fortune-500® company, and only eight remain. That represents roughly 1.6%, while African Americans make up roughly 14% of the American workforce. According to Fortune magazine, whites make up over 73.4% of Fortune-500® board seats. This phenomenon is often dismissively labeled by corporate boards, politicians, and the mainstream American media as a "lack of diversity." Let's be frank; what it is, is racial bias

---

[13] American Psychological Association, July 15, 2016 / http://www.apa.org/research/action/stereotype.asp
[14] Aronson, J., & Inzlicht, M. (2004). The ups and downs of attributional ambiguity: Stereotype vulnerability and the academic self-knowledge of African-American students. *Psychological Science, 15*, 829-836.
[15] Harrell, David Edwin and Gaustad, Edwin S.; Unto A Good Land: A History Of The American People; Wm. B. Eerdmans Publishing; Sep 15, 2005; p. 1163

and discrimination…pure and simple. There is no other honest explanation for this disparity?

As further evidence of covert racial biases, research by Robert W. Livingston and Nicholas A. Pearce of Northwestern University's Kellogg School of Management revealed that the handful of Black Fortune-500® CEOs that have existed were mostly lighter-skinned and/or more likely to possess so-called "baby-faces" than their Black colleagues. Livingston and Pearce theorized that these superficial physical features made some Black individuals appear less threatening to White people than others. Such surreptitious race-based disparities were first branded "Institutional Racism" in the 1960s by US Civil Rights activist and future Black Panthers leader Stokely Carmichael.

America's One-Drop Rule, its history of institutional racism, and its failure to recognize African Americans as equals have helped sustain a system of bias, racism, and economic exploitation of its Black citizens. Citizens who have been historically denied an economic and educational support structure to rely on for their survival, security, and growth. Furthermore, the arrogance and biases still very much present among many White Americans have nurtured a collective attitude of neocolonialist entitlement – White Privilege. This delusional sense of superiority has romanticized the actions of barefaced thieves, who, in the name of "cultural heritage and preservation," raided, ransacked, and plundered the sacred sanctuaries of the most vulnerable and marginalized African Americans. These outlaws, masquerading as friends, advocates, and supporters, gained entry to sacred places of worship, then, while their victims' heads were bowed, filled their pockets with priceless cultural treasures and walked away millionaires.

Yes, I *was* flying high with President Barack Obama in office—a man of color with exceptional education, character, empathy, intelligence, wisdom, and communication skills. It was encouraging to know that enlightened Americans of *all* hues had come together to elect him—to validate him. People were desperately seeking higher ground. But it wasn't until I discovered a remarkable photograph taken before the November 2008 presidential elections that a much deeper, spiritual connection to President Barack Obama and Robert's grandmother, Louise Shropshire, was forged.

Barack Obama in prayer with ministers of the African American Christian Church

# The Saints

I was still floating on the effervescent cloud of President Obama's first year in office when, out of the blue, I received an email from my former bandmate, Robert Goins. 17 years had passed since I had seen or heard from him. After catching up a bit, Robert reported that since our last conversation seventeen years earlier, he had become a Christian minister and was now happily married. This was a 180-degree change from the Robert I had known before. I could not have been happier to hear this news, as his path had, in the past, taken quite a few treacherous turns. Unlike earlier, when our lives could not have been more different, he and I now shared much more in common. –Not to mention some gray hair.

To no surprise, Robert informed me that he was still making music and had even formed his own independent music label, *Longevity Entertainment*. He said he was working on a CD for his *Soft Ministry* collection—a project featuring original spiritual songs—marketed and distributed independently by him. He reported that this venture had proven a great blessing to him—bringing him great spiritual satisfaction while also helping him provide for his family's financial needs. Before long, however, his mood dimmed as he shared with me how he had recently suffered a financial setback, leaving him discouraged and disillusioned.

In an effort to distract him from his melancholy, I reminded him of our conversation years earlier about his grandmother, and We Shall Overcome. I suggested we revisit the matter. It was then that I first learned of his beloved grandmother's passing. Changing the subject, however, proved quite effective, and for several hours, Robert reverently shared details of the eighteen treasured years he spent with his grandmother before her death. At one point, he broke down in tears... his powerful voice crumbling as he recalled a very painful and life-altering event from his past. I'll never forget his tear-filled words: *"She stood in the gap for me, Ike. She stood in the gap for me."* Robert was referring to a violent 1984 automobile accident in which he and three others, riding in a *two*-passenger convertible sports car, plunged off a cliff in the San Bernardino Mountains of California.

It was a sunny June afternoon, the day that might have been Robert's high school graduation ceremony. He was depressed and hungover that day—finally feeling the consequences of the many foolish decisions he had made while in, but mostly out of, school. Those decisions included his habitual inclination to skip class, drink heavily, and partake of *"those funny cigarettes,"* as his grandmother, Louise, used to call them. As a sobering consequence, a then-nineteen-year-old Robert had nowhere *near* the academic credits needed to graduate alongside his high school peers, and he was all too eager to try to drink away his sorrows.

At the time, Robert lived with his mother, Darlene, and stepfather, "Big Mike". They were renting their garage to, as Robert described him, *"this White-dude named Dee"*. Dee was *one of* Big Mike's running buddies and not precisely a role model, having successfully encouraged Robert on many occasions to share in his insatiable appetite for drugs, alcohol, and pornography. Not surprisingly, Dee suggested that Robert drown his graduation-day blues in a bottle of whisky, then offered to drive him and a couple of cronies up to Mount Baldy for his own private pity-party. Dee had a groovy little red MG-Midget convertible in which all four would ride that fateful day. True to form, Robert accepted the invitation, and off they went. Before heading up the narrow mountain road, however, they stopped to pick up the two *other* geniuses and, while there, polished off two twelve-packs of beer between the four of them (six beers apiece, according to my calculations). Well, apparently not feeling quite intoxicated enough for their excursion, the four stooges then drove to the local grocery store, *stole* two large bottles of Jack Daniels whiskey, and then, with Billy Idol's *"Rebel Yell"* blaring from the car stereo, proceeded to weave a crooked path up the twisted mountain road—passing the whisky bottle around the entire way. Indeed, Robert's reckless decisions were adding up quickly.

MG Midget Convertible

As the sporty MG was only a two-seater, Robert volunteered to sit facing forward on its rear trunk, with his legs wedged behind the driver's seat—just like the Grand Marshall of a fool's parade. Alongside Robert, another passenger did likewise, and before they knew it, they were on top of the world… eight thousand feet above reality, with a whole bottle of Jack Daniels left. Having arrived at their intended destination, they parked the car, tumbled out, grabbed the last bottle of booze, and staggered off into the woods. There, Robert—the guest of honor—proceeded to drink himself blind in a miserable attempt to forget his academic humiliation. Once the last drop of liquid stupidity was drained from the bottle, Dee decided it was time to leave. This time, however, Robert was feeling a bit dizzy and, instead of sitting on the trunk, asked Dee—still the driver—to slide the driver's seat up so he could squeeze his body in behind it. I guess he figured he'd be safer there. Yes, said Dee, drunk as skunks. The four day-trippers poured themselves back into their convertible, cranked up the engine, and then attempted to corkscrew their way back down the treacherous mountain road.

Before long, Dee—their pickled pilot—began slipping in and out of consciousness and drifted onto the wrong side of the road, sideswiping an oncoming car. Momentarily wide-awake and fearing prosecution, Dee panicked and floored the gas pedal in an attempt to flee the scene. Within seconds, however, he missed a sharp turn and sent the tiny red convertible nose-diving over the cliff, with all its horrified passengers flying like rag dolls in every direction—except Robert, who was now inescapably wedged behind the driver's seat. As the car plunged downward, all but Louise's grandson were thrown clear of the vehicle, sparing them life-threatening injuries. Robert and the MG, on the other hand, would tumble 200 feet together down the rugged cliffside, with both their mangled bodies finally coming to rest at the base of a tree—one roll away from a 1,000-foot drop. Somehow still conscious, Dee staggered down the hillside to check on Robert, called 911, then passed out. Within about an hour, all four were being rushed to the nearest hospital—Dee in handcuffs.

Robert was in critical condition, with a severely lacerated liver and numerous other internal and external injuries. His midsection had been completely carved up. Robert's mother, Darlene, and grandmother, Louise, were notified of the accident and immediately rushed to the hospital in a state of distress. Grave news awaited them there. Upon arrival, the ER doctor informed them that Robert's injuries were not survivable and advised them to say their goodbyes. Devastated and overwhelmed, Robert's mother accepted the prognosis, entered his hospital room, and bid farewell to her son. Robert's grandmother, Louise, however, would not accept the doctor's opinion. With a Bible in hand, she shook her head, turned around, and left the hospital, broadcasting to all, *"I'M GONNA GO GET THE SAINTS!"*

The "Saints" she referred to were a highly potent, twelve-person prayer group composed of members of her church, the Greater New Light Baptist Church in Pomona, California. Shortly afterward, Louise returned to the hospital with all twelve *Saints* in tow. Upon crossing the hospital lobby's threshold, they formed a circle, locked hands, and dropped their heads in prayer. As Robert lay bleeding, unconscious, and on the brink of death, Louise and the Saints held a 14-hour prayer vigil right smack in the middle of the hospital lobby, the likes of which I suspect the hospital had never seen. For safety reasons, hospital security asked them to disperse on several occasions, but this sanctified circle of prayed-up Baptists would *not* be moved.

During her vigil, Louise desperately appealed to God to spare her grandson's life, promising on his behalf that, in return, Robert would offer his life to God in service. Later that night, Louise also donated blood for her beloved grandson, whose utter recklessness had left him teetering on the brink of death.

Robert survived the night and by the next day showed signs of recovery. He was going to make it. Robert's mother, Darlene, who stayed by his bedside during his weeks of recovery, shared stories of Grandmother's remarkable faith and the extraordinary spiritual event. A month later, Louise Shropshire would call him her "miracle boy." He left the hospital, stitched, bruised, and broken, but still alive.

Robert Anthony Goins Sr. (Pictured far-left) shortly after his release from the hospital. Mother, Darlene Reliford is pictured at center next to unnamed family friend / Courtesy Louise Shropshire Foundation

Years would pass after that fateful accident and although by his own admission Robert often fell considerably short of his grandmother's pledge, he would spend many treasured years with her before her death.

# A Call to Service

While still on the phone, Robert choked up again as he recalled the last words his grandmother said to him before her death:

*'One day, somebody's gonna do somethin' with all my music.'*

"I just can't get those words outta my head," said Robert. Then came his request. Robert asked if I, then a songwriter and music producer by trade, might help him fulfill his grandmother's dying wish by proving her story to the world. After giving him a few moments to settle, I asked whether his grandmother had left any physical proof—photographs, sheet music, documents, or other items related to her possible connection to "We Shall Overcome." As 17 years earlier, Robert didn't know of anything specific, but he added that his grandmother, Louise, had bequeathed all her remaining physical possessions to her daughter, Darlene—Robert's mother. Darlene, however, had died a few years earlier, having bequeathed her estate—which included the items left to her by her mother, Louise—to Robert. These items, Robert said, were now housed in a storage facility not far from where he lived. He recalled that when his mother, Darlene, passed, he helped move her personal effects to the storage unit and remembered seeing some old photo albums there, along with an old suitcase containing what appeared to be sheet music. This sounded promising. I admit, however, that I was still rather skeptical.

I advised Robert to visit the storage facility as soon as possible to search for and secure any items that might support his grandmother's story. He did exactly that, and a week later I was on my way to Riverside, California, to meet him at his home and survey the items he had recovered. Halfway there, I got a call from Robert asking if I could pick him up on the way. Following his directions, I pulled off the freeway and drove about fifteen minutes out of the way into Pomona, California. During his visit to the storage facility, Robert had learned that the old suitcase containing sheet music had been moved to his Aunt Thelma's home in Pomona and was now stored in her garage. I assumed I would be picking him up from there, but instead I found him walking along White Avenue, lugging a large, well-worn suitcase. Seeing this image of Robert, 17 years later, like myself, a few pounds heavier, with less hair on his head and patches of gray about his face, I was reminded not to take time for granted. After exchanging a big "man-hug," we climbed into my truck and continued on to his home in Riverside... reminiscing all the way.

As we walked up the stairs to Robert's apartment, I still had doubts about whether this would lead to anything. I mean, all of us have heard incredible tales from relatives, haven't we? – amusing family folktales handed down from generation to generation? More often than not, these stories turn out to be more fiction than fact. And given the widely published information available at the time regarding the alleged origins of We Shall Overcome—information that made absolutely no mention of Louise Shropshire—it occurred to me how much more likely it was that Robert's grandmother, though a wonderful hymn writer and human being, had no actual connection to We Shall Overcome. Well, that was before "Precious Lord".

Upon arriving at Robert's apartment, we walked to the dining area, paused for a moment, then lifted his grandmother's old suitcase onto the dining table. As heavy as it was, there had to be *something* important inside. Almost ceremoniously, we snapped open the rusty latches and slowly raised the lid. The first thing I saw was a soggy, yellowing sheet of staff paper stuck to a thick mound of paper just like it. It was blank on the upward-facing side, but, being wet, I could see the horizontal staff lines peeking through from the other side. Concerned about possible water damage to these materials, I asked Robert how the items inside the suitcase had gotten wet. He said the suitcase had been soaked by a recent thunderstorm, which had leaked rainwater into his aunt Thelma's garage, where it had been stored. After taking a moment to ponder that, I reached down and slowly, carefully peeled away the first damp page of what I hoped was sheet music. Upon turning it over, staff lines and musical notes came into focus, and as my eyes found their way to its title, my jaw dropped. "Take My Hand, Precious Lord," written by Thomas A. Dorsey–a first edition copy. Although I never met her, I can honestly say I felt Louise Shropshire's presence in that moment and the love she must have had for the beloved, monumental hymns of glory and praise she had kept sheltered in this suitcase for some 50 years.

*"Take My Hand, Precious Lord" is a well-known Gospel hymn, but not just any hymn. It is, by and large, considered the most beloved Gospel hymn ever written. It has been performed by a who's-who of renowned singers, including Elvis Presley, Pat Boone, Mahalia Jackson, Little Richard, Aretha Franklin, Tennessee Ernie Ford, Jimmy Dean, B.B. King, Ike and Tina Turner, Whitney Houston, Gladys Knight, Beyonce, Chaka Khan, and many others. The author of this hymn was Rev. Thomas A. Dorsey, who is universally considered the "Father of Gospel Music".*[16]

---

[16] Edited by Emmett G. Price, III, Tammy L. Kernodle, Horace J. Maxile, Jr.; Encyclopedia of African American Music, Volume 3; C-CLIO, Dec 17, 2010; p. 303.

We Shall Overcome: Sacred Song on the Devil's Tongue

# TAKE MY HAND, PRECIOUS LORD

SPECIAL ARRANGEMENT
FOR MIXED VOICES
WITH DUETT AND TRIO

by

THOMAS A. DORSEY

*Price 25¢ each*

PUBLISHED BY
THOMAS A. DORSEY
4154 S. ELLIS AVE.,    CHICAGO 15, ILL.

Sheet music to Take My Hand, Precious Lord.

I asked Robert whether he knew of the hymn or its author. He did not. I took a breath and paused to consider what might have happened to that old, banged-up suitcase had it not been rescued that very day. Then, unexpectedly, in that moment, a flood of memories came over me as I recalled three distinct childhood experiences: 1. hearing my father recite the Lord's Prayer on his knees at my bedside; 2. ringing the Sanctus bells during Mass as an altar boy; and 3. passing around a red velvet-lined collection plate in Baptist Sunday School. (As a child, I alternated churches each month, as my father was a devout Catholic and my mother, a faithful Baptist) Somehow, in that exact moment, I felt the muted thunder of a gentle yet authoritative call to service. I can't say I understood it, but somehow I knew the contents of this suitcase would point me toward the truth... the truth about Louise Shropshire and her connection to We Shall Overcome. Standing over this extraordinary collection of artifacts, I felt time stand still. Page after sodden page, I removed more than one hundred pieces of sacred African-American music from Louise Shropshire's sturdy old treasure chest. – Music that I later found included many of her own original hymns; *Behold the Man of Galilee* (written with Rev. Thomas A. Dorsey); *I'm Tryin' My Best To Get Home To See Jesus*; *Whom Do Men Say That I Am?*; *I Know Jesus Pilots Me*; *Are you Worthy to Take Communion?*; *Come on: Jesus Will Save You Right Now*; *I've Got The Big Seal Of Approval; Mother's Beautiful Hands; His Precious Blood; and If My Jesus Wills*. The titles alone spoke to the great depth of Louise Shropshire's love of God.

On the long drive back home, the magnitude of what I had just discovered began to sink in. I recognized that this precious collection of artifacts held extraordinary, unmistakable historical, spiritual, and cultural significance. These hymns told the story of how African Americans, with God at their side, have clung to their faith through the very worst of times—slavery, rape, the bullwhip, lynching, bombings, shootings, beatings, humiliation, degradation, discrimination, and abuse. In my mind, that beat-up old suitcase and another we would later discover held the key to what inspired Rev. Dr. Martin Luther King to preach, *"I just want to do God's will."* To me, these sacred songs were like the Dead Sea Scrolls of the African American Civil Rights Movement. But it was the lyrics to one of Shropshire's own hymns, **"If My Jesus Wills,"** that carried a very intimate reminder of the promise made to African Americans by God—that with *His* help and in *His* time, they would indeed "Overcome Someday".

The lyrics to "Verse-1" of, If My Jesus Wills:

***"I'll overcome, I'll overcome, I'll overcome someday***

***Oh yes, if my Jesus wills, I do believe, I'll overcome someday."***


The lyrics to the "Verse-1" of, We Shall Overcome:

***"We shall overcome, we shall overcome, we shall overcome someday,***

***Oh, deep in my heart, I do believe, we shall overcome someday."***

This wasn't rocket science. Upon first reading the lyrics to "If My Jesus Wills," I immediately found the striking similarities between *it* and "We Shall Overcome" breathtaking. There had to be a connection. Then something else sank in. I couldn't help but notice that aside from the change in pronouns—*"I'll"* to *"We Shall"*—the words *"If my Jesus wills, I do believe…"* now read *"Deep in my heart, I do believe…."* All of a sudden, there was this theological question staring me in the face; **How could African Americans, who once submitted to God's authority, will, and power for liberation from slavery, "overcome" racism, discrimination, and oppression in America without, once again, trusting in God's authority, will, and power to help achieve this objective?**

In the Christian bible, when **Moses** confronted **Pharaoh** in Egypt *demanding* he liberate the Hebrew slaves, did he say, "' Pharaoh, deep in my heart I do believe' you should 'let my people go?" –Certainly not. Here is what Moses said to Pharaoh:

## The First Plague: Waters Become Blood

### Exodus 7:14-18 (NKJV)

*"So the Lord said to Moses:' Pharaoh's heart is hard; he refuses to let the people go. Go to Pharaoh in the morning, when he goes out to the water, and you shall stand by the river's bank to meet him; and the rod which was turned to a serpent you shall take in your hand. And you shall say to him, 'The Lord God of the Hebrews has sent me to you, saying, "Let My people go, that they may serve Me in the wilderness," but indeed, until now you would not hear! Thus says the Lord: "By this you shall know that I am the Lord. Behold, I will strike the waters which are in the river with the rod that is in my hand, and they shall be turned to blood. And the fish that are in the river shall die, the river shall stink, and the Egyptians will loathe to drink the water of the river.'"* (see also, Shemot 7 / Orthodox Jewish Bible)

Here, we see Moses clearly and dutifully invoking *God's* authority, will, and power—not his own; 1. **"The Lord God of the Hebrews has sent me** (God's authority);

2. **"Let My people go**, that they may serve Me in the wilderness" (God's will), and

3. **"Behold, I will strike the waters** which *are* in the river with the rod that *is* in my hand, and **they shall be turned to blood**…" (God's power).

Thus, removing the deeply meaningful words "If My Jesus Wills" from Shropshire's Christian hymn was an attempt, conscious or otherwise, to remove God's name, authority, will, and power from it as well. How could a non-violent movement based on moral principles proceed without God? But what would motivate anyone to do such a diabolical thing? -Money? There was clearly something deeper at work here. Whatever it was, I was convinced that whoever chose to replace Shropshire's *"If My Jesus Wills"* with *"Deep in my heart"* was not a person of faith. Something felt very wrong to me now. A dark cloud had been cast over this illuminating moment of discovery. However, despite growing suspicions, I had no meaningful evidence that Shropshire's hymn was used to create "We Shall Overcome," and I knew that jumping to conclusions without any proof was a waste of time.

Nevertheless, like an essential archaeological find, I was filled with an almost childlike sense of exuberance and wonder. But was this the Rosetta Stone, or just some old bones? Either way, from a practical standpoint, there would be considerable raw physical evidence and information for me to excavate, catalog, process, and analyze. Not to mention the research required to place it in context. The world had the right to know and understand the facts surrounding the *true* history of We Shall Overcome. However, I also understood that such an endeavor would require an extraordinary amount of my time and resources—likely more than I could afford. From a spiritual and cultural perspective, I had numerous questions about what the discovery of Louise Shropshire and her hymn, "If My Jesus Wills," would mean for the African American community if it were the antecedent of "We Shall Overcome." Truly overwhelmed, I wondered if I was the man for this job.

Although exhilarated by what I had found, I had not yet accepted this undertaking as my *own* spiritual charge, but I sensed there was much more here for me to do than met the eye. I was beginning to feel a powerful spiritual undertow that seemed to pull me in or under. So many things were running through my head. If Louise Shropshire's hymn had in fact been co-opted by Pete Seeger and his associates, what effect would the revelation of these facts have on African Americans? There had to be others much better qualified than I to process and disseminate such a culturally important find. My apprehension led me to contact a man who, without question, would know exactly what to do – **the Reverend Dr. Cecil "Chip" Murray.**

In 2010, the distinguished Rev. Dr. **Cecil "Chip"** Murray retired after 27 years as senior pastor of First African Methodist Episcopal Church (F.A.M.E.) in the West Adams area of Los Angeles, California—a few blocks from my childhood home. Since retiring in 2004, Rev. Murray had been appointed John R. Tansey Chair of Christian Ethics in the School of Religionat the **University of Southern California (USC)**, in addition to serving as a Senior Fellow of the Center for Religion and Civic Culture at Murray held a doctorate from the Claremont School of Theology and had many years of experience as a highly respected advocate, activist, and senior statesman in the Los Angeles African-American community. He was also a professor of theology at USC and had just published his new book, *"Twice Tested By Fire."* Indeed, he was the man for *this* job.

Rev. Murray became a household name during the 1992 Rodney King riots in Los Angeles for his very public efforts to end the violence and destruction. He was recognized as a voice of peace, reason, and reconciliation in the African-American community and had been a featured guest on the Oprah Winfrey Show and interviewed on numerous television and cable network broadcasts. I contacted Rev. Murray to ask whether he would be willing to lead this very spiritual project to its divine destination, but I was truly unprepared for his response. The following is an excerpt:

*"Precious son, you seek nothing and are a one-of-a-kind spirit. This is the combination that God constantly seeks, as in the case of Moses. You are brilliant. You can do it. The issue is big, but it was given to you by God, so it cannot fail. And you will not fail it."*
-Rev. Dr. Cecil Chip Murray

I still cannot find the words to express my feelings that day. I was profoundly humbled by Rev. Dr. Murray's response, and, thanks to his God-given wisdom and guidance, I now knew that this divine mission was mine and mine alone. And as the good Reverend had affirmed, I would *not* fail it.

The Rev. Dr. Cecil Chip Murray

Although I had not yet fully grasped the historical implications of this discovery, I somehow knew that communicating it to the world would be challenging, given the wealth, influence, fame, and power that this internationally treasured song had conferred on its current copyright claimants. People, who like hermit crabs, had, for more than 50 years, lived deep inside their comfortable We Shall Overcome shell and would not likely go without a fight. I felt I had embarked on a voyage to discover something America probably did not want found—that an African American woman was, in truth, the original author of We Shall Overcome, not the four Caucasian folk singers now credited. And that Louise Shropshire's sacred hymn, If My Jesus Wills, by another name, was now considered the most influential song of the 20th century.

Over the course of the next three years, I interviewed Robert Goins extensively... two to three times a day. Ultimately, I would cast my nets of exploration, research, and investigation far beyond those initial interviews, consulting and interviewing university professors, copyright experts, attorneys, musicologists, ministers, historians, Freedom-Marchers, folk-singers, Gospel-singers, music-publishers, copyright-administrators, personal assistants, record-producers, politicians, presidential-librarians, government-archivists, and even the FBI. In due course, I would obtain astonishing historical information from these and other irrefutable sources, but would it be enough to corroborate such a historically unprecedented claim? Could this evolve into the most controversial music copyright-infringement case in American history?

Having decided to take on this challenge, I would now set sail in search of... well, anything. Anything that could lead me to the truth. My very first expedition, however, would not only threaten to deflate my sails once again but also almost cause me to abandon ship!

## Chapter 3

# A Time to Search

*"Truth alone will endure; all the rest will be swept away before the tide of time. I must continue to bear testimony to truth even if I am forsaken by all. Mine may today be a voice in the wilderness, but it will be heard when all other voices are silenced -if it is the voice of truth."* [17]

**-Mohandas K. Gandhi**

After returning home from Robert's place, I did what many information seekers do—I ran a Google search, which led me to Wikipedia. Wikipedia is a widely used online encyclopedia that allows users and contributors to create, submit, and edit content. Its most notable and often controversial feature is that virtually anyone with access can anonymously edit its pages, which can enable unprincipled individuals to upload erroneous information for dishonorable reasons. In today's age of instant, continuous information flow, it has become increasingly challenging to find the truth amid the misinformation, disinformation, and lies found online. Sir Winston Churchill famously said, "A lie gets halfway around the world before the truth gets a chance to put his pants on."

There is much to be said for having data scrutinized and verified by many people rather than an elite few. Without unbiased discernment, the truth tends to suffer. The vast majority of Wikipedia entries are contributed by tens of thousands of volunteer, well-qualified editors who routinely check the site for errors, omissions, and misinformation. As you might imagine, this online resource is continually embroiled in controversy, but without independent alternative sources, it can be inherently unreliable as a sole academic or historical source. That said, perhaps because of the speed with which you can access its material and the seemingly infinite number of entries found there, the cyber resource is considered the most popular general reference resource in the world.

Not surprisingly, Wikipedia had a lot to say about "We Shall Overcome" and, at first glance, appeared to be a one-stop resource on the subject. Were it not for possibly

---

[17] Gangrade, K.D.; Moral Lessons From Gandhi S Autobiography And Other Essays; Concept Publishing Company; Jan 1, 2004; p. 131

incompatible information I had, I suspect I'd have found the Wikipedia content on the song more than sufficient to satisfy my informational needs. Curiously, however, everything Wikipedia had to say about We Shall Overcome seemed to have been contributed by one or more of the folk-singers currently drawing royalties from the song—Pete Seeger, Frank Hamilton, Guy Carawan, and Zilphia Horton—or, as I've come to refer to them, "The Folk-Four". At the end of its We Shall Overcome entry, Wikipedia listed its suggestions for "Further Reading". A closer look at this section revealed that all seven resources listed were either written by or contributed to by Pete Seeger, Guy Carawan, their wives, or family members. Something didn't smell right. Having worked in the music business for the better part of thirty years, I understood the tremendous financial value of music publishing and, having had my first original song published while I was still in my teens, had fallen victim to more than my share of shady characters and crooked publishing deals. I now had far more questions than answers, but felt I was on to something. I had work to do.

Not knowing exactly where this path would lead, I began interviewing Robert extensively about his grandmother, Louise Shropshire. However, because his knowledge was based primarily on the many years of oral stories shared with him, these interviews would need to be supported by additional independent sources. I began setting up meetings and interviews with various surviving members of Shropshire's family, former church members, and friends, most of whom affirmed that they had always known and believed that Louise Shropshire was the author of "We Shall Overcome." How could everyone be wrong? After seeing her lyrics for myself, I knew there was more to this than family folklore, and the possibility that someone may have infringed on Shropshire's hymn began to seem increasingly plausible. Could a song as important and well-known as "We Shall Overcome" have been stolen in plain sight? I felt I might benefit from an expert legal opinion.

After some investigation, I discovered a prominent music-copyright attorney, whom I'll refer to as "Mr. J". Mr. J was considered a "super-lawyer" in the business and was well known for having won a well-publicized music copyright-infringement case between a popular 1970s Black Funk band, and a very successful 1990s White male Pop-Singer. Mr. J. and I had been playing phone tag for a few days, and just as I was considering camping out on the doorstep of his law firm, the phone rang. I could not have anticipated the conversation we were about to have.

It was a sunny Saturday morning in California, and Mr. J was calling me from his high-performance sports car as he sped along the Pacific Coast Highway toward Malibu for breakfast. I thanked him for returning my call on a weekend, then gave him the rundown. Without naming names, I provided a brief overview of the circumstances and nature of the situation. At first, he, like many to follow, expressed genuine interest in the prospect of a provable, profitable, and newsworthy undertaking. However, when I told him that the song in question was *"We Shall Overcome"* and that I suspected it had, in fact, been written by an African American woman, not Pete Seeger, he appeared to downshift. When I suggested that the potential case would likely implicate Seeger and his publishing company for plagiarizing the legendary protest song, he lost it. Mr. J launched a minor tirade—citing Pete Seeger's many honors, accolades, and achievements—and rebuked me for "attempting to tarnish Pete Seeger's legacy." He continued, referring to Seeger as a "legend" and even hurling the classic: "How dare you!!" at me. By Mr. J's reaction, it was clear to me that, quite inadvertently, I had touched the "third rail" of American history, politics, and ideology—race.

Mr. J then declared, "No copyright attorney worth a damn would take this case for less than a six-figure retainer." Surprisingly, however, for all his indignation, he managed to include himself in that 'worth-a-damn' category—asking whether I wanted to "move forward" with the case. Now, as a general rule, I am considerably slow to anger, but let's just say I declined his generous proposal and, remembering he had a date with a plate of eggs, decided it was best not to take up any more of his time.

It was now very clear to me how difficult it must be for a person with little money or education to vigorously defend their intellectual property rights, a vulnerability that, for many generations, would enable a parasitic feeding frenzy of misappropriation and exploitation of African American music and culture. My voyage of discovery had already carried me far from home, but after my conversation with the attorney, I had passed my point of no return. I knew now that the truth I sought to unearth would not be welcomed by everyone, and the explosive cargo I now possessed carried with it the potential to trigger and engage volatile racial sensibilities and undercurrents. After taking the rest of the day to process Mr. J's remarks, I understood more than ever the need to responsibly collect, examine, and protect the information I had exhumed, and whatever more was to come. I had to consider that for over a century, White men of great power and influence had, with a great sense of entitlement and impunity, freely plundered African American cultural assets and treasures. We Shall Overcome and its principal propagator, Pete Seeger, had become as prized a part of America's whitewashed history and self-image as the Star-Spangled Banner. And perhaps for this reason, the song's provenance had never been seriously questioned or challenged. To do so would require faith, endurance, and resolve, tempered by patience, understanding, and a dogged commitment to learning everything I could about this hallowed hymn's true historical background.

# Chapter 4

# A Time to Mend

*"Facts are stubborn things; and whatever may be our wishes, our inclinations, or the dictates of our passions, they cannot alter the state of facts and evidence…"*
**~ John Quincy Adams**

In researching a particular subject, context, and objectivity are vital to a rational understanding of the relevant facts and other information to be considered or evaluated. Without these elements, you cannot truly form an educated, unbiased conclusion or claim to have *true* knowledge or understanding of the subject. To illustrate this point, consider these two suggestive hypothetical headlines:

*"Girl Kills Old Woman on First Day in New City"* and

*"Girl Kills Again—This Time with Three Accomplices"*[18]

These two headlines appear to suggest a serial killer on the loose; however, what you just read are factual descriptions of events dramatized by the character *Dorothy* in the MGM musical *The Wizard of Oz*. Without the proper context, however, these words suggest an entirely different idea from the story's intended narrative.

Given America's history of oppression, subjugation, and discrimination, I understood that without an appropriate historical context to support my findings, it would be irresponsible to propagate the extraordinary and, in some cases, shocking revelations contained in these pages. This realization made it necessary that I address the truth about the song's powerful connection to Africa, slavery, and God.

To be certain, however, examining these skeletons in America's closet would mean revisiting some difficult and indefensible chapters of its past. This process would not and perhaps *should not* be painless, as the concealed, scarred back of America's past had now

---

[18] Source: Marin County (California) newspaper's TV listing for "The Wizard of Oz"

become infected—left unhealed and untreated. In the case of We Shall Overcome, the lies, half-truths, and omissions fed to the American people by its rock stars and folk heroes had burrowed deep into the American psyche.

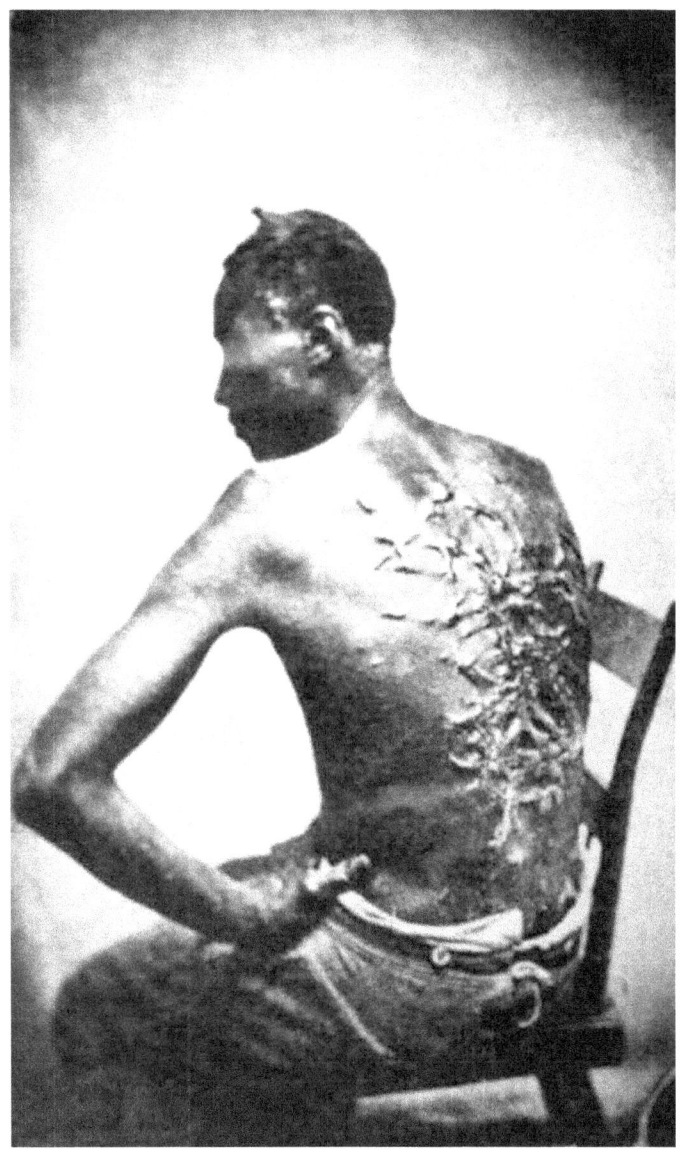

The bullwhipped back of an unknown American Slave/ Baton Rouge 1863, Library of Congress / War Department/National Archives, via Time & Life Pictures, via Getty Images

## No Direction Home

Researching Louise Shropshire's ancestry was deeply disheartening, as, like most African Americans, she had virtually no official records of her family history prior to the 1870 census, a mere seven years after the Emancipation Proclamation.

In the American South, prior to the abolition of slavery, African slaves were not considered human and therefore were not deemed worthy of the same degree of human treatment or consideration as Whites. With few exceptions, no vital records, i.e., birth, marriage, or death certificates, were recorded at the time, as they were not considered legally legitimate. As a result, I had to rely heavily on oral history, photographs, funeral programs, family records, and other family keepsakes to gain background on Louise Shropshire's ancestral past. Unlike most White Americans, few African Americans find trails that lead back to their ancestors without ending with slavery and fading into disenchantment, discouraging many from ever searching at all.

In America, the very popular genealogical research website, **Ancestry.com** dedicates five entire sentences to this topic:

"1870 is a critical date for researchers of African American genealogy. It represents the beginning of an extremely difficult research period: the pre-1870 world of enslaved African Americans. Success in researching this period actually depends on how thoroughly one has researched records created after 1870. The researcher must use every available post-1870 source to work methodically back in time from the present to build a strong foundation of evidence before trying to conduct pre-1870 work. [-Merely] using census records, as many novices do, is not enough."[19]

I didn't expect it to be easy to search for remnants of Louise Shropshire's past, but I was taken aback by this particular hindrance. I found this disproportionate lack of Black ancestral genealogical material sad, dehumanizing, and disheartening. In a world where DNA tests are used to establish paternity and free unjustly accused prisoners, why hasn't America done more to help Black people recover the precious fragments of their scattered cultural legacies? Why hasn't America begun to atone for its actions?

I considered that slavery was more than just a part of America's past, but part of *its* ancestry, and that the mindsets that enabled American slavery to exist in the first place were akin to what may have led to We Shall Overcome being misappropriated. Were oppression, injustice, and exploitation genetic strands of America's DNA? Perhaps this was more than a simple case of literary theft.

# The Hallmark Moment

---

[19] Source: Ancestry.com; http://www.ancestry.com/wiki/index.php?title=Overview_of_African_American_Research

Five months after President Barack Obama's 2009 inauguration, Iowa Democratic Senator Tom Harkin, a White man, called for a measure before the U.S. Senate, apologizing to the descendants of 4 million enslaved Black people for slavery and for the racist and repressive Jim Crow laws that followed. Harkin's resolution affirmed:

*"A national apology by the representative body of the people is a necessary collective response to a past collective injustice… So, it is both appropriate and imperative that Congress fulfill its moral obligation and officially apologize for slavery and Jim Crow laws."*[20]

The Senate passed the resolution by a voice vote, an anonymous voting method often used by legislators seeking political secrecy when voting on a controversial measure. When a voice vote is used, no identifying names or numbers of its participants are recorded. Harkin's resolution specified that the congressional "apology" was made to African Americans on behalf of the people of the United States for *"the wrongs committed against them and their ancestors"*; however, the resolution drew sharp criticism for a condition that accompanied it, stipulating:

*"…nothing in this resolution authorizes or supports any claim against the United States; or serves as a settlement of any claim against the United States."*[21]

-In other words, **there would be no reparations**.

Surprisingly, few African Americans I questioned about this resolution were even aware of it, and those who were did not appear affected by it. Initially, I found this unresponsiveness confusing and, frankly, a little disturbing. Before long, however, I would come to understand it much better.

As I began sharing the story of Louise Shropshire and "We Shall Overcome," I encountered generally low enthusiasm among the very people I thought would embrace this remarkable story. However, I later discovered this was not a case of simple indifference. I came to understand that "We Shall Overcome" evoked a particular chapter in American history that many, if not most, Black Americans found too painful and disheartening to revisit. It was as though the heart-crushing murder of Black America's noblest hero, the Rev. Dr. Martin Luther King Jr., was an emotional wound still unhealed in their hearts and minds.

Perhaps, like slavery, Dr. King's brutal, racially motivated assassination by a White man was perceived as a heavy blow to their own minds and spirits, a curse upon their futures and those of their children, and a mockery of their hopes and dreams. Perhaps their tragic hero's zealous goal to achieve love, brotherhood, compassion, understanding, and equality through nonviolent dissent extended beyond the reach of human nature and exposed this great Black leader's worldly, fatal flaw; his unwavering belief in the teachings of Jesus Christ, who taught that the only way to achieve true peace and fulfill God's will

---

[20] Warshauer, Matthew; Civil War: Slavery, Sacrifice, and Survival; Wesleyan University Press; Apr 4, 2011; p. 221.
[21] Source: US Senate Judiciary Report; US Senate Apologizes for Slavery; June 19, 2009; http://www.judiciaryreport.com/us_senate_apologizes_for_slavery.htm

was to actively demonstrate love for one another and one's enemies through acts of compassion, self-denial, faith, and forgiveness.[22]

After all, if Dr. King could fall to the devil's foil, why *should* African Americans hope for a happy ending to Louise Shropshire's story—a woman who, like Dr. King, lived faithfully by the teachings of Jesus Christ? Was this quest for justice tethered to Dr. King's dream? And was the intoxication of hope worth the hangover of failure and disillusionment? I wondered whether every hateful lash of abuse, violence, discrimination, and bigotry—like open welts on a young slave's back—had left scars of doubt and cynicism among American Blacks, causing so many to give up on so many dreams, or, in many cases, not dream at all.

Would Louise Shropshire's story have a different ending? Was there palpable, justifiable hope that the world was any different now than when Dr. King was struck down? To be certain, New generations of Americans, White and Black, have never learned to hate or discriminate against each other to the degree that their forefathers may have, but was that enough for real change to emerge and grow from America's festering past?

Perhaps the election of Barack Obama had signaled a new era and a new promise. Perhaps the "arc of the moral universe" Dr. King spoke of had finally begun its bend towards justice. And perhaps it was time for African Americans to reignite a torch that was snuffed out on the balcony of the Lorraine Motel.

In the words of American author and poet **Maya Angelou**:

*"I can be changed by what happens to me, but I refuse to be reduced by it."*

I came to understand that Louise Shropshire's powerful narrative of injustice, adversity, and inequity was still, for many African Americans, a deeply painful recollection. I also realized that this condition could at least partially explain how the knowledge I now possessed had remained suppressed all these years.

These realizations caused me to reflect on Senator Tom Harkin's 2009 resolution and contemplate the answer to an important question: If, by the U.S. Congress's unanimous admission, slavery and injustice had been committed against African Americans by the United States, how could a simple apology alone be considered an execution of justice or a fulfillment of America's so-called "moral obligation"? Since when has America, or the world, for that matter, accepted simple regret as atonement for acts involving kidnapping, torture, murder, false imprisonment, and rape? Aren't these universally considered atrocities of the lowest order?

Among other things, Harkin's "non-binding" resolution states:

*"African Americans continued to suffer from the consequences of slavery and Jim Crow—long after both systems were formally abolished—through enormous damage and*

---

[22] Source: The Holy Bible; Galatians 5:22-23, Matthew 5:44, Colossians 3:13

*loss, both tangible and intangible, including the loss of human dignity and liberty, the frustration of careers and professional lives, and the long-term loss of income and opportunity,"* [23]

Don't get me wrong; a genuine admission of guilt would have been a step in the right direction. However, without remediation, Harkin's proposition is disingenuous at best—nothing more than lip service and rather worthless to American Blacks. If contrition were the honest sentiment of the U.S. government, reparations would have been proposed. After all, isn't the "long-term loss of income" quantifiable in a personal-injury lawsuit? This is America, isn't it? To simply say I'm sorry and walk away as if slavery never happened is insulting and condescending to all Americans. At the very least, the so-called "loss of human dignity" has resulted in the near annihilation of the two-parent African American family. – You break it…you buy it…this is America. Without offering reparations, Senator Harkin's proposition was nothing more than banal political showboating…never intended to heal such a deep wound. –But it gets deeper.

We must insist that our congressional representatives explain the following:
On August 10, 1988, President Ronald Reagan signed the *"Civil Liberties Act of 1988"* into law. This legislation, passed by Congress, effectively apologized to Japanese Americans on behalf of the U.S. government for the internment of approximately 150,000 Japanese Americans in prison camps during World War II. The legislation acknowledged that America's actions were based on *"race, prejudice, war hysteria, and a failure of political leadership."* As a result, the U.S. government approved and disbursed more than $1.6 billion in reparations to former Japanese American internees and the heirs of those deceased. Each eligible claimant was paid approximately twenty thousand dollars.

Years later, President George H. W. Bush would offer the following written apology to these same people:

*"A monetary sum and words alone cannot restore lost years or erase painful memories; neither can they fully convey our Nation's resolve to rectify injustice and to uphold the rights of individuals. We can never fully right the wrongs of the past. But we can take a clear stand for justice and recognize that serious injustices were done to Japanese Americans during World War 11. In enacting a law calling for restitution and offering a sincere apology, your fellow Americans have, in a very real sense, renewed their traditional commitment to the ideals of freedom, equality, and justice. You and your family have our best wishes for the future."* [24]

With no disregard for the cruelties suffered by Japanese Americans, were not the nearly three centuries of atrocities endured by African American slaves more deeply devastating? *Why*, then, is America, having admitted to the profound physical, psychological, and economic damage done to African American slaves and their

---

[23] Source: US Senate Judiciary Report; US Senate Apologizes for Slavery; June 19, 2009;
http://www.judiciaryreport.com/us_senate_apologizes_for_slavery.htm

[24] Murphy, Sean D.; United States Practice in International Law: 1999-2001; Cambridge University Press, 2002; p. 98.

descendants, unwilling to provide Blacks with reparative atonement for its actions, as it did with WWII internees? As far as the U.S. government is concerned, are Japanese Americans somehow more worthy of restitution than Blacks? The likely truth is yes, and unfortunately, many U.S. politicians are unwilling to address financial remediation related to slavery for fear it would prove polarizing to their political party and detrimental to their political careers. Ultimately, however, the cost of not doing so will prove far greater.

> *"Find out just what any people will quietly submit to, and you have the exact measure of the injustice and wrong which will be imposed on them."*
>
> **~Frederick Douglass**

In 2003, during a visit to Goree Island in Senegal, Africa, a port from which hundreds of thousands of enslaved people were shipped to America, President George W. Bush declared slavery "One of the greatest crimes in history," adding: "Liberty and life were stolen and sold." I suppose it is unreasonable to expect the United States of America to penalize itself for the atrocities it has committed and admitted to, but perhaps there is an alternative solution.

# ACTION ITEM # 1: REPARATIONS

## The United States African American Restoration Act

As a meaningful gesture of atonement, I propose that the U.S. Congress, having openly acknowledged responsibility for the generational damage caused by slavery, sponsor and pass the U.S. African American Restoration Act.

### "The U. S. African American Restoration Act

Experts worldwide agree that education is the key to cultural transformation. African Americans are not a broken people in need of reparation; they are a distressed, oppressed, and suffering people in need of restoration. To survive and prosper, African Americans must build their own futures on a deeply embedded foundation of education—something that has been systematically denied them since their abduction from Africa.

The devastating generational byproducts of slavery in America are well documented and have resulted in crippling emotional and psychological damage to the descendants of those once thriving Africans, who were kidnapped, brutalized, and enslaved for profit. The vestiges of Slavery in America have now manifested themselves into mass incarcerations, noxious racial polarization, and profound damage to the overall psychological and ideological state of the African American people.

Among other effects, the malignant horrors of slavery, Jim Crow, and institutional racism in the U.S. have metastasized into a five-to-one ratio of incarcerated Black men to Caucasian men (according to the U.S. Bureau of Justice Statistics). Countless studies have shown that African Americans do not commit more crimes than White Americans. However, due to racial profiling by police, African Americans are arrested and incarcerated at far higher rates than non-African Americans, decimating the lives and futures of their descendants.

Although African Americans make up roughly 14 percent of the U.S. population, they make up nearly 40 percent of America's prison population. These statistics should be a clear sign to all Americans that something is terribly wrong—that more than 150 years after the Emancipation Proclamation, Black Americans are still under the yoke of racial bias, marginalization, abuse, discrimination, and oppression. Disturbingly, in a 2014 study published in the journal Psychological Science, Stanford University psychology researchers Rebecca Hetey and Jennifer Eberhardt found that *"White participants who were exposed to higher racial disparities in incarceration rates reported being more afraid of crime and more likely to support the kinds of punitive policies that exacerbate these racial disparities."*

So now what? If seeing more African American men in prison makes White Americans more fearful of Black people, how can these truths set America free from racial and economic inequality? Perhaps this explains why H.R. 40, the so-called "reparations bill' sponsored by Rep. John Conyers of Detroit, Michigan, which sought to study the effects of slavery on African Americans, has, for nearly 40 years, been effectively ignored by Congress—a Congress, according to Pew Research, that, as of 2025, was 74 percent White.

In presenting his bill to Congress, Senator Tom Harkin added the following:

*"While the reconstruction amendments, the 13th amendment banning slavery, the 14th amendment granting full citizenship to all slaves, and the 15th amendment guaranteeing the right to vote supposedly signaled equality for all, widespread oppression continued. Jim Crow laws, African-Americans were denied voting rights, denied employment opportunities, denied access to public accommodations, denied entry into military service, denied criminal justice protections, denied housing, denied education, denied police protection, denied due process. In short, denied their very humanity.*

*"Not until the passage of the Civil Rights Act of 1964 and the Voting Rights Act of 1965 and other federal protections did legal -- legal -- segregation effectively cease in this country. The destructive effects of both slavery and Jim Crow remain, however. As President Bush noted, 'the racial bigotry did not end with slavery.' President Clinton stated that the racial divide is 'America's constant curse.' Today many African-Americans remained mired in poverty. Average incomes remain below that of white Americans. There remains an achievement gap in education and, for many, health conditions. African-Americans bear a disproportionate burden of disease and injury and death and disability. African-Americans are more over disproportionately involved with the criminal justice system in our prisons."*

I propose that the U.S. government, having admitted responsibility for the generational damage caused by slavery, fully underwrite the post-secondary education of ALL African Americans for a period of 40 years. Regardless of age and at no cost to African Americans, this federally funded program will, without prejudice, provide full academic scholarships, books, and materials to all African Americans with a high school diploma, G.E.D., or equivalency certificate for post-secondary and vocational institutions.

As a meaningful gesture of contrition and atonement by the US for the atrocities of slavery, once passed, the "U.S. AFRICAN AMERICAN RESTORATION ACT" will restore the hope, lives, fortunes, and futures of American Blacks by providing college and vocational scholarship vouchers, rather than direct cash disbursements. This historic legislation will, among other things, save US taxpayers billions of dollars by furnishing African Americans with the educational resources they need to take advantage of educational opportunities and truly overcome the historical denial of such resources. –Resources necessary to restore all African Americans willing and able to put in the time to study and train, to their earned positions of cultural relevance, generational productivity, prosperity, and self-sustainability.

To be clear, once passed, this historic legislation will not represent a "free" education for Blacks. These proposed entitlements have already been paid for in full with the blood sweat and tears of those African Americans enslaved, abused, murdered, exploited and dishonored in the US. Moreover, this act will require a full and sustained scholastic commitment from each recipient, who, to redeem scholarship benefits, must attend classes and/or training and earn passing grades. By signing this bill into law, the US government can finally, meaningfully atone for the atrocities committed against Black Americans, and in doing so, exchange an abominable past for a bright future. -At long last, a quality education for all Blacks will become a reality. This is the "Promised Land" for African Americans, as Rev. Dr. Martin Luther King Jr. called it. We are still one nation under God, and this is the righteous, just, and moral thing to do.

*"The Negro has no room to make any substantial compromises because his store of advantages is too small. He must press unrelentingly for quality, integrated education, or his whole drive for freedom will be undermined by the absence of a most vital and indispensable element—learning."*   -Martin Luther King, Jr.

There is strong evidence that new generations of enlightened Americans of all colors and ethnicities will support this just legislation and think and act for themselves in electing those who support it. However, given the US's long history of bigotry, racism, and exploitation, it would be foolish to assume that all Americans will support it. Such an unprecedented initiative will never take place without the strength and resilience needed to endure struggle, sacrifice, and suffering. Without unrelenting, non-violent action, manifested through voting, boycotts, protests, and other effective methods to access and leverage the considerable political and economic power of African Americans, the caged bird's song alone will not liberate her.

We Shall Overcome: Sacred Song on the Devil's Tongue

☙

# Chapter 5

# Circling the Drain

*"It is easier to build strong children than to repair broken men."*
-Fredrick Douglass

As difficult as it was to admit, I had to accept that the misappropriation of a song as culturally significant as We Shall Overcome was likely motivated by forces that have plagued America since its inception—racism and greed. Racism could explain why Louise Shropshire's sacred hymn was not considered off-limits to its abductors in the first place, and greed explained the rest. It wasn't the first time in American history that men have risen to wealth by exploiting Black people.

In America, the country that once invoked religious ideals to justify its independence from Mother England, capitalism is now king. Times have changed since the Revolutionary War, and what was once submission to the laws of God has been replaced by the principles of wealth accumulation. The profit motive reigns supreme, and anything that gets in its way, including truth, equality, and justice, is often slain under the weight of power, self-indulgence, and selfish ambition.

Under just circumstances, any man looking to make his fortune would employ his *own* or fairly paid labor as a means to achieving his ambitions. Such was not the case with American slavery. White slave owners, not believing that Black men, women, and children were their equals, chose to exploit *their* unpaid labor instead. Was this not also what was done with We Shall Overcome?

For the most part, I had always understood that the enslavement of Black men, women, and children in America was very much about racism and greed, but I was now beginning to recognize how the acts of Pete Seeger and his comrades may not have been much different.

American slavery caused *profound* generational damage, not just to the enslaved themselves but also to their descendants and the future psychological, cultural, and emotional well-being of the African American family model. But what effect did American slavery have on future generations of *White* Americans? This bloody, profitable era of American economic growth at the expense of Black people seems to have left a savory taste in the jowls of future American profiteers. Perhaps this was due to White America's belief that African Americans were not their equals—a belief put forth in one of the US's most celebrated documents.

As beloved and revered as it may be, the US Constitution did not even define Black people as people. In 1857, Supreme Court Chief Justice Roger B. Taney ruled that the US Constitution had been written for Whites only and that Black people were not citizens and *"had no rights which the white man was bound to respect."* Additionally, Justice Taney stated:

*"In the opinion of the court, the legislation and histories of the times, and the language used in the Declaration of Independence, show that neither the class of persons who had been imported as slaves, nor their descendants, whether they had become free or not, intended to be included in the general words used in that memorable instrument."*[25]

Ok... 1857 was a long time ago, but these attitudes, passed down from generation to generation, still exist in the minds and hearts of many Americans. For Black Americans, the end result has been social, economic, and cultural devastation. By the time the stench and horrors of slavery had abated, the African American family was in ruins... shattered and scattered into millions of pieces.

Government statistics show that approximately 70 percent of African American children are born to unmarried mothers, most of whom also grew up in fatherless homes. These women are heavily burdened with economic and emotional responsibilities, which, in a pre-slavery West African patrilineal society, would have been shared with the village and the birth father. Statistics further associated with the lack of a father figure are shocking:

- **63 percent of youth suicide victims come from fatherless homes**
- **90 percent of all homeless and runaway children come from fatherless homes**
- **80 percent of rapists with anger problems come from fatherless homes**
- **71 percent of all high-school dropouts come from fatherless homes**
- **85 percent of all youths in prison come from fatherless homes**

(Source: U.S. D.H.H.S., Bureau of the Census)

These alarming figures disproportionately affect African American households and are the malignant, congenital byproducts of racism and greed.

In 2009, Black non-Hispanic males were incarcerated at a rate of 5,525 inmates per 100,000 U.S. residents of the same race and gender. By comparison, White males were incarcerated at a rate of 671 inmates per 100,000 U.S. residents of the same race and

---

[25] Lane Sr., Ambrose I.; For Whites Only; How and Why America Became a Racist Nation; AuthorHouse, Nov 5, 2008; p, 33-34.

gender, and Hispanic males at a rate of 1,146 inmates per 100,000 U.S. residents of the same race and gender.

**African Americans Encarcerated in America**

America's Prisoners per 100,000 Population, by Race 2010 (males only)

Source: U.S. Bureau of Justice Statistics / Public Policy Institute of California

These statistics graphically illustrate that African American men are dramatically more likely to be imprisoned than other racial or ethnic groups in America. Author Michelle Alexander, in her book "The New Jim Crow: Mass Incarceration in the Age of Colorblindness," notes that more African Americans are in the penal system now, either in prison, on probation, or on parole, than were enslaved in 1850. It cannot be denied that these shocking indicators are symptomatic of the generational effects of slavery, unless, of course, you believe that Blacks are somehow genetically predisposed to criminality.

I've also found that many African Americans suffer from yet another form of emotional and psychological damage, causing them to sever the social, cultural, and economic ties that bind other successful cultures. As a result of the negative consequences imposed on American slaves for helping one another escape from bondage or avoid abuse on the plantation, Blacks in America struggle to foster a sense of political and economic loyalty to one another that could lead to the merging of their knowledge, experience, and resources to achieve economic and political influence.

Most African American adults have heard the well-known "Crabs in a Barrel" parable. One version of it goes something like this:

Two men are standing on a pier after each has caught a huge barrel full of live crabs. Neither barrel is covered. The first man is having great difficulty, as his crabs keep crawling out of the top of their barrel and scattering all over the pier. On the other hand, not one of the second man's crabs has crawled out of its barrel. Unable to ignore this phenomenon, the first man asks the second man to share his secret for keeping *his* crabs in their barrel. The second man replies:

*"It's really quite simple... your crabs are white crabs and, not wanting to be boiled alive, simply make their escape up and out of the barrel as quickly as possible. My crabs, on the other hand, are black crabs... when one gets to the top of the barrel, the others claw him back down, trying to get themselves out."*

For far too many African Americans, climbing out of poverty and hopelessness has become extremely difficult. As a product of slavery and its repressive aftermath, many African Americans have developed a self-preserving *"I got mine—you get yours"* mentality, resulting in the mistaken belief that, in order to achieve financial success, they must claw their way to the top of the barrel at the expense of leaving others behind.

# The Wash

In 1994, I was approached by an African American businessman seeking assistance with his struggling car wash in Culver City, California. With 55 employees, the once-successful business was on the brink of bankruptcy and needed help—fast. The car wash was composed primarily of African American employees, most of whom could not find employment elsewhere due to felony or misdemeanor convictions. There were also five or six Latino employees. The owner and I negotiated my compensation and terms of employment, which included a measure of autonomy over the car wash's financial, human resources, and operational decisions. As a contracted "Takeover Specialist," I immediately assumed the role of interim general manager of the business.

The very next day, I called a meeting with all 55 employees, during which I introduced myself and my objectives. I communicated my intent to carefully observe each worker's work ethic and skill level over the next two months, then promote, retain, or discharge employees accordingly. I received very little response or reaction to my announcement and was asked no questions. I didn't know how long it would take to turn this business around, but I knew it wouldn't happen overnight.

I was a single parent of three at the time and, to maximize time with my kids, chose to move to an apartment complex next door to the car wash. With support from a wonderful nanny, I worked 10-hour days, seven days a week, for the next two months, observing, learning, and practicing every function of the car wash's daily operations. From taking orders, vacuuming interiors, and scrubbing tires to drying, detailing, and cashiering, you name it—I did it all, side by side with the other workers.

During this two-month assessment period, I was the first to arrive and the last to leave. This helped me not only learn the business but also earn the respect and friendship of the other employees while trying my best to identify the true source of the car wash's problem. It didn't take long for me to recognize that one of the core factors contributing to the business's distress was its owner.

To begin with, the employees, almost all of whom had children, had no work schedules. The acting manager, a real tyrant, would simply hand-pick his favorite workers from whoever happened to show up that morning. Except for himself, none of the other 54 employees knew how many hours, if any, they might work in any given day or week. In addition, none were given enough hours to receive any health benefits whatsoever. Adding to all the other morale issues, the employees were given *only one* blue t-shirt, bearing the car wash's name and logo, and told to wear their own black pants to complete the required uniform. Not surprisingly, most of the employees' t-shirts and pants were faded, frayed, tattered, and torn from being washed three or more times a week. Others were simply wrinkled and filthy from being laundered much less often. This was truly bad business.

The second critical issue I encountered was that most of these 55 employees weren't very good employees at all. All the way down the line, I witnessed everything from unbelievable rudeness and disrespect toward customers to workers stealing coins and valuables from cars, doling out free washes to their friends, pocketing cash for extra services, and leaving inexpensive vehicles spotted out in the sun while spending twice as much time on luxury automobiles (hoping for higher tips). The list went on and on. Well, I had seen enough and knew what had to be done.

At the end of the initial two-month period, I called ten employees into my office—workers who had demonstrated to me a strong work ethic, a positive attitude, and/or strong leadership skills. I sincerely thanked them for their exceptional service to the company and then promoted each to a supervisory position. These positions were accompanied by a pay increase. I then informed them that by the end of the day, they would be the *only* employees left at the car wash. There was a distinct reaction to *this* statement, as many of the other employees were close friends of these ten. I spent the rest of the day calling the remaining staff into my office one at a time, and when the smoke had cleared, I had discharged 45 of the car wash's 55 workers, giving each a detailed explanation of why. Prior to their leaving, however, I informed some of them that I would offer them another chance and that if they were willing to show up bright and early the next morning with new attitudes, I would rehire them.

The next morning, to everyone's surprise, about thirty of the forty-five previously-fired employees returned to work and, as promised, were re-hired. The previous manager was asked to return. Next, I handed out a weekly work schedule, which granted hours to employees based on work performance, punctuality, and customer service. –Something they never had before. But I had one more surprise in store.

To the "new" staff's delight (and the owner's frustration), I had ordered 110 crisp, new powder-blue jumpsuits emblazoned with the Car Wash's red logo across the chest and shoulders. For me, this relatively small investment yielded the greatest return, as my new crew was now a proud, cohesive team that worked together effectively, efficiently, and harmoniously. A few months later, an Inglewood superior-court judge decided to patronize the car wash after hearing about it from a parolee employed there. After witnessing firsthand the pride, competency, and organization demonstrated by the 40 mostly African American workers, the judge approached me and confessed that had she not seen it with her own eyes, she would not have thought it possible, given the criminal histories of many of these men and women.

Soon, things really started picking up. Weekends at the car wash were a sight to behold, with celebrities, professional athletes, businesspeople, high-rollers, and neighbors coming from all over to patronize it. People came to see and be seen, snack and chat, listen to soul music, and relax while their cars were attended to by the well-groomed, friendly, highly motivated, and proud staff. This Black-owned and operated business became well known around town and was the pride of Los Angeles, with some patrons coming as far as 20 miles away to partake in this very unique car-wash experience.

One of the car wash's regular patrons, filmmaker and rap-music producer "DJ Pooh," appeared inspired there and spoke with the owner on several occasions about producing a car-wash movie. A few years later, he wrote, produced, and directed the film *"The Wash,"* starring rappers Snoop Dogg and Dr. Dre. In the film, the workers wore the same powder-blue jumpsuits. As a result of the incredible employees there, within twelve months the car wash had gone from redlining to very much "in the black."

Thrilled by his business's financial turnaround, the owner of the car wash called me in for a meeting, during which he commended me for my efforts and, to my absolute astonishment, then stated the following:

"You've done a good job, Isaias, and we're making money now, but you know, I've been thinking…we're paying these "niggas" too much. We need to get some Mexicans in here who will work "under the table" for less and not complain as much." I didn't see that one coming. For once, I was speechless.

He then asked me to fire a disabled African American employee whom I had hired to perform light janitorial work a few days a week, saying the man wasn't "pulling his weight".

During that meeting and over the next few days, I fought hard to convince the owner of the many reasons he should reconsider. I reminded him of the many benefits to the African American community of allowing these well-trained workers to keep their jobs and feed their families. Unfortunately, my appeals fell on deaf ears. Soon afterward, I relinquished control of the car wash, said goodbye to the employees, and moved on with my life. A little more than a year later, the car wash went bankrupt and closed its doors. Although there are numerous noteworthy exceptions, it was all about the money for this owner, not about helping others succeed.

Aside from a deficiency in character, I witnessed how ill-equipped this particular business owner was to meet the needs of his 45 African American employees—men and women from broken families who, as a result of neglect and a scarcity of positive role models, became America's walking wounded. Without help and support, they lacked the social, economic, and emotional tools needed to rebuild their lives and escape a cycle of poverty and despair—a perpetuating legacy likely passed down to their descendants.

## Crippling Affects

Louise Shropshire's hymn was composed to spread the Gospel and help her distressed brothers and sisters bear and overcome the anguish of hatred and discrimination that wounded their hearts, minds, and spirits. It seems Pete Seeger and his associates saw no value in helping African Americans through these spiritual attributes. They weren't the first.

One of the most influential Black activists and intellectuals of the 20th century, **W.E.B. Dubois** held that slavery was the fundamental cause of social disorganization among Black families. He also recognized important differences between the familial structures of slaves selected as house servants and those of field workers. In addition, Dubois noted that the religious and marriage rites of slaves among the families of the domestic servants, although not legally acknowledged, were much more valued and even encouraged by slave owners than those of field hands. This was not necessarily beneficial. In many cases, house servants became objects of their master's regard and were treated with so-called "affections" not unlike those given to a family pet. Among *female* slaves, however, there was generally the likelihood that these "affections" on the part of slave owners would degenerate into sexual abuse and rape.

Dubois wrote that among the farm and field hands, especially those with particularly cruel and sadistic overseers, "there was no family life, no meals, no marriages, and no decency..." to say nothing of the torture and abuse. Field slaves were treated no better than plantation cattle, and on many of the larger estates, the slaves' owner was seldom, if ever, present to direct or control the treatment of field slaves, leaving them alone and helpless with their sadistic overseers.

Though it was clearly in the financial interests of the slave owner to treat his slaves better, overseers lacked the same financial motivation and self-interest as owners to dispense humane treatment to the slaves. Aggravating these conditions, slave owners would often encourage and induce the overseers to overwork the slaves during certain agricultural seasons in hopes of increasing production, of course, for greater output and higher profits. Only high character on the part of an overseer, a paradox if ever there was one, might result in less-brutal treatment of slaves on a large plantation. Typically, however, the overseer was considered one of the least principled men in the community, known for a violent disposition and an all-around low grade of character. Given full control of the plantation's agricultural slave population and without another White man for miles, an overseer could impose a living hell on plantation slaves, with no one but God to hear the cries or bear witness to the atrocities committed upon these helpless men, women, and children.

Dubois observed that the effects of slavery had a profoundly negative psychological and emotionally crippling effect on enslaved men, who lacked any real authority to lead or protect their families, adding:

*"...his wife could be made his master's concubine; his daughter could be [raped], his son whipped, or he himself sold away without being able to protest or lift a preventing finger".*[26]

W.E.B. Dubois (Courtesy US Library of Congress)

---

[26] Dubois, W.E.B. / The Negro American Family (The Atlanta University publications series)

The emasculation of the male African American slave would result in the disintegration of his former African family social organization, as well as the moral codes and values by which his African ancestors had once thrived. Even after the abolition of slavery, African Americans would remain cultural outcasts within a White social order, no longer conscious of their cultural value, purpose, or ancestry.[27] –Tragically ironic for a people from whom all civilization was born.

# Far From Home

In 1997, the skulls of two adults and one child, dating back 160,000 years, were discovered buried in the golden sands near a small Ethiopian village. These relics are still considered by experts to be the oldest human remains known to man. This historic find confirmed to the scientific world that human civilization evolved from Africa. This extraordinary discovery overruled the previously held theory that Neanderthals, thought to be direct human ancestors of European origin, were anything more than an offshoot of pre-human evolution that remained isolated in Europe. This historic find proved that the very beginnings of familial structure, culture, and civilization were African.

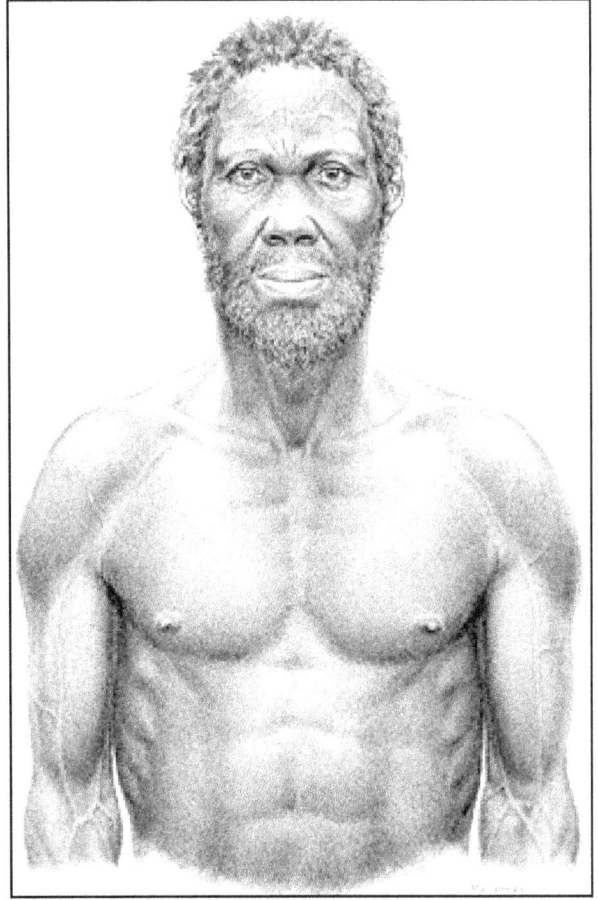

University of California, Berkley, A Reconstruction of an Adult Male Homo Sapiens / Photo: Jay Materness

---

[27] Johnson, Leanor Boulin and Staples, Robert, Black Families At The Crossroads: Challenges and Prospects; John Wiley & Sons, 2005; p. 25-26

In West and Central Africa, from where the bulk of African American slaves were kidnapped, Africans had been accustomed for thousands of years to strictly regulated family structures and rigidly enforced moral codes. These vital pillars of cultural organization helped shape their thriving civilizations and encouraged Africans to value and respect their well-established customs. However, once captured, brutalized, and transported to America by Whites, the relentless torture and dehumanization of the once-free Africans all but obliterated their sense of pride, identity, and social conduct. Within a few generations, thousands of years of tradition, social organization, and cultural sanctions were stripped from them.

For example, as mentioned earlier, American slaves were not legally permitted to marry, which rendered all slave births legally illegitimate and all slave children bastards in the eyes of Southern Whites. This resulted in a distorted value system among slaves that, by necessity, refrained from stigmatizing the offspring of slave women. This culturally and socially distorted value system persists to this day. Evidence of this is demonstrated by the nearly 70% rate of African American children born out of wedlock—a more than three-to-one ratio compared with the 22% rate of White children born out of wedlock. (Source: National Vital Statistics Report, U.S. Centers for Disease Control / 2020.)

Additional substantiation for this social ailment was found in a 2011 University of Michigan study conducted by Professor Cassandra Dorius. The study revealed that 59% of African American mothers reported children with multiple fathers, compared with 22% of White mothers and 35% of Hispanic mothers. Most of these Black women, already poorer than others, expressed little hope for a better future and, with little to no cultural support network, were more likely than women of other ethnicities to accept their socioeconomic circumstances as permanent. As a direct consequence of a value system distorted by slavery, many African American women were economically forced to submit to their circumstances.

Most people agree that it takes two emotionally and psychologically healthy parents to *best* raise a child. However, the staggering number of incarcerated African American men in America has made that goal virtually impossible to achieve in the Black community. This lack of father figures has produced a domino effect, causing millions of single African American mothers to bear the financial responsibility of raising their children alone. As a result, many of these women remain poorly educated and impoverished.

Among African American single-parent families, 31% now live in poverty, compared with 16% of Whites. This disparity is largely due to the lack of economic support from African American fathers, who, among other factors, have been disproportionately imprisoned. After release, they seldom secure employment above the minimum wage. Those fortunate enough to find work are rarely granted sufficient hours to meet their households' economic needs or to qualify for insurance benefits. As a result, African Americans "lead" the nation with an overall poverty rate of 17-20%, compared with 8-10% for Whites. (Source: US Census Statistics)

The institution and practice of slavery in America, by design, critically weakened and destabilized the pre-slavery African family model, forcing American slaves to involuntarily abandon their native cultures and adopt White-American customs by force. With no viable substitute for their African traditions, these culturally malnourished slaves were left to grovel and fight for unfamiliar, indigestible crumbs of social sustenance, dignity, and self-identity on the threshing floor of the American ethos.

By virtue of the color of their skin, following the Emancipation Proclamation, the European-based customs and sensibilities that Blacks were forced to accept would not provide the reciprocity of social acceptance and esteem usually linked with fellowship in a particular ethnic or cultural group. Like it or not, Blacks had become White America's unwanted foster-children and, through violence, abuse, segregation, and discrimination, were not allowed to forget this fact. African Americans would be fated to suffer a post-slavery legacy of destructive social and cultural disarray at the very hands of their former White captors, a legacy that exists to this very day.

Their plight, however, did not go unnoticed by some spiritually enlightened White Christian colonists from the North, whose Bible-based values and morals had not been compromised by the materialistic objectives that motivated Southern Whites to subjugate American Blacks and exploit their labor.

*"Before the victory is won, even some will have to face physical death. But if physical death is the price that some must pay to free their children from a permanent psychological death, then nothing shall be more redemptive."*
-Rev. Dr. Martin Luther King Jr.

## Chapter 6

## A Great Awakening

*"Truth, crushed to earth, shall rise again."*

**-William Cullen Bryant**

Divine inspiration in the African American church community is often channeled through songs of faith, such as Louise Shropshire's "If My Jesus Wills." Having spent many childhood Sundays in African American churches, I can attest that hymns like hers were, and still are, considered powerful vessels of ministry. In fact, in many, if not most, Black churches, the choirs spend far more time singing to the congregation than the ministers do preaching. From pulpit to pew, I've witnessed these sanctified songs mend many a suffering heart, mind, and soul with divine lyrical and melodic stitches. I can only imagine how comforting hymns such as "If My Jesus Wills" might have been to the mother of a bullwhipped slave child. These songs were God's gifts of strength and hope to a suffering people who sang prayers to God from their lips to protect them from the Devil at the whip.

Beginning in the 1730s, a worldwide religious revitalization movement known as **"The First Great Awakening"** swept the American Colonies and brought Christianity to American slaves. Publicly led by the prominent colonial-era theologian Jonathan Edwards, this important Christian movement sought to move away from ritualistic and ceremonial worship and to emphasize the importance and power of a more deeply personal and active relationship with God. In America, the movement focused heavily on the religious conversion of Black people. This was the first recognized American evangelical revival and inspired sermons of a more powerful, dramatic, and emotional style. This new style of preaching and its message of salvation breathed new life into American religion and called on Christians to become more passionately involved in their faith. Those affected by the revival began to study the Bible at home and committed themselves to a new standard of personal morality.

In the Southern colonies, revivalist Baptists and Methodist missionaries were instrumental in spreading the Word of God among enslaved people. These Baptists and Methodists, however, did not merely welcome Black members into their denominations; they also encouraged and empowered them to assume active leadership roles in the church, including deacons and preachers. By comparison, Presbyterians typically required would-be ministers to undergo formal schooling and licensing, effectively excluding Black people from leadership roles. They were also uncomfortable with what they perceived as the "excesses" of the revivals.

In Virginia, Baptist preachers challenged the established Anglican Church, which had many slave-owning members and held that the White, rich, and powerful should govern. Preachers in the movement emphasized God's covenant with America and repudiated the materialistic, corrupt practices of the affluent American colonial culture. Revivalists asserted that the source of this corruption lay in England. They also believed that severing ties with the "mother country" would bring God's blessing and rededicate America to the making of God's Kingdom. This great movement provided a new form of radical American nationalism, which, in turn, laid the foundation for the American Revolution.[28]

In the late eighteenth century, White Baptist and Methodist preachers traveled across the American South to evangelize the core Christian belief that all were equal in the sight of God. This message resonated deeply with enslaved people, offering much-needed optimism and spiritual "manna," if you will. Enslaved people, whose numbers had increased by as much as fifty percent since the early 1700s, were now overwhelmingly converting to Christian Evangelical denominations such as the Methodists and Baptists. These conversions were also motivated by the fact that, in addition to their Christian message of freedom, these denominations worshiped in ways many first-generation enslaved people found similar to West African worship patterns. This included high-spirited singing, dancing, chanting, clapping, and sometimes even spirit possession. Jesus' crucifixion also resonated deeply with enslaved people because of the similar, brutal treatment they endured.

Far from ideal, however, numerous White-controlled churches, many of which owned slaves themselves, restricted slaves' worship to segregated areas within their sanctuaries, fearing that Blacks would plot rebellion against their owners if allowed to worship independently. As if quarantined, during Sunday services, Blacks were crammed into hot, humid, overcrowded, and poorly ventilated balconies. Many Blacks considered these White churches, where ministers promoted obedience to one's master as a high religious ideal, a mockery of God's true "Gospel" message. The Gospel message, as articulated in the first four books of the New Testament, was one of love, compassion, and

---

[28] Ferguson, Robert A.; The American Enlightenment, 1750-1820; Harvard University Press, 1994; p. 18

righteousness, as demonstrated through the life and teachings of Jesus Christ. This message was certainly inconsistent with the deeds of these White men.

As they learned more about Christianity, American slaves began to feel unduly constrained in White churches and desperately longed to worship God in their own separate gatherings. Slaves wanted to sing, shout, and clap their hands, but feared punishment for doing so in White churches, where such expressions were forbidden. It was very difficult for them to feel the Christian message of brotherly love under the weight of repression and subjugation. These frustrations would ultimately motivate slaves to take their longing for independent worship into their own hands.

Newly converted slaves soon began organizing their own secret gatherings known as "Camp Meetings," "Bush Meetings," and/or "Hush Harbors." Meetings were usually held in the backwoods of the forest after dark, where they could worship exuberantly and openly practice their newly adopted religious traditions. The locations of these clandestine gatherings varied so as to avoid detection and the brutal lashing that would surely follow if they were caught praying without White supervision. Through signals, passwords, and coded communications, indiscernible to Whites, slaves summoned other newly converted believers to join them, where they would covertly incorporate African rhythms, jubilant singing, and passionate preaching into their own unique form of Christian worship. These meetings were effectively the very first African American churches and served as starlit sanctuaries of joyous worship in the cruel, heartless world of slavery. It was here that **Negro Spirituals**, with their double meanings of religious salvation and freedom, were born.[29]

It was also here that the first Black itinerant preachers, believing that God had "called" them to speak His Word, developed their unique, rhythmic, chanting sermons and colorful, extemporaneous styles of preaching. This calling, however, would come at a price, as many Black preachers were whipped and even sent to prison for preaching the Gospel to slaves. While serving as a spiritual asylum, communal jamboree, and psychological sanctuary, these spiritual gatherings would also serve as secret meeting places for organizing occasional acts of rebellion.[30]

---

[29] Source: The Christian Work and the Evangelist, Volume 88; Anonymous; Biblio Bazaar, 1923, 2011; p. 25
[30] The Black Church in the African American Experience / Lincoln, C. Eric; Mamiya, Lawrence H. / 1990/ Duke University Press; p. 1

"Camp Meeting" (Artist Unknown, Courtesy Library of Congress)

## Nat Turner

The Baptist Church continued to lead the way in welcoming Black preachers and in other roles within the church. Some of these spiritual leaders were also leaders in the fight for freedom. One such man was Nat Turner, a slave and Baptist preacher during **"The Second Great Awakening"**, an early 19th-century revival in which previously unchurched Blacks were converted to Christianity.

Nat Turner often preached and conducted Baptist services in fields and forests for fellow slaves. In 1831, he led 70 enslaved people and free Blacks in a violent rebellion, during which an estimated 60 White people were killed. Turner avoided capture for several months but was eventually caught, tried, and hanged.

Turner's hanging was lawful at the time, as the laws of the land superseded the laws of God, but in truth, he was murdered. By today's standards of justice, he and the other runaway slaves would have been justified in taking the lives of those who tried to kidnap, enslave, or kill them.

The aftermath of this violent uprising led Virginia state legislators to pass new laws strictly prohibiting the education of slaves and free blacks and to restrict the rights of assembly and other civil rights for free blacks. White ministers were now also required to be present at Black worship services. In addition, Turner's rebellion would cause Whites to feel justified in banning the education of blacks. In Lacy K. Ford's book, Deliver us from Evil: The Slavery Question in the Old South, Ford notes that Alabama, where Louise was born, had existing laws "prohibiting the education of slaves as well as free Blacks." She adds: "This ban on the education of slaves and free Blacks represented a self-conscious attempt by Alabama lawmakers to limit black literacy."

Although widely publicized for the number of whites killed, Nat Turner's rebellion was not the first carried out by slaves and certainly not the last.

"Nat Turner's Rebellion", Courtesy, U.S. Library of Congress

# Chapter 7

# Woman's Work ~ Harriet Tubman

Although the Black enslaved woman tended not to engage in outright rebellion, as Nat Turner did, there were exceptions to this rule. **Harriet Tubman** was one such exception.

Harriet Tubman / Courtesy: National Portrait Gallery

Born a slave, Araminta Ross, or "Minty" as she was called, later changed her name to Harriet after her mother. Her parents were Harriet "Rit" Green and Ben Ross. Minty and her mother, "Rit," were owned by Mary Pattison-Brodess and later by her son, Edward. Minty's father, Ben Ross, was owned by Anthony Thompson, who became Mary Pattison's second husband. When Mary Pattison-Brodess and Anthony Thompson married, they combined their slaveholdings, which is how Rit and Ben were brought together.

As a young child, Minty's mother was assigned to "the big house" as a servant and given little time to tend to her own family. This left a five-year-old Minty to care for herself, a younger brother, and a baby. By the time Minty was six years old, her owner, Mary Pattison-Brodess, recognizing Minty's ability to care for young children, hired her out as a nursemaid to a woman named "Miss Susan". This would be Minty's third job. Among other duties, Miss Susan ordered Minty to keep watch on her baby as it slept. Whenever the baby woke and cried, little Minty was whipped, sometimes four or five times before breakfast. She would carry those physical and emotional scars for the rest of her life. Minty was eventually sent back to her owner for the offense of eating a cube of Miss Susan's sugar.

Minty's mother, Rit, struggled in vain to keep her family together as slavery tore it apart. Edward Brodess, Mary's son, had sold four of Rit's daughters, separating them from their family forever. When a slave trader from Georgia approached Edward Brodess about buying Rit's youngest son, Moses, Rit was alerted by a fellow slave and, with help from other slaves, managed to hide little Moses for an entire month. One day, however, Edward Brodess and the Georgia trader surprised Rit and approached her slave quarters to seize young Moses. Upon seeing them, Harriet opened the door, stood tall, and roared, "You are after my son, but the first man that comes into my house, I will split his head open." Brodess backed away and abandoned the sale. Although Minty was too young to remember the incident, stories of it spread like wildfire and later influenced her belief in the possibility of resistance and perhaps freedom.

Rit had very little time to care for Minty because of her responsibilities in the master's house. As a result, Minty spent most of her early childhood with her maternal grandmother, Modesty, who was a great source of strength, wisdom, and inspiration. Although Minty and her mother, Rit, were born into slavery, her grandmother was born free among the great Ashanti people of West Africa before being kidnapped and brought to America.

Marriage and family were fundamental to the Ashanti's cultural existence, social structure, and communal life. An Ashanti child was said to inherit the father's soul or spirit and the mother's flesh and blood.

The Ashanti were described as a fierce, organized people whose king could assemble an army of 200,000 warriors on the battlefield and were known for their fierce resistance to British attempts to subjugate them. Ironically, the British regarded the Ashanti as one of the more "civilized" African peoples, carefully documenting their religious, familial, and legal systems. -A far and painful cry from the so-called civilization that awaited these proud African people in America.

On Minty's eleventh birthday, she would begin wearing a bright-colored cotton bandana around her head. This ritual of plantation life announced her transition to womanhood and honored traditional African customs. Minty would also take the name Harriet, after her mother. This name-changing tradition was passed down by Harriet's grandmother, Modesty, and was among the few customs to survive from her Ashanti heritage.

Harriet's intolerance of slavery eventually led her to escape north to Philadelphia, but before her flight, she secretly sent word of her plans to her beloved mother, Rit, in the form of a coded farewell song, sung to a trusted fellow slave; "I'll meet you in the morning"..."I'm bound for the Promised Land". Following her escape with the help of the network of anti-slavery activists and safe houses known as the Underground Railroad, Harriet, now a wanted fugitive, made numerous trips back into the South, personally escorting over 300 slaves to freedom. Legend has it that by 1856, the South had placed a $40,000 price on her head. - An extraordinary sum, considering Abraham Lincoln's own presidential salary was $25,000 per year.[31]

# And Still She Rose

For female slaves, early adolescence was a difficult and grim period. For many young slave girls, puberty marked not only a coming of age but also the beginning of a lifetime of physical, sexual, and emotional abuse by their masters, their masters' sons, overseers, male slaves, and others. The psychological and emotional effects of these devastating abuses would drive *some* slave women to rebel in unsettling ways. By law, any child born to a slave woman became the property of her master. In this way, slave owners would increase their slave holdings and wealth over time. Many of these newborn slave children, some of whom were the products of rape by the master, would be sold to other plantations to conceal the master's infidelities from his wife, settle debts, or simply punish an insubordinate slave.[32]

Some enslaved women, as a personal form of rebellion, resorted to infanticide...killing their infants. Some believed that in doing so, they could free their babies from the suffering and horrors of slavery. Others felt that by committing this act, they alone could decide their child's fate and deny their masters' ownership of their babies. This deeply troubling manifestation of the enslaved woman's will testified to her profound emotional scars and psychological disfigurement. It also reflected her lifelong struggle against physical and sexual abuse, oppression, and objectification by Whites.

It was clear that while enslaved, the plantation could provide no emotionally and psychologically healthy mother or father figure to the enslaved child. There was no legal wife for the enslaved man or husband for the enslaved woman. The independent Black Church would ultimately serve as an important emotional and spiritual refuge for these men, women, and children, and for their now broken, dysfunctional families. Enslaved mothers who had converted to Christianity taught and instilled in their remaining children the need to become active in the church... one of the few places where they might find surrogate male role models. Through their commitment and devotion to the Black Church, women, both enslaved and free, would pass down Bible-based morals and values, as well

---

[31] Henry Jarvis Raymond, Francis Bicknell Carpenter, Abraham Lincoln; Lincoln, his life and time; Thompson & Thomas, 1891; p. 600

[32] Lee, Debbie, Slavery and the Romantic Imagination / University of Pennsylvania Press / p. 197 / 2004

as newly developed cultural traditions. Along with this, they would also provide a sense of love and guidance from a "heavenly father" to otherwise mostly fatherless children.[33]

Black women, both enslaved *and* free, wove together their maternal love, incomparable work ethic, worldly suffering, and spiritual optimism to form a durable fabric of love, faith, and hope with which to feed, nurture, and defend present and future generations. The independent Black Church would become the communal backbone of a body of African American Christian believers and a wellspring of faith and culture for their moral and social hydration.

---

[33] Thompson, Jerry D.; Civil War to the Bloody End; The Life and Times of General Samuel P. Heintzelman; Texas A&M University Press; 2006

Baptist Congregation, Alma Plantation - False River, La., U.S. Library of Congress

# The Negro is Free

*"Dictatorship naturally arises out of democracy, and the most aggravated form of tyranny and slavery out of the most extreme liberty."*  **-Plato**

In 1863, the Emancipation Proclamation is signed into law. Although President Abraham Lincoln is hailed as "the Great Emancipator," empirical evidence shows that Lincoln could not envision a biracial America and, for more than a year after the proclamation, sought to deport newly freed slaves to British colonies in Central America and the Caribbean to work on "Free Labor Plantations."[34]

It's 1865, and Georgia Johnson, Louise Shropshire's maternal grandmother, is born on a cotton plantation in Georgia. On April 9 of the same year, Confederate General Robert E. Lee surrenders to Union Army General Ulysses S. Grant, marking the end of the American Civil War. Five days later, on April 14, 1865, Abraham Lincoln is assassinated by Confederate sympathizer John Wilkes Booth. Later that year, in response to the Emancipation Proclamation, the Ku Klux Klan is formed in Pulaski, Tennessee, by veterans of the Confederate Army.

Contrary to popular belief, the Emancipation Proclamation did not free *all* enslaved people; it applied only to those in the 11 Confederate states that had seceded from the United States. In order of secession, these states were South Carolina, Mississippi, Florida, Alabama, Georgia, Louisiana, Texas, Virginia, Arkansas, Tennessee, and North Carolina. Although there were other "slave states" besides the 11 Confederate ones, President Lincoln felt a political instinct not to provoke the so-called "border states" (Delaware, Kentucky, Maryland, and Missouri), which were still loyal to the Union, by freeing *their* slaves. By 1870, however, the ratification of the Fifteenth Amendment abolished slavery in all states. African American *men* were now informed they could legally vote…a promise that would not truly be kept for another century.

The Fifteenth Amendment was followed by the Reconstruction Era, a period between 1865 and 1877 after the Civil War, during which the U.S. economy and its social and infrastructural systems were redesigned and rebuilt. Poor, illiterate, yet skilled former slaves would now seek living wages for their labor, while many former slave owners were forced to work their own land and redefine their standards of living. This was a new and unfamiliar world for emancipated Blacks, who would now need the support of the Black Church more than ever.

Just in time, free Christian Blacks from the North would come to the rescue, welcoming former slaves into their religious communities by transplanting their newly formed independent Black churches throughout the South. Though possessed of great

---

[34] Hannings, Bud; Every Day of the Civil War; A Chronological Encyclopedia; p. 525,526; McFarland; 2010

faith, these missionaries had little notion of how to meet the many practical needs of their newly freed brethren. Their mission to organize stable religious communities proved more complex than anyone could have imagined. Nevertheless, these churches would fan out across the South in an epic endeavor to help emancipated Blacks reconstruct their lives, reunite families, find jobs, and cope with what it meant to live in the United States as free citizens rather than as personal property.

Some argued that the first "Christianization" of the American slave by the *White Christian Church* restored a sense of family and morality among them. Ironically, though, this new religion, which many Whites expected to ensure the compliance and docility of slaves, actually inspired them to reject the very essence of bondage as they came to know their true value in God's eyes, as evangelized by the very object of Christian devotion, Jesus Christ. This enormous Christian missionary campaign led to the rapid proliferation of independent black churches in the Southern states between 1865 and 1900.

Emancipation from slavery created many practical challenges for African Americans in the South. Although the Black church was of immeasurable assistance, African Americans still lacked a stable psychological, social, or cultural foundation on which to build their new way of life. There was little time now, however, to focus on what they didn't have. Now that freed Blacks could *earn* a living, they needed jobs; however, this was complicated by their distrust of Whites. This distrust hindered their efforts to communicate with prospective White employers and negotiate favorable terms for their labor. Freedom was accompanied by frightening uncertainties, as many former slaves who chose to leave their masters found themselves homeless, hungry, and with few possessions. In these uncertain times, with families to feed, many former slaves made the agonizing choice to stay on plantations, in some cases with their former masters and slave owners. In return for their labor, unscrupulous plantation owners offered them a meager yet reliable source of sustenance for their families. This promise of security from starvation and homelessness, however, would come at a high cost. To ensure their survival, many African American families chose to continue working on Southern land as sharecroppers. Louise Shropshire's kin were one such family.[35]

*"I have observed this in my experience of slavery, - that whenever my condition was improved, instead of its increasing my contentment, it only increased my desire to be free, and set me to thinking of plans to gain my freedom. I have found that, to make a contented slave, it is necessary to make a thoughtless one. It is necessary to darken his moral and mental vision, and, as far as possible, to annihilate the power of reason. He must be able to detect no inconsistencies in slavery; he must be made to feel that slavery is right; and he can be brought to that only when he ceases to be a man."*

— **Frederick Douglass**

---

[35] Rodriguez, Junius P.; Slavery in the United States; A Social, Political and Historical Encyclopedia Volume 2; p. 142; ABC-CLIO 2007

We Shall Overcome: Sacred Song on the Devil's Tongue

Frederick Douglass (Courtesy National Archives)

Isaias Gamboa

A Southern Lynching / Image: Library of Congress

# Chapter 8

## Strange Fruit

*"Southern trees bear strange fruit,*
*Blood on the leaves and blood at the root,*
*Black body swinging in the Southern breeze,*
*Strange Fruit hanging from the poplar trees.*

*Pastoral scene of the gallant South,*
*The bulging eyes and the twisted mouth,*
*Scent of magnolia, sweet and fresh,*
*Then the sudden smell of burning flesh!*

*Here is fruit for the crows to pluck,*
*For the rain to gather, for the wind to suck,*
*For the sun to rot, for the trees to drop,*
*Here is a strange and bitter crop."*
-Abel Meeropol

Nineteen thirteen is not the best of times in Coffee County, Alabama. The red Alabama clay stains the bare, hardened soles and ragged clothes of local sharecropper children. The same rust-colored earth, though, is striking against the fresh, green Alabama grass and baby-blue southern sky. Majestic Magnolia and Poplar groves crisscross the countryside and, by day, are a magnificent sight to behold. By night, however, they stand mute, bystanders to unspeakable horror, as their torch-lit trunks witness infernos of darkness and cruelty—by dawn's light, bearing the lifeless fruit of hatred and ignorance. That year, eighty-five African Americans were lynched in Alabama alone.

It is a difficult time to be born Black, but apparently no one told baby Louise Jarrett. Born February 15th, 1913, to father James "Papa" Jarrett and mother Ollie Johnson-Jarrett, respectfully known as "Big Mom". Louise is one of thirteen brothers and sisters, six of whom died at birth and were buried in an old slave cemetery near the cotton fields, but still counted.

Louise and her family are second-generation sharecroppers, a byproduct of post-Civil War Reconstruction, and, like many others before them, scrape out barely enough to survive. Millions of former slaves and their descendants entered into sharecropping contracts in which they would pay rent to former slave owners and their descendants in the form of crops and labor, in return for a share of the crops, food, and housing. These onerous agreements proved economically disastrous for Black families, as they were designed to perpetuate a cycle of dependence on the landowner and to guarantee sharecroppers a life of poverty and debt.

Sharecroppers brought to a farm, their only sought-after resource—labor. However, they needed much more than labor and land to farm and survive. They also required seed, fertilizer, mules, plows, food, clothing, and living expenses to survive until the crop was harvested. To obtain these items, they were forced to borrow heavily from the landowner, who demanded sky-high prices for everything, usually at his own high-priced plantation store. The plantation owner would then levy the debt against the poor sharecropper's share of future harvests.[36]

Although sharecropper agreements varied widely, in a typical arrangement the landowner would receive three-fourths of the crop's yield in return for the sharecropper's labor. However, by the time sharecroppers tallied their debts to the heartless landowners, most ended up not only surrendering 100 percent of the crop but also going into debt...for life. In most cases, this debt was passed on to the sharecropper's children and grandchildren. To further ensure the sharecropper's reliance on the landowner, sharecroppers were rarely paid in cash. Instead, they were paid in scrip or crudely fashioned metal tokens, which had value only at the landowner's plantation store. This made it all but impossible for a sharecropper to save money toward securing their family's financial independence. The sharecropping system bound generations of poor and illiterate Blacks to a life of poverty and hard labor and to an endless cycle of debt.

World War II and the Industrial Revolution would eventually break the sharecropping system as the United States sent 2.5 million African American men to war. Meanwhile, other Black men secured jobs in Northern shipyards and other defense-related industries. The G.I. Bill also helped dismantle the sharecropping system by providing educational opportunities and home loans to ex-servicemen after the war. Once out of the sharecropping system, few would return. Like many others, Louise Jarrett's family is barely hanging on. - Something's gotta give.

Good news! The Industrial Revolution is well underway. It's 1914, and Henry Ford's Model-T is king. Ford claims a forty-eight percent share of the automobile market, announces an unprecedented minimum wage of five dollars for an eight-hour day, and introduces a profit-sharing plan. Ford is hailed as a friend of the working man, and this news is the talk of barber shops, general stores, and cotton fields across the country. Key to Ford's success is his perfection of the assembly-line process, which allows him to assemble a complete Model T in 93 minutes. This system relies heavily on a large unskilled

---

[36] Interview with Alice Jarrett McCloud and Robert Anthony Goins Sr.; 2-22-2012; San Dimas, California

labor force, and Ford experiences high turnover among employees because the work is fast-paced, physically demanding, monotonous, and repetitive. In 1913 alone, Ford hires 52,000 workers to maintain a workforce of 14,000. No matter, though, for Papa Jarrett. This is very good news. It means JOBS and the prospect of leaving the cruel Southern existence he and his family have always known.

Ford Model-T Factory Cir. 1915 / Library of Congress

In an effort to attract Black workers from the South, many northern industries advertise for labor in Southern newspapers, and some even offer to pay moving expenses and the first month's rent. Good news travels fast. The Jarretts hear about the northern jobs, but with seven children, they are concerned whether their family could ever afford such a move. Conditions were tougher than ever, as the low-quality soils on the plantations where sharecroppers lived and worked had been depleted of nutrients from repeated plantings of cotton and other crops. This resulted in dismal harvests, and because the sharecropper was responsible to the landowner for a minimum yield, the shortfall came out of their portion. To make ends meet, many sharecropping families would travel across the Alabama-Georgia state line in search of additional agricultural work.

Rumors of blacks leaving the South and finding work in the North were spreading like wildfire. Three years would pass, though, before Louise's family, 15 in all, packed up and began their journey north to Ohio. They would travel by way of the Cincinnati Southern Railway. The Cincinnati Southern Railway featured a wood-burning locomotive and would later inspire the song "Chattanooga Choo-Choo" by Glen Miller, nicknamed for its nonstop route to Chattanooga, Tennessee.[37] It would carry them from the Northern Georgia-Alabama border all the way to Cincinnati…leaving behind the only life they had ever known.

"Colored Waiting Room" of Cincinnati's Union Terminal / Courtesy Library of Congress

---

[37] Rebecca Goodman, Barrett J. Brunsman; This Day In Ohio History; Emmis Books, Mar 1, 2005; p. 218

Cincinnati Southern Railway Locomotive / Cir. 1900 (Library of Congress)

## Deliverance

*"Following the light of the sun, we left the Old World."*

- Christopher Columbus

**"The Great Migration"** has begun, and from 1910 to 1930, two million African Americans leave the South for the Midwest and the Northeastern United States. This exodus causes a massive demographic shift across the United States, as New York, Detroit, Chicago, and Cleveland see their populations and economies grow by as much as 40 percent. The number of Black workers employed in industrial jobs nationwide doubles during this period.[38]

The Jarretts are now *former* sharecroppers, and, led by their Christian faith, they plow north into an unknown industrialized world and an uncertain future, trusting only in God's promise of guidance and provision. As is their custom, throughout their journey out

---

[38] Wilkerson, Isabel; The Warmth of Other Suns: the Epic Story of America's Great Migration; Random House Digital, Inc.; 2010; p. 190

of the South, the family sings Negro Spirituals the whole way north. They, along with extended family, find great inspiration in biblical accounts of Moses leading the Israelites from Egypt. The popular Negro Spiritual "Go Down Moses," also sung by runaway slaves for hope and inspiration, is intoned by young and old during their voyage from the bowels of the South.[39]

## "Go Down Moses"

*"When Israel was in Egypt's land,*
*Let My people go!*
*Oppressed so hard they could not stand,*
*Let My people go!*

*Go down, Moses,*
*Way down in Egypt's land;*
*Tell old Pharaoh*
*To let My people go!..."*

(author unknown)[40]

The lyrics to "Go Down, Moses" carried powerful coded messages. "Israel," for example, represented the slaves, while "Egypt" and "Pharaoh" stood for the slave owners. "Down" was understood to mean "down the Mississippi River" (in a southerly direction), where conditions for slaves were known to worsen the farther south one traveled. From this powerful association, the American idiom "selling someone down the river" was born.

With considerable help from northern Black congregations founded by freed slaves, six million Black people decided to no longer live under the racist and oppressive system of the South into which they were born. This decision would devastate the South's agricultural economy and profoundly affect American music, politics, culture, and education. The cities, districts, neighborhoods, and slums that emerged and grew as a result of the racial, social, and economic margins shaped by the Great Migration still exist today.

---

[39] Liebergen, Patrick M.; Singer's Library of Song; Medium Voice; p.143; Alfred Music Publishing; 2005

[40] http://www.sccs.swarthmore.edu/users/08/ajb/tmve/wiki100k/docs/Go_Down_Moses.html

African Americans Leaving the South during the Great Migration

Isaias Gamboa

Jarrett family listing / Inset from 1920 United States Census Report

# Chapter 9

# Amazing Grace

It's 1917, and World War I has begun. The US has declared war on Germany as the first US troops arrive in France.[41]

Louise is now four years old, and her family, having endured the long, difficult trip north from Coffee County, Alabama, has arrived in Cincinnati, Ohio. The Jarretts have traveled from Alabama with two other families, the Wades and the Whiteheads. They are met at the train station by a welcoming committee from the Tried Stone Baptist Church. The town is abuzz with activity... this is the big city, and the entire Jarrett clan is wide-eyed at the spectacle. Big Mom, needing a strong sense of assurance in these unfamiliar surroundings, finds comfort in the church to lean on. Her parents, Georgia and Robert Johnson, have also made the long, grueling trip out of the South, but both are old, with little formal education, and in no condition to work. As the rest of the family takes in the sights of Cincinnati, Big Mom takes a private moment to bow her head in a silent prayer of thanks. Papa Jarrett also takes a moment to assess the needs of his large, newly migrated family and says his own prayer. He must find a job... and fast.

With the Church's help, Louise's family finds lodging at 827 W. Fourth Street in the overcrowded "West End" of Cincinnati. The West End is a slum across from the rail yard and next to slaughterhouses and factories. Three families, totaling 17 people, occupy the run-down row house where the Jarrets live. Before long, Papa, who is also illiterate, secures a job as a factory laborer, and Big Mom, a factory packer. Both jobs require long hours and back-breaking labor, but a job is a job, and they are grateful to be able to feed and shelter their family. Migrated Blacks are often illiterate and typically offered the most difficult and lowest-paying jobs. Consequently, most of the migrated Black families find themselves living in overpopulated, filthy, and segregated slums with outdoor bathrooms and open sewers. Many of these families would descend into a mire of poverty, hopelessness, and disillusionment.[42]

Most of these severely underprivileged neighborhoods become overcrowded with disheartened, out-of-work men and women, who, in desperation, sometimes turn to crime, drugs, and alcohol to pay the bills and ease their pain. The West End is one such neighborhood. Fortunately, Louise's family is a churchgoing tribe, which helps keep the

---

[41] Lawrence Sondhaus; World War One: The Global Revolution; Cambridge University Press, Mar 31, 2011; p.259.

[42] Source: Personal Interview with Alice Jarrett McCloud; April 21, 2012 / Louise Shropshire Obituary/ Personal Interview with Thelma Jarrett; 2-22-12; Pomona, Ca.

children out of trouble…most of the time. Frolicking their way to Sunday school, Louise, along with her band of brothers, sisters, and cousins, sings church hymns all the way. Encouraged by Big Mom, this musical family also sings as they scrub clothes on washboards and sweep the floors of their overcrowded row house. Holidays are also filled with melody and verse as Louise and her family sing to celebrate Easter and Thanksgiving, and on Christmas Eve, they join hands to share choruses of "Nearer My God to Thee".

There were times, though, when the Jarrett boys got out of hand, especially Louise's older brother, James, or "Pig Meat," as he was called for his love of pork. Big Mom, however, was a firm believer in the biblical lesson: "Spare the rod and spoil the child."

Cir. 1930 / Image Courtesy Library of Congress

**January 16th, 1920**. Prohibition goes into effect following the ratification of the Volstead Act.[43]

---

[43] Jack S. Blocker, David M. Fahey, Ian R. Tyrrell; Alcohol and Temperance in Modern History: An International ..., Volume 1; ABC-CLIO, 2003; p. 440

We Shall Overcome: Sacred Song on the Devil's Tongue

In **February 1921,** Marcus Garvey speaks to a large crowd at the Universal Negro Improvement Association (UNIA) Hall on George Street in Cincinnati. The UNIA, a Black nationalist organization founded by Garvey a decade earlier, promotes a so-called "Back to Africa Movement." Marcus Garvey, a Black West Indian, passionately advocates Black economic self-sufficiency, political action, unity, and pride. The Cincinnati chapter of the UNIA is particularly large, boasting 8,000 members. The Jarretts are there and join the UNIA, where they also attend worship services.

Marcus Garvey (Courtesy Library of Congress)

Isaias Gamboa

It's 1929, and twelve years have passed since the Jarrett family first arrived in Cincinnati. Now seventeen, Louise accepts the Lord and is baptized at the New Prospect Baptist Church in the West End of Cincinnati, first under Rev. S. Williams and later under Rev. A.L. Collins.

Soon afterwards, Louise organizes *"The Humble Three"* choir, consisting of herself, Big Mom, and her younger sister, Alice.[44]

The Humble Three (left to right Ollie Johnson-Jarrett "Big Mom"; Alice Jarrett, Louise Jarrett) / Courtesy Louise Shropshire Foundation

Though things are anything but easy, the Jarretts somehow manage to get by. Papa and Big Mom work extra hours to feed their family, but as a result, they spend little time with the children. The last thing the family needs now is another worry or expense, but sure enough, Louise's brother, "Pig Meat", failed to come home last night, and that was never a good sign.

---

[44] Source: Louise Shropshire Obituary / History of the New Prospect Singers, Document #3

It's early morning, and although Papa and Big Mom are worried sick about their oldest son, these are tough times. Papa, not wanting to risk losing his job, leaves for work. Calling Pig Meat's friends is not an option, as only about a third of American households have telephones in the late 1920s. For African Americans, that number was closer to seven percent. The Jarretts are certainly not among that privileged class. Louise is also awake now and, shortly afterward, hears a knock at the door. She answers it to find one of her big brother's cohorts, who nervously tells Big Mom that he has been arrested for running moonshine. With no time to waste scolding his accomplice, Big Mom and Louise scramble down to the local bail-bonds office to see what might be done to bail Pig Meat out.

James "Pig Meat" Jarrett Cir. 1928
Courtesy   Louise Shropshire Foundation

Isaias Gamboa

The owner of **Bob Shropshire Bail Bonds** is **Robert "Bob" Shropshire**, a very successful Black businessman who dresses "to the nines" and is highly regarded in the community. At the local barber shop, however, he is known as a hard-nosed, pistol-packing man with powerful connections and a keen eye for the ladies.

Robert "Bob" Shropshire (on right) with a young Theodore M. Berry (Cir. 1925)
Courtesy Louise Shropshire Foundation

Robert Shropshire was born on March 24, 1900, in Georgetown, Kentucky, the only child of the union of Newton and Susie Lewis Shropshire. Obliged by his mother, he attended Sunday school at the First Baptist Church in Georgetown as a boy and was later baptized there. He remained an active member until he left to make his home and fortune in Cincinnati. Even then, he continued his affiliation with the church and contributed to its financial support. Being only 60 miles away from Cincinnati, he also attended services whenever possible.

Upon arriving at Shropshire Bail Bonds, Big Mom, without the cash to bail her son out, pleads with Shropshire to extend her family some form of credit. Shropshire agrees. He was well known in the community for helping those in need. It doesn't take Big Mom long to notice that Shropshire has taken an interest in Louise. No time to think about that now, though. Big Mom signs the necessary papers, and Pig Meat is out on bail.

Ever grateful to Mr. Shropshire, Big Mom invites him to church services at New Prospect Baptist Church that Sunday. Shropshire accepts. Later that night at home, Big Mom tells Papa about Shropshire's kindness and his attraction to Louise. Although obliged to give him credit and relieved that Pig Meat is out on bail, Papa does not like being in Shropshire's debt. Tired from a long, hard day of work, he has little time to ponder Shropshire's generosity and instead spends the rest of his energy putting his work boot to Pig Meat's britches. This is the last straw. Papa kicks Pig Meat out of the house, warning him not to return. This would not be Pig Meat's last run-in with the law.

That Sunday, true to his word and sharp as a tack, Robert Shropshire sits in the Jarrett family pew. During the service, he is visibly preoccupied with Louise as she exuberantly directs the youth choir and later sings a heartrending solo. In many ways, Louise reminds him of his own mother back in Kentucky. Later, as the collection plate is passed, all eyes are on Shropshire as he makes a generous offering to the church. Everyone is impressed—everyone, that is, except Papa. Nevertheless, at Big Mom's request, after church, Papa invites Shropshire to supper at the humble Jarrett home.

That night, Shropshire asks Papa and Big Mom for permission to court Louise. Although Louise is only 16 and Shropshire is 29, such a relationship was not uncommon. But everyone knew Louise was Papa's "special girl," and, as a patron of the local barbershop, Papa would need to know Shropshire's true intentions. After dinner, Papa asks Shropshire to take a walk with him so they might talk, man to man. During their conversation, Shropshire does not deny his reputation but offers an earnest account of himself, his business, and his intentions. Impressed by his authenticity, Papa gives his consent for Shropshire to court Louise.

Courtesy Louise Shropshire Foundation

With Papa's blessing, Robert and Louise begin a whirlwind courtship. Their relationship, however, would have to take a back seat to what would soon overwhelm the Jarrett family.[45]

---

[45] Personal Interview with Robert Anthony Goins Sr.; Riverside, Ca.; 5-6-2010 / Personal interview with Alice Jarrett McCloud; 2- 22, 2012; San Dimas, Ca.

# The End of the Beginning

October 29, 1929 - Black Tuesday. The New York Stock Exchange has crashed, sending stocks plummeting. This unprecedented economic catastrophe profoundly affects the lives and fortunes of millions of Americans, driving bankrupt former millionaires to leap to their deaths. Highly educated men now stand in bread lines, unable to secure employment to house and feed their families. The Great Depression has begun.

"Black Tuesday" Panic outside the New York Stock Exchange, October 29, 1929

Unemployed men during the Great Depression

Ironically, the Jarretts' financial status is relatively unaffected by Wall Street's financial chaos. They're just as poor as they were before the crash. All the same, everything was about to change.

In an interview with Louise's younger sister, Alice Mcloud, the sister vividly describes what happened next:

*"I remember one Sunday. It was raining, and Papa had to work. Papa got off of work, and I was at church. My daddy worked for the gas company, and if there was a leak, he had to work until he found the leak. Well, anyway, this Sunday, my sister [Lara] had carried me to church. Well when church started, me and a friend of mine were playing games around the back of the church, and my sister came around and said 'come on, Alice, we got to go home'. And I said 'go home?' She said 'yeah, somethin's wrong with Papa'. And she didn't have to tell me no more. That was my friend—my daddy. Anyway, when we got home, Lara and I saw Papa sittin' up in the chair, and a lot of people [was] there. I said, 'What [all] these*

*people doin' in here?'—you know…to myself. I better not have let no grown-ups hear me say that…you know I was in trouble."*

*"Well, anyway, I had run in the house, and with Papa sittin' in the chair, I went to go with Papa, eh (choking up)…but they wouldn't let me come to 'im. -And they had a fight on [they] hands…they had a fight on [they] hands. But I didn't know he had passed (whispering)…he had died. That Sunday; he died that Sunday, and it was raaainiiiin', rainin', rainin'. And he had died. He was sittin' in the chair. He was throwin' up blood. That's what he had: the sickness. I guess it was Tuberculosis or whatever. I used to say, 'When I get grown, I'm not workin'. I'm not working for nobody.' I said, 'Work killed my daddy, and it ain't gon' kill me.' And I thought that it was because he worked on a Sunday. But…I was young."*[46]

On November 10, 1929, the beloved James Papa Jarrett passed away. He was fifty-seven, just below the average life expectancy for men at the time.[47] The entire Jarrett family is in agony and, during the worst economic times, is left with few resources to survive. Big Mom has no money to bury her cherished husband, but without hesitation, Robert Shropshire insists on paying all funeral expenses, and the much-loved Papa Jarrett is laid to rest. That day, Big Mom's dress is sodden with tears from the agony of her seven fatherless children.

Soon after that day, Louise and Robert Shropshire inform Big Mom of their intent to be wed. She quickly discerns their circumstances but—physically and emotionally drained—she simply shakes her head and gives the two her blessing. To avoid legal complications given Louise's age, the two are married in Tijuana, Mexico, on November 29, 1929.

During their long trip to Mexico, Louise sheds many tears over Papa's passing but finds great comfort in Robert, who shares with her very personal stories from his life and childhood. She is delighted to learn that her soon-to-be husband is a real jokester with a side–splitting sense of humor. In fact, he makes Louise laugh so much throughout their trip that she gives him the pet name "Funny". Together, Robert and Louise form a powerful and lasting emotional bond.

Upon Louise and Robert's return to Cincinnati, Big Mom, still numb from her husband's death, is comforted by her daughter's new marriage but laments that Papa was not alive to see his special girl marry. Big Mom dries her eyes, hugs her new son-in-law, and now looks forward to a new grandchild. She would have to wait, however, as, to the sorrow of all, Louise takes a fall, and Robert's first child is stillborn.

Now, a married seventeen-year-old woman, Louise, moves into her new residence with Robert. In addition to being the wife of a successful bail bondman and caring for her new husband, she must take on a more active role in caring for her brothers and sisters as Big

---

[46] Personal interview with Alice Jarrett McCloud; 4-21, 2012; San Dimas, Ca.
[47] Sutton, Bettye. "1930-1939"; *American Cultural History*; Lone Star College-Kingwood Library; 1999. Wed. 7 Feb. 2011

Mom looks for additional work. As was customary for older children, Louise dropped out of school in the sixth grade to help with her family's practical needs. Although she can read and write, her lack of education would affect her later in life. Big Mom finds work cleaning houses, but Robert Shropshire won't hear of it. He assumes financial responsibility for Louise's family and purchases a home for Big Mom. This gesture allows Big Mom to stay home and properly care for her family and also affords Louise some extra time to spend in church, where she can develop her musical talents.

Louise remains deeply affected by her father's death and channels some of her grief into church and music. She enters a self-imposed emotional retreat, emerging with a collection of songs she calls "His Precious Blood." The collection includes "His Precious Blood," "Crucified For Me," "I Know Jesus Pilots Me," "Are You Worthy To Take Communion," "I'm a Child of Christ The King," "I'm Longing To Go There Someday," and the very popular "If My Jesus Wills." Although the exact date cannot be determined, multiple living witnesses report that the songs were composed between 1932 and 1942.

Young Louise becomes a valued musical leader at the **New Prospect Baptist Church** and gains some notoriety by performing her compositions during Sunday services and at the **National Convention of Gospel Choirs and Choruses** with her choir, "The Humble Three". At times, she slips away to find quiet time alone, hiding in her favorite place behind the big church organ, where she rests her head and cries. She often thinks of Papa and her lost child, and during this difficult time, finds great comfort in sacred music and her hiding place. Younger sister Alice knows all about Louise's hiding place and, at times, watches her gaze up at the big wooden cross above the altar, with the same adoring look she used to give Papa.

Although Robert's financial support is truly a God-send, Big Mom still has mouths to feed and little time to process *her* loss. At times, though, late at night, the kids hear her weeping into her pillow. She's never had to make so many decisions on her own, and now she relies more than ever on her church and her faith in God to keep her remaining children away from drugs and crime. Her daughters, Louise, Lara, Alice, and Jimmy-Mae, stay close to the church and out of trouble. Her son, Garland, does the same. Sadly, however, she is unsuccessful with her two older boys, Pablo "Pap" and Pig Meat, who turn their grief over Papa's death into anger and rebellion and take to the streets.

With her father gone, Louise is a tremendous help to Big Mom, taking on extra chores and responsibilities. By nature, she has always been a serious, hardworking young woman, but hearing everyone say "you got a lot of Papa in you" gives her great comfort. She continues to rely on the church for her social and spiritual needs and is seldom idle in mind or hand. Her musical gifts are beginning to shine, but they, along with her numerous acts of service to her church and family, go unnoticed by Big Mom, who, as a single mother, has her hands full.

Times are tough all over, and though most Americans struggle financially during this period, Louise and Robert are doing very well, able to provide considerable support to her family in their time of need. —No small feat for former sharecroppers.[48] [49]

## Powerful Friends

1929 has come and gone, and The Great Depression has hit America hard. Complicating matters, Prohibition is wreaking havoc on the nation. Nine years earlier, the country went "dry" when the Volstead Act was passed, banning the sale and manufacture of alcohol. This was followed by the closing of all US breweries, saloons, and distilleries. The Prohibition movement was led in part by the Anti-Saloon League and the Women's Christian Temperance Union, which linked alcohol consumption to a variety of social ills, such as spousal and child abuse. Henry Ford and other powerful industrialists also played a role in the passage of the Volstead Act by touting the negative impact of drinking on labor productivity. Mandated by the Eighteenth Amendment, Prohibition indirectly spawned organized crime, fueling the rise of the American Mafia. In the process, it made millionaires out of gangsters like Al Capone, Dutch Schultz, and the undisputed king of the bootleggers, George Remus.[50]

Unscathed by the October 29 stock market crash, the ten-year-old Bob Shropshire Bail Bonds business is booming. The overindulgent "Roaring Twenties" have been extremely good for business, and now, thanks to Prohibition and the crime it spawned, Shropshire prospers, making big bucks and powerful friends by bailing out the criminal associates of Cincinnati-based kingpin George Remus and lesser-known bootlegger Joseph Kennedy.

Robert "Bob" Shropshire Sr. Cir. 1920

---

[48] McCloud, Alice Jarrett interview 2-22-2012'; San Dimas. Ca.
[49] Recorded interview with Robert Anthony Goins Sr. #4; Riverside, Ca.; 5-6-2010
[50] Martin Gitlin; The Prohibition Era; ABDO, Sep 1, 2010; p. 90

Robert "Bob" Shropshire Sr.

George Remus

# George Remus

George Remus was a former criminal-defense lawyer who entered the bootlegging business after witnessing many of his clients amass huge fortunes selling illegal liquor. In 1919, Remus chose Cincinnati to launch his lucrative bootlegging business—the same year Robert Shropshire founded his bail bonds business. Remus chose Cincinnati in part because 80% of America's bonded whiskey was produced in Kentucky, within a few hundred miles of the city, and Cincinnati itself contained many distilleries. He also knew that mobsters like Al Capone and Dutch Schultz had monopolized the bootlegging racket in other big cities, such as Chicago and New York. In Detroit, Ohio's neighbor to the west, bootlegging was controlled by the infamous Purple Gang. Cincinnati, however, was still wide-open.

Remus ultimately purchases nine whiskey distilleries in Kentucky, Cincinnati, Indiana, and Missouri, putting himself in a position to make a fortune in illegal booze. Operating with a fleet of 147 trucks in nine states, Remus runs twenty-four hours a day, seven days a week. Using his legal acumen, Remus discovers a loophole in the Volstead Act that permits pharmacies to legally purchase alcohol from distilleries for medicinal purposes. Before long, Remus purchases several pharmacies and then sells liquor to himself. This "medicinal" liquor is then hijacked by Remus' own cronies and distributed to major cities like New York and Chicago…to the extreme irritation of his competitors, Al Capone and Dutch Schultz.

With all of the legal Cincinnati bars closed, Remus sets up shop in illicit "speakeasies" and "after-hours" nightclubs. There, he resells watered-down whiskey shots and home-brewed "hooch" at tremendous markups to anyone who whispers the secret password through the little sliding peephole door. A shot of watered-down whiskey goes for 50 cents, and the supply never lasts long. As a result, one truckload or boatload of contraband can carry as much as $200,000 worth of illegal liquor at a time. – This at a time when $50 a week is considered a good salary.

These shipments, by land and water, were typically handled and distributed by the most expendable employees in Remus' organization. These men were called "rum-runners" (by water) or "bootleggers" (by land). As an occupational hazard, they were frequently arrested by honest cops and Prohibition agents—sometimes as a result of an "anonymous tip" from a competitor or to divert attention from a larger shipment coming in at another point. This is where the Bob Shropshire Bail Bonds company came in. Shropshire's business was consistently fed large sums of cash to bail out these bootleggers on a virtual revolving-door basis. "Bob" Shropshire was known as a reliable and discreet businessman and, as a result, became one of the most successful and influential men in the city, making powerful friends during this period. Among trusted friends, Shropshire is sometimes heard sharing stories of bailing out "those Remus and Kennedy boys".

For Remus, managing such a massive criminal enterprise required a sophisticated transportation network, a large workforce, and reliable protection from police interference. He also needed safeguards against ruthless competitors like Al Capone and Dutch Schultz.

In less than three years after arriving in Cincinnati, Remus would amass over forty million dollars in profits and add thousands of personnel to his criminal operation. This included judges, police, and prohibition agents. His entire bootlegging empire, however, relied on "The Fix"... bribes, including an alleged $500,000 paid to the U.S. Attorney General. By his own accounts, Remus estimated that during his heyday, he spent over twenty million dollars in cash bribes. To keep so many palms greased, he was known to deposit huge sums of money in various banks, including $2,700,000 in a single Cincinnati bank in 1921. His net worth was estimated at $70 million.

Business associates like Shropshire are offered many fringe benefits by Remus, who, among his friends and associates, has a well-earned reputation for hosting lavish parties at his Cincinnati Hermosa Avenue mansion, dubbed "The Marble Palace". It is said that at one notable New Year's party, 100 of Remus' "well-connected" invitees were pleasantly surprised when, at dawn, Remus presented 100 male guests with diamond-studded watches and each guest's wife with a brand-new car.

Unfortunately, Remus' web of crime eventually ensnares Louise's older brother, Pig Meat, who takes a job as a blues pianist at one of Remus' back-alley clubs. He plays for food, booze, tips, and whatever other gratuities may be offered. Pig Meat learned to play piano in church; however, while Louise polished her musical gifts for sacred purposes, Pig Meat's talents were sold to the highest bidder. Although he is now a legitimate and sought-after blues musician, Pig Meat can't seem to get his fill of wooden nickels. Wanting to bring in extra dough, he accepts an offer from Remus to run moonshine. On one such run, he is chased down and shot by the police but escapes capture and is treated for his wounds across state lines by a veterinarian in Kentucky. Fortunately for Pig Meat, Prohibition ends in 1933, enabling him to pursue legitimate musical engagements. He eventually goes on to play alongside blues luminaries Bessie Smith and John Lee Hooker.

Over the next 8 years, Robert and Louise are blessed with two children, Robert Jr. and Jackie. The bail-bonds business is as busy as ever, and Louise, now 28, is much more active at New Prospect Baptist Church. She becomes a church board member, teaches Sunday school, and takes the principal choir director responsibilities. She also shows interest in a new style of church hymn called "Gospel Music" and spends much of her free time composing.

☙

# Chapter 10

# A Time for War

**December 17, 1941** – In a surprise military strike by the Imperial Japanese Navy, 353 Japanese fighters, bombers, and torpedo planes attack the United States Naval base at Pearl Harbor, Hawaii. The attack is a massive blow to the U.S. Pacific fleet, killing 2,402 servicemen and wounding 1,282. 188 U.S. aircraft are destroyed. The next day, the United States declares war on Japan and enters World War II.

Pearl Harbor Attack, Dec. 7, 1941, taken from a Japanese plane, Courtesy Library of Congress

Meanwhile, Louise's younger brothers, Garland and Pablo Jarrett, head off to war.

Garland "Brother" Jarrett with Ollie Johnson Jarrett "Big Mom", 1942

Pablo "Pap" Jarrett, Circa 1942, Courtesy Louise Shropshire Foundation

**December 11, 1941** – Adolf Hitler declares war on the United States. President Franklin Delano Roosevelt asks Congress to declare war on Germany—passionately asserting, "Never before has there been a greater challenge to life, liberty, and civilization." The United States then enters the war in Europe and concentrates nearly 90 percent of its military resources on defeating Hitler.[51]

Adolph Hitler, standing with his arm extended, is pictured; his military commander, Heinrich Himmler, in a dark uniform, is just below him. / Courtesy Library of Congress

**January 1942** – As ordered by Hitler, mass killings of Jews with poisonous "Zyklon-B" gas begin at the Auschwitz concentration camp.[52]

## Precious Blood

**December 1942** – Louise is now 29, and deeply affected by the war's death and destruction, and the possibility that her younger brothers, Garland and Pablo, might be killed. She calls upon her faith for strength.

---

[51] Conrad Black; Franklin Delano Roosevelt: Champion Of Freedom; PublicAffairs, Mar 16, 2005 – 1280; p. 691, 692, 693
[52] Adam LeBor, Roger Boyes; Seduced by Hitler: The Choices of a Nation and the Ethics of Survival; Sourcebooks, Inc., Feb 1, 2004; p. 160

## We Shall Overcome: Sacred Song on the Devil's Tongue

In 1943, Louise forms "The Shropshire Singers," a gospel choir comprising herself, Big Mom, her niece Mary Thomas, and her younger sister, Alice McCloud, Mary's mother. Together, they perform at the National Convention of Gospel Choirs and Choruses in Cincinnati and are a rousing success. While there, Louise is approached and complimented by Rev. Thomas A. Dorsey, the convention's founder. Encouraged by her choir's popularity, Louise and the Shropshire Singers tour the South, performing songs from the "His Precious Blood" collection at various churches to raise funds for her Cincinnati church. During the trip, they are denied access to public restrooms and to water designated for White people. Although there are segregated schools in Cincinnati, this is Louise's first personal encounter with the South's hateful Jim Crow racism since leaving Alabama at the age of four.

**In 1944, as WW II rages on,** Louise joins the **Greater Cincinnati Choral Association** and the **National Association of Gospel Singers of America**.[53] Americans are rationing food, planting "Victory Gardens," and recycling rubber and scrap metal for the war effort.[54]

**April 29th, 1945** – Just after midnight, in a small civil ceremony, Adolf Hitler, having cowered in his Berlin bunker for more than three months, is married to his longtime lover, Eva Braun. Later that day, he receives word that his ally, Benito Mussolini, has been slain. Mussolini and his mistress have been executed by enraged Italians, hung by the heels, and then mutilated. By now, Berlin is surrounded, and Hitler's Nazi Third Reich has all but disintegrated. The "Axis Powers" have also collapsed, and finally, Hitler admits defeat to those in his bunker.

**On April 30th**, with Soviet forces less than 500 meters from his bunker, Hitler puts a gun to his temple, bites down on a cyanide capsule, and commits suicide. His wife, Eva Braun, whom he had married less than 48 hours earlier, swallows a cyanide capsule and also kills herself. Per Hitler's request, both his and Eva Braun's bodies are doused with gasoline, burned, and buried.

**On May 7, 1945,** the World War II Allies formally accept the unconditional surrender of the armed forces of Nazi Germany. Japan, however, will not surrender.[55]

**On August 6, 1945,** at 8:15 AM, the American B-29 bomber Enola Gay drops **"Little Boy,"** the world's first atomic bomb ever used in war, on **Hiroshima, Japan.** An estimated 120,000 innocent civilians are killed. Hundreds of thousands suffer agonizing burns, leukemia, and infections for the rest of their shortened lives.

**On August 9, 1945**, the U.S. drops the world's second atomic bomb, **"Fat Man,"** on **Nagasaki, Japan**, killing 74,000 innocent civilians. Another 75,000 were injured, and several hundred thousand are left sick and dying from nuclear fallout

---

[53] Source: Louise Shropshire Obituary
[54] Bill McWilliams; Sunday in Hell: Pearl Harbor Minute by Minute; E-reads/E-rights, Nov 3, 2011; p. 870
[55] Michael Burgan; Shima: Birth of the Nuclear Age; Marshall Cavendish, Sep 1, 2009; p. 12, 13, 16

and illnesses caused by the bomb's radiation. The bomb was intended to be more destructive than the one dropped on Hiroshima, but it landed a mile off target.

**On August 15, 1945,** Japan's **Emperor Hirohito** announces Japan's surrender. World War II is over, and Louise's brothers, Garland and Pablo, come home.[56] Later that year, the Shropshire Singers perform at the Detroit meeting of the National Convention of Gospel Choirs and Choruses. During the event, Louise shares the stage with Mahalia Jackson. Rev. Thomas Dorsey asks her to direct the "Mass Choir" portion of the convention. The Mass Choir helps conclude the week-long convention and is a highly anticipated event where the various choirs in attendance come together to rehearse and perform popular sacred and Gospel songs. After the convention, Rev. Dorsey and Louise establish a collaborative musical association and a lifelong family friendship.

Louise Shropshire, pictured standing, Rev. Thomas A. Dorsey, seated at the Piano

Courtesy Louise Shropshire Foundation

---

[56] Recorded Interview # 44, with Thelma Jarrett; February 2, 2012; Pomona, Ca.

# Chapter 11

# Georgia Tom

Seven-year-old Thomas A. Dorsey, Left-front and Family

Thomas Andrew Dorsey, who would one day be known as the Father of Gospel Music, was born on July 1st, 1899, in rural Villa Rica, Georgia. The son of sharecroppers, he had a father who was an itinerant Baptist preacher and a mother who was a church organist and piano teacher. Although he showed a great love and talent for music, young Thomas was spiritually conflicted during his formative years, torn between his love of secular "Blues" music and his family's strict religious traditions. This did not go over well at home and led to many bouts of discord between Thomas and his father, the Reverend Thomas Madison Dorsey, who believed Blues to be the Devil's music. Unbeknownst to his father, by age eleven, Thomas secretly dropped out of school and accepted a job at a local Vaudeville theater. Six years later, he would leave Georgia to seek fame and fortune in Chicago, contributing to The Great Migration north.

A young Thomas A. Dorsey

In Chicago, Dorsey is an instant success. Branded the "Whispering Piano Player," he provides musical entertainment at illegal Prohibition-era speakeasies, where he masters the art of playing quietly to avoid police attention. By age twenty-one, however, his overindulgent nightlife leads to a breakdown, forcing him back to Georgia to recover. While there, his mother urges him to stop playing the blues and serve the Lord with his musical gifts. Dorsey ignores her advice.

Following his recovery, Dorsey returns to Chicago and, before long, secures a gig playing with Ma Rainey, a very popular blues singer. While there, he meets a young girl named Nettie Harper, with whom he shares a Chicago boarding house. Before long, the two fall deeply in love. Dorsey secures a job for Nettie as Ma Rainey's wardrobe mistress, and soon afterward, he and Nettie are married. Dorsey, however, continues his fast-paced, after-hours lifestyle, now performing under the moniker "Georgia Tom". In 1925, he suffers another breakdown, leaving him temporarily unable to play music. Nettie cares for him during this difficult period. Three years pass before an emotionally and spiritually renewed Thomas A. Dorsey commits himself to composing sacred music. He does so by uniquely *marrying* his rhythmic piano blues style to modern choral arrangements and scripture-based themes and lyrics.

For African American churches of the time, Dorsey's musical deviations from the traditionally arranged hymns were not always welcome. The spiritual solemnity and reverence evoked by the more traditional hymns of the time reflected the hard lives of rural Southern Blacks, who had endured slavery and its difficult aftermath. These long-revered hymns were curative in nature and, given the prevailing culture of violence, hatred, racism, and segregation in America, served a vital spiritual purpose. Dorsey's new "Gospel Music," however, although based on biblical doctrines, was considered by some traditional churchgoers to be spiritually divisive. They felt that his music reflected the fast-paced, big-city lifestyle in which Dorsey had once peddled his Blues. Unlike traditional spirituals and hymns, which emphasized the need to manage suffering with "patient endurance," as did the biblical Gospels, Dorsey's Gospel Music provided a form of musical escapism for the masses, leading them away from the comparatively grim biblical message of suffering and endurance toward an arguably more superficial and aesthetic sense of jubilation and euphoria.

> *"And we boast in the hope of the glory of God. Not only so, but we also glory in our sufferings, because we know that suffering produces perseverance; perseverance, character; and character, hope."* **~Romans 5: 2-5**

Dorsey, however, who had never won his spiritually unyielding parents' endorsement of his music, would now seek validation from a new breed of urban Baptists, who might find his modern music more palatable. Much to his disappointment, however, the ambitious piano arrangements featured in many of his new songs initially caused urban, Southern-styled churches to reject his newest compositions. Even in the big city, the piano was not a traditional component of Southern-Baptist choral singing and was initially considered by Baptist preachers and congregations a distraction from the true message of the Gospels. This tide, however, would inevitably turn, as the Great Migration meant that Black urban congregations now greatly outnumbered the more traditional, Southern-style churches. As such, a new generation of younger, big-city churchgoers sought to worship in ways that reflected their fast-paced urban lives. Thomas A. Dorsey had finally found his calling. His ambitions would have to take a detour, however, as Nettie soon became pregnant, prompting Dorsey to take to the road to sell and perform his music. Tragically, in August of 1932, Dorsey's life was shattered while on a road trip in Saint Louis, Missouri, when he received the following message: "NETTIE'S DEAD."

Thomas's beloved wife, Nettie, had died during childbirth… his newborn son, however, had survived. Devastated, he rushed home and, though deeply distraught, found comfort in holding his newborn son. That night, however, his infant son also died. He later said he found some measure of peace in believing that his wife had returned for his son and was now together with the Lord. In his grief-stricken state, he turned to music for relief and composed "Take My Hand, Precious Lord." He would always claim that the song came "direct from God."

Years later, in a rare moment of emotional catharsis, Dorsey shares the story of "Take My Hand, Precious Lord" with Louise, along with his typewritten testimony. Part devotional prayer, part sermon, and perhaps a confession, this remarkable historic document was found among Louise Shropshire's sheet music and is now housed in the University of Cincinnati's Rare Books Archives. "Precious Lord, Take My Hand" would become universally recognized as one of the most beloved and successful Gospel Hymns of all time.

Unhappy with the unfair business practices of established White music publishers or the time, Dorsey established the first independent Black Gospel music publishing company, "Dorsey House of Music." This would prove to be one of the best business decisions he would ever make. Black music—both secular and sacred—had now been discovered by White men calling themselves "Ethnomusicologists," and self-proclaimed "song-hunters." Like the first glimmer of gold flake found at Sutter's Mill nearly a century earlier, there would be no turning back. No longer would these precious African American treasures—these sacred hymns, plantation melodies, prison work songs, and street-corner symphonies- find sanctuary in the temples of Christian reverence or the halls of human decency. Kidnapped, chained, gentrified, and renamed, they would now be bought and sold to the highest bidders by ruthless White profiteers on America's musical auction block…"Tin Pan Alley".

Tin Pan Alley was a nickname for a small district in New York that housed the most influential collection of music publishers of that era. Originally situated on West 28th Street in Lower Manhattan, Tin Pan Alley was considered the center of the American music-publishing industry from the late 1800s to well into the 1950s. From there, some unscrupulous songwriters and music publishers made their fortunes by publishing and exploiting lyrics, melodies, and songs that were misappropriated from poor and uneducated Black people who knew little or nothing of their rights under complex U.S. Copyright laws. Those Black people who understood copyright law could not afford the high cost of defending their rights in court.

Many Tin Pan Alley millionaires were also rewarded by publishing racially belittling and demeaning compositions known as "Minstrel Music" and "Coon Songs." It was clear that, on many fronts, African Americans were fair game.

In his book, *Tin Pan Alley: A Chronicle of the American Popular Music Racket*, one of America's most successful and respected composers, **George Gershwin**, asserts the following:

*"From the first, the white has been under some [psychological] compulsion to mimic the [Negro], at first in ridicule and superiority, then in understanding and sympathy. The [Negro], at almost every step, has participated in the making of our popular song…*

> *"Before the various types of jazz was the modern coon song; before the coon song was the minstrel show; before the minstrel show was the plantation melody and the spiritual. It is safe to say that without the Negro, we should have had no Tin Pan Alley…*
>
> *"The Negro is a symbol of our uninhibited expression, of our uninhibited action. He is our catharsis. He is the disguise behind which we may, for a releasing moment, join that part of ourselves which we have sacrificed to civilization. He helps us to a double deliverance. What we dare not say, often we freely sing. Music, too, is an absolution, and what we would not dare to sing in our own plain speech, we freely sing in the [Negro] dialect or in terms of the Black…"*[57]

It was widely known then (and now) among African American songwriters, including Thomas A. Dorsey, that many White music publishers and songwriters had been amassing great fortunes by appropriating their songs. It was also known that, in most cases, the true authors of the misappropriated songs would remain "unknown" and, of course, unpaid.

In her book, "Rage to Survive: The Etta James Story," the late legendary jazz singer **Etta James** spoke candidly about this issue:

> *"Like Green cash and flashy diamonds, songs get stolen. Books have been written about the thieves that ran the R&B business. The History of Black Music is filled with tales of exploitation.* **Bessie Smith**, **Fats Waller**, **Billie Holiday**—*they all got ripped off, songs swiped, money squandered, one-sided contracts, no royalties, and God knows what else."*[58]

Rev. Thomas A. Dorsey is considered the first successful independent African American music publisher, and in 1933, established the **National Convention of Gospel Choirs and Choruses (NCGCC).** Six years later, he teamed with **Mahalia Jackson,** and together they ushered in what is known as the "Golden Age of Gospel Music." He was later ordained a Baptist minister and recognized as the "Father of Gospel Music".[59]

---

[57] Goldberg, Isaac; Gershwin, George; Tin Pan Alley a Chronicle of the American Popular Music Racket; The John Day Company, Kessinger Publishing; 1930, 2005; pgs. 32,33,34,35.

[58] Etta James, David Ritz; Rage to Survive: The Etta James Story; Da Capo Press, Jun 5, 2003; p. 50

[59] Source: National Convention of Gospel Choirs and Choruses, Inc.

Rev. Thomas A. Dorsey

# Chapter 12

# New Prospects

It is now 1946, and the Shropshire family continues to thrive. Louise and her husband decide to rent their existing home and purchase an expansive residence at 141 Huntington Place, in Cincinnati's exclusive Mount Auburn area...three houses away from the former home of President William Howard Taft. Mount Auburn is known as a hilltop retreat, where Cincinnati's social elite can escape the sweltering summer heat, dusty roads, and raucous clatter of the city below. At their new home, the Shropshires are known to host judges, politicians, dignitaries, prayer groups, choir rehearsals, church meetings, and other events. Thanksgiving and Christmas at the so-called "big-house" are a sight to behold, with sumptuous 12-course meals served upon fine china and silver. The Shropshires are considered one of Cincinnati's most influential African American families.[60]

The Shropshire's Mount Auburn Home Cir. 1946 / Courtesy Louise Shropshire Foundation

Also in 1946, Mary Thomas, the nine-year-old daughter of Louise's sister, Alice, begins singing with the Shropshire Singers. Soon afterward, Louise's brother, Garland Jarrett, is discharged from the Navy and adds a much-needed baritone voice to the group. Shortly thereafter, Louise joins forces with select vocalists from the New Prospect Baptist Church and expands the "New Prospect Singers". The success of the New Prospect Singers grows rapidly, due in large part to Louise's very popular, If My Jesus Wills, which is sung

---
[60] Personal interview with Mel Carter, September, 2011; Los Angeles, Ca. / Personal interview with the King Sisters; October, 2011; Cincinnati, Ohio

with an upbeat Gospel arrangement. The song title is often mistakenly referred to as **"I'll Overcome"**, for its memorable chorus:

*"I'll overcome, I'll overcome, I'll overcome someday-*

*If my Jesus wills, I do believe, I'll overcome someday."*

Louise's singing group continues to grow in popularity and is sought after in many cities and towns across the US. They now require larger auditoriums to accommodate their audiences and, on some occasions, are forced to turn people away because standing room is unavailable. The New Prospect Singers travel across the country, performing in churches large and small. Louise is pleased, feeling she is hard at work for the Lord. Aside from expenses, all proceeds from these performances go to the New Prospect Baptist Church, as Louise feels strongly that saving souls should be their only reward.

**NEW PROSPECT SINGERS** OF CINCINNATI, OHIO

FIRST ROW, LEFT TO RIGHT:
Cornelia Kirkland, Pianist, Soloist and Pianist, Secretary; Mary Current, Baritone; Louise Shropshire, Lead Singer and Manager.
SECOND ROW:
Mary L. Thomas, Tenor and Treasurer; Alice McCloud, First Lead Singer; Ollie Jarrett, Bass Singer and Chaplain.
For engagements, call Louise Shropshire, Manager, AV. 0544.

Courtesy Louise Shropshire Foundation

It's **May 13th, 1947,** and **Jackie Robinson** has broken the color barrier, becoming the first Negro professional baseball player in America. When the Brooklyn Dodgers come to town to play the Reds on their first road trip of the season, the Shropshires and many other Black residents of Cincinnati proudly pack **Crosley Field** to get a glimpse of the famous first baseman.

    Mr. Robinson receives several death threats that day but does his best to keep his mind focused on the game ahead. During infield practice, however, racial slurs are hurled at the first baseman by both Cincinnati fans and players from the dugout, a few yards from first base. Then, unexpectedly, Dodger shortstop Pee Wee Reese, a slim, white man born and raised on the segregated sandlots of Louisville, Kentucky, raises his hand and stops practice. He then crosses the field to first base and places his hand on Robinson's shoulder. The jeers and insults continue, however, until Reese turns around and, without a word—never ever taking his arm from Robinson's shoulder—stares into the Cincinnati dugout and grandstand, where the rabid slurs are coming from. In this extraordinary moment, those who were there say a hush fell over the entire stadium and the racial slurs were silenced. For the rest of his life, Robinson would say that thanks to Pee Wee Reese's extraordinary gesture, he never felt alone on the baseball field again. A monument commemorating this remarkable event was later erected in Brooklyn.

Brooklyn Monument commemorating Pee Wee Reese's Gesture to Jackie Robinson
(Pee Wee Reese on left)

    Later that year, at the National Convention of Gospel Choirs and Choruses in Huntington, West Virginia, Louise and the New Prospect Singers perform alongside **Mahalia**

**Jackson.** Church choirs and choruses from congregations across the United States attend. Louise also directs the Mass Choir portion of the convention.[61]

In 1949, Louise gives birth to a daughter, Darlene, and is overjoyed by this blessing. Two years later, she begins to hear whispers of her husband's infidelity but tries to ignore them, accepting that his irregular hours are part and parcel of the family's bail-bond business. Years later, however, she discovers evidence of her husband's unfaithfulness. Deeply hurt, humiliated, and downright furious, in a rare display of raw emotion, Louise charges down to the bail-bond office and, by all accounts, tears the place apart. Immediately afterward, perhaps humiliated by having lost her self-control, she spares the office further injury and returns home, only to slip into a state of depression that lasts several months. As always, however, Louise clings to her faith and, aside from occasional episodes of grief and anger, works to forgive her husband's transgressions. She pours herself into the church and her music more than ever now.

## Reds, Whites, and Blues

It's now 1952, and Pete Seeger's folk group, The Weavers, releases a highly successful song titled "Wimoweh," later known as "The Lion Sleeps Tonight." The song becomes a huge hit for the Weavers. Although the song was written by a Black African man, Seeger and his music publisher exploit the copyright and reap the financial rewards. Celebrations would have to wait, however, as Seeger has other things to worry about. This is the Cold War era, and America is on the hunt for "Commies."

The United States House Un-American Affairs Committee has its sights set on the entertainment industry. At a hearing in Washington, D.C., Pete Seeger—at the time an admitted communist—has the misfortune of being named by a loose-lipped former comrade, Harvey Matusow. Matusow had worked with Seeger for an underground Communist organization called "Peoples Artists," which sent folk singers like Seeger to agitate on picket lines and at union meetings. Matusow would testify that Communists were "preying on the sexual weakness of American youth" to lure young recruits into their movement, and he was naming names—among them, three members of the popular folk group The Weavers, including Pete Seeger.

Newspapers report the testimony, and soon after, nightclub owners refuse to book Pete Seeger or the Weavers. Almost overnight, the Weavers are finished, and Pete Seeger is back to teaching "Kum-baya" to grade-schoolers. -Or is he?[62] [63]

---

[61] Source: National Convention of Gospel Choirs and Choruses, Inc.

[62] LaFraniere, Sharon; "In the Jungle, the Unjust Jungle, a Small Victory"; March 22, 2006; New York Times

[63] Malan, Rian; In The Jungle; Rolling Stone Magazine; May 24, 2000

The Weavers, Pete Seeger standing top left

On April 8, 1952, Louise Shropshire copyrights her sacred composition, **"Whom Do Men Say I Am**." Copyright number: EU270766.

In 1954, Louise establishes Shropshire's Religious and Music Center, which offers music and singing lessons and rooms for club meetings, teas, weddings, and receptions. Following the close friend Rev. Thomas A. Dorsey's advice, Louise prints and publishes 1,000 copies of sheet music from her ever-popular **"His Precious Blood" collection of songs**. The sheet music is widely disseminated through public performances. She buys several hundred three-cent stamps and mails copies to churches and choir directors all over the United States. She also sells copies at the National Convention of Gospel Choirs and Choruses, and while the New Prospect Singers perform the songs onstage, her niece Marylyn sells copies in the convention center lobby. Louise advises young Marylyn to pin the money to the inside of her dress, cautioning her, "They'll steal money, but they won't steal a child." She also features the popular collection in her music store, increasing the price from twenty-five to fifty cents. [64]

*As sung by the New Prospect Singers, Cincinnati, Ohio.*

His Precious Blood

Crucified For Me

I Know Jesus Pilots Me

Are You Worthy To Take Communion

I'm A Child Of Christ, The King

I'm Longing To Go There Some Day

If My Jesus Wills

By

LOUISE SHROPSHIRE

Price 50¢

Published by
LOUISE SHROPSHIRE
141 Huntington Place, Cincinnati 19, Ohio.

Courtesy Louise Shropshire Foundation

---

[64] Alice Jarrett McCloud recorded interview; February 22, 2012, San Dimas, Ca.

Having composed sacred music all these years for the pure joy of sharing the Gospel message, Louise never considers copyrighting most of her music until a church member hears a recording of her song "If My Jesus Wills" on Cincinnati's WCIN Sunday-morning Gospel-music radio show. Louise consults with Rev. Dorsey and contacts her family attorney, Sam Rubenstein, who helps her submit her songs to the U.S. Copyright Office in 1954.

On July 13, 1954, Louise is granted a copyright for ***If My Jesus Wills,*** which is assigned the registration number EU 364306.

Page from 1954 US Music Copyright Registration Book

That same year, Louise is also granted copyright for the following songs: "Are You Worthy to Take Communion," "Behold the Man of Galilee," "Crucified for Me," "I Know Jesus Pilots Me," "I'm a Child of Christ the King," "I'm Longing to Go There Someday," "Let Us Walk on the Hilltops of God," and "Mother's Beautiful Hands."

Not one to let the grass grow beneath her feet, Louise establishes the "U-Name-It Song Shop" at 1571 Central Avenue in Cincinnati, Ohio, in January 1955. The business specializes in the sale of religious sheet music.

We Shall Overcome: Sacred Song on the Devil's Tongue

Courtesy Louise Shropshire Foundation

1955 – Dr. Martin Luther King Jr. enters the national spotlight when he is arrested while leading the **Montgomery Bus Boycott**. Louise is deeply moved by Dr. King's words, which draw on the Gospels to call for strong action through peaceful protest.

Montgomery, Alabama, Sheriff's Department booking photo of The Rev. Martin Luther King Jr., Feb 22, 1956

Louise and the New Prospect Singers are growing in popularity and are featured regularly on the WCIN Gospel Hour. They continue to perform their popular suite of songs in various Cincinnati churches and at Gospel music conventions across the US.

**HE'S COMING BACK**
**Singing SAMMY LEWIS**
*CROWN PRINCE OF GOSPEL SINGERS*
And Cincinnati's
**New Prospect Singers**
JONES TABERNACLE CHURCH -- Lincoln Pk. Dr.& Freeman
Sunday, June 19, 1955      8 P.M.
Ted Byrd, M.C.                       Adv. $1.10
(W.C.I.N.)
Grow Printing – 8th and John

Courtesy Louise Shropshire Foundation

**1957** – Louise Shropshire and Rev. Thomas A. Dorsey collaborate on a new version of **"Behold the Man of Galilee"**.[65] Dorsey adds new lyrical and melodic components, and the song is copyrighted in the same year, published by Dorsey and distributed to churches nationwide through "Shropshire's Religious and Music Center".

---

[65] Behold the man of Galilee: for choir, chorus or solo / words and music by Louise Shropshire and Thomas A. Dorsey; Chicago Public Library Document Archives

# Behold the Man of Galilee

For Choir, Chorus or Solo

Words and Music by

Louise Shropshire

and

Thomas A. Dorsey

PRICE 20 CENTS

Distributed by
LOUISE SHROPSHIRE
141 Hunting Place, Cincinnati, Ohio

Published by
THOMAS A. DORSEY
4154 S. Ellis Avenue, Chicago 15, Illinois.

Made in U.S.A

Courtesy Louise Shropshire Foundation

That same year, Louise is introduced to the Reverend Fred Shuttlesworth by Rev. Dorsey at the annual National Convention of Gospel Choirs and Choruses (NCGCC).[66] As a result of their meeting, Shropshire's and Shuttlesworth's lives would be changed forever.

Photo taken in 1957 at the National Convention of Gospel Choirs and Choruses: Louise Shropshire is pictured 2nd from right; Thomas A. Dorsey is pictured 4th from right; Rev. Fred Shuttlesworth is pictured standing 4th from left.
Courtesy Louise Shropshire Family Papers Collection, University of Cincinnati

ღ

---

[66] Personal interview with Alice Jarrett McCloud; February 22, 2012 San Dimas, Ca.

# Chapter 13

## The Battlefield General

Rev. Fred Shuttlesworth / Courtesy Library of Congress

 On March 19th, 1922, in rural Mount Meigs, Alabama, Fred Lee Green was born to Vetter Green and Alberta Robinson. Although Vetter and Alberta were in love, Alberta's father, March Robinson, a tough, hard-working tenant farmer, did not approve of Vetter, who lived in a broken-down shack outside of town and scraped out a living keeping dogs and cleaning guns. Although Alberta's father would not give his permission for her and Vetter to marry, she continued the relationship behind his back. Before long, however, to her father's great discontent, Alberta became pregnant with Vetter's child. Her father would now have to take matters into his own hands, and soon after baby Fred was born, March Robinson moved Alberta, her new baby, and the rest of his family away from Mount Meigs to Birmingham, Alabama, in search of a better future.

 In Birmingham, Alberta, raised Fred alone for five years but would eventually marry William Nathan Shuttlesworth, a hard-drinking man 23 years her elder. Alberta urged Fred to accept his new stepfather and to legally change his last name to Shuttlesworth. Unlike Alberta and her father, March, "Will" Shuttlesworth, as he was called, was a violent man and religious only in his *avoidance* of church or anything related. There was little peace and even less harmony in the Shuttlesworth home, as frequent arguments between Fred's mother and his heavy-handed, philandering stepfather escalated into violence. On one such occasion, a domestic clash resulted in Alberta's eye being gouged out by a splintered chair. Fred never forgave his stepfather for this violent act that left his mother permanently blinded in one eye.

Unfortunately, violence remained a fixture in young Fred's childhood home. In addition to Will Shuttlesworth's violent nature, he inflicted toxic doses of verbal and physical abuse on Fred and his siblings. Although he resented his stepfather, young Fred was repeatedly told by his mother that "the man who takes care of you is your daddy." This uncritical view of paternity would enable levels of physical, psychological, and sexual abuse among many young Black children, a largely untreated social disorder that, sadly, was all too common in the African American community, where positive male role models and father figures are scarce. These conditions are generationally linked to the physical and psychological abuses of slavery. In this reflection, African American author **James Baldwin**, who, like Fred Shuttlesworth, was also a preacher and the victim of an abusive stepfather, noted the following:

*"The actions of the White republic, in the lives of Black men, have been, and remain emasculation. Hence, the Republic has absolutely no image or standard of masculinity to which any man, Black or White, can honorably aspire. Likening this condition to a disease he calls 'sorriness', it is transmitted by Mama, whose instinct—and it's not hard to see why—is to protect the Black male from the devastation that threatens him the moment he declares himself a man. All of our mothers, and all of our women, live with this small, doom-laden bell in the skull, silent, waiting, or resounding, every hour of every day. Mama lays this burden on Sister, from whom she expects (or indicates she expects) far more than she expects from Brother; but one of the results of this all too comprehensible dynamic is that Brother may never grow up—in which case, the community has become an accomplice to the Republic."*[67]

As could have been expected given his home life, young Fred Shuttlesworth had a troublesome childhood, by his own accounts a "devilish boyhood," and more than his share of trouble in school. As a result, he would suffer more than his share of cloak-room "strappings" to his backside, inflicted by his teachers. A cloak-room was a small coat closet located within the classroom, but even with the door closed, Shuttlesworth's whippings could be overheard by all his classmates. These floggings generally concluded with a humiliated child emerging from the cloak-room in tears, to the restrained amusement of his snickering peers. Not "Freddy" Shuttlesworth, though.

On one particular occasion, while sitting in the corner for penance over a behavioral infraction, undetected by the teacher, young Freddy managed to set the classroom clock forward by 45 minutes. This caused the teacher to release the entire class early. Upon being alerted by an amused colleague to her mistake, the enraged educator called the class back

---

[67] Carbado, Devon W.; Black Men on Race, Gender, and Sexuality: A Critical Reader; Quoting Author James Baldwin; p. 240, New York University Press, 1999

into session and promptly escorted Freddy to the infamous cloak-room, where she might avenge her dignity. After a rather harsh strapping, however, Shuttlesworth refused to produce the requisite tears of contrition for his schoolmaster and instead, to the great amusement of his classmates, emerged from the tiny torture-chamber wearing his biggest grin. Not surprisingly, Freddy's irreverent performance infuriated the teacher even more, resulting in several more thrashings, most of which were delivered to the same regions of his exposed legs and buttocks. During his fifth cloak-room session, Shuttlesworth—fearing his teacher might end up killing him—extracted some saliva from his mouth and smeared it down his face to emulate tears, thus ending his ordeal. He claimed not to have given anyone the satisfaction of seeing him cry that day.

Shuttlesworth's steel hide, fearless inner strength, and resolute disposition would lead to a challenging public and private life. These same traits, however, would one day join with those of the Rev. Dr. Martin Luther King Jr. in the struggle for equality, justice, and Civil Rights.

Despite the negative experiences with his stepfather and the emotional frustrations of not having a relationship with his biological father, Fred Shuttlesworth found a stern yet warm-hearted role model in his grandfather, March Robinson. March Robinson was a respectable, hardworking man and a faithful, dedicated member of his congregation, the Saint Matthew AME (African Methodist Episcopal) Church, as was Fred's mother, Alberta. Because his stepfather was incapable of doing so without abuse, Alberta was forced to take on the role of hard-nosed disciplinarian in Fred's life. Although she was no saint…proving her knowledge of salty language and fisticuffs in various altercations with her husband, Fred nonetheless grew to manhood viewing his strong African American mother as a loving and dedicated woman, and, for the most part, uncritically. Arguably, this reflects the prevailing view of maternity within African American culture.

In a desperate attempt to keep their "fatherless" children alive and out of prison, alarmingly disproportionate numbers of single Black mothers are forced to shed softer maternal instincts in favor of tougher, stricter parental models. However, this improvised familial structure can have debilitating consequences, particularly when it comes to raising boys.

In Stephen W. Smith's book, *The Transformation of a Man's Heart: Reflections on the Masculine Journey*, he discusses the relevance of a father's influence in a boy's life compared with a mother's. Smith asserts:

> "Just as life requires input, manhood requires fathering. The father shapes a boy's sense of himself more deeply than any other person in his life. Even the father's absence, whether emotional or physical, has destructive effects…There are two ways, after all, to kill a plant; you can cut it down, or just not water it."

Speaking to the effect on many African American men from not having been raised with father-figures, Smith also shares the following poignant illustration:

"Catholic priest Richard Rohr tells the story of a nun ministering in a men's prison. One day early in May, an inmate asked the nun to get him a Mother's Day card. Happy to oblige, the nun went into town and bought it for him."

"The inmate told others, and word spread like wildfire throughout the prison. Soon, dozens of inmates were knocking on the chaplain's office door, asking for their own Mother's Day cards. Overwhelmed, the nun wisely called Hallmark's national office for help. The company donated 1,000 cards to the prison. A week before Mother's Day, the prison warden invited inmates to the chaplain's office to pick up their cards. By the end of the day, all the cards had been distributed."

"The nun was delighted. Soon after this great success, she checked her calendar and saw that Father's Day was approaching. This time, she planned ahead and contacted Hallmark again, which sent her a thousand Father's Day cards. The warden repeated his announcement on the Sunday before Father's Day. 'Father's Day came, and Father's Day went,' the nun reported in dismay. 'Not one inmate asked me for a Father's Day card.' She returned all the cards unused." Smith astutely contends, "…the wound that develops in a man's boyhood festers within and among men today."

Certainly, both boys and girls of all races suffer the negative consequences of lacking strong paternal role models during their formative years. Fortunately, there *are* male surrogates—brothers, uncles, grandfathers, and others—who help raise otherwise fatherless boys and girls. Fred Shuttlesworth was blessed to have had one such man in his childhood.

By the grace of God, Fred managed to make it out of high school with most of his backside intact and went on to graduate from college. He continued his education, becoming an ordained minister and was appointed pastor of the First Baptist Church in Selma, Alabama. In 1953, he accepted the position of pastor at the Bethel Baptist Church in Birmingham, Alabama.[68]

As a pastor, he was widely admired yet criticized for his autocratic management of church affairs. In some cases, he refused to allow the church's deacon board to make decisions without his consent and participation. Many wealthy church patrons felt they should have a say in church affairs, given their substantial financial contributions; however, Shuttlesworth believed these matters should always yield to God's will, not the worldly will of the congregation or deacon board. In most cases, he succeeded in convincing the congregation to stand with him.

Rev. Shuttlesworth soon became a leading Civil Rights figure in Birmingham and, as such, the enemy of Birmingham's Commissioner of Public Safety, Theophilus Eugene Conner, better known as "Bull Conner". Despite the city's many attempts to thwart his efforts, Fred Shuttlesworth's church was the first Black church in Birmingham to register all its members to vote. Soon, however, deeply affected by the brutal murder of a young black boy named Emmett Till, Shuttlesworth would switch to a more explosive brand of

---

[68] Manis, Andrew M. (1999) *A Fire You Can't Put Out: The Civil Rights Life of Birmingham's Reverend Fred Shuttlesworth.* Tuscaloosa: University of Alabama Press; p. 19, 20, 39, 40, 41

social activism and come onto the radar of the treacherous Southern White political power structure.

## The Bus Boycotts

On November 13, 1956, the U.S. Supreme Court upheld the ruling in Browder v. Gayle, affirming that bus segregation was unconstitutional. The ruling was a response to the Montgomery Bus Boycott, which began on Thursday, December 1, 1955, when Rosa Parks was arrested for refusing to give up her seat to a white bus patron. The Montgomery boycott would greatly affect Birmingham's and Rev. Fred Shuttlesworth's destinies.

Rosa Parks was not the first African American to protest in this manner. Earlier that same year, African American Claudette Colvin was arrested for refusing to give up her seat to a white man. At the time, the local president of the N.A.A.C.P. was E.D. Nixon. Nixon had initially intended to use Colvin's arrest to challenge segregation on Montgomery buses, but changed his mind upon learning that 15-year-old Claudette was pregnant. Conceding that young Claudette would not have been considered worthy of protest by the Black community, he chose to bide his time. Then, along came Rosa Parks, whom Nixon felt projected a more positive image because of her employment history, marital status, and good standing in the community. Nixon believed that Parks was someone the entire community would get behind, and he was right.

News of Rosa Parks' arrest spread quickly, and that very night, E.D. Nixon organized a meeting of local ministers at the Dexter Avenue Baptist Church—the parish of a young, unknown minister named Rev. Dr. Martin Luther King Jr. Once again, the Black Church would serve as a spiritual command center. Initially, Nixon and some of the ministers present disagreed on the scope and effectiveness of a bus boycott. As a result, it was decided that a larger meeting of African American clergy would convene that same night to help resolve this important matter.

At the second meeting, several ministers, perhaps fearing that their congregations would suffer financial hardship or that their own lives would be at risk, voiced their reluctance to support the boycott. Exasperated, Nixon offered a humbling reminder to the reluctant ministers that their secure pastoral lifestyles depended on shepherding their respective disadvantaged congregations, and that now was the time to stand up for their flocks. It was then that Rev. King stood and, reasserting the need to support this cause, agreed to lead the Montgomery, Alabama bus boycott—a position for which there was no competitor.

Impressed by Rev. King's courage, E.D. Nixon understood that the young minister was willing to risk his and his family's lives. He also saw Rev. King as an excellent choice to lead this campaign, recognizing that, being fresh out of Boston University, young, intelligent, and new to Montgomery, King would be less likely to be intimidated by the city's powerful White racist establishment. Dr. King also had a fresh voice and preached Christian love—not worldly revenge or retribution—as the only means of resisting hate.

King's spirit of selfless volunteerism truly galvanized the ministers gathered at the Dexter Ave. Baptist Church that evening. Together, they agreed to support the Boycott and encourage their respective congregations to stay off Montgomery buses that Monday. They also elected to organize the bus boycott campaign under the intentionally benign-sounding name, the **Montgomery Improvement Association** (MIA). However, the conditions the MIA sought were more of a request for compromise than a demand for desegregation.

Under King's leadership, the MIA proposed a citywide boycott by Black residents of public transit to demand a fixed dividing line for the segregated sections of the buses, ostensibly allowing Black passengers unrestricted access to their own *segregated* rear section of the bus. In other words, the MIA was asking Montgomery to uphold the Jim Crow "Separate but Equal" law, promised to Black residents by the Supreme Court in Plessy v. Ferguson.

At the time of Rosa Parks's arrest, she was seated in the front row of the "Colored Section" of the bus, which was still located at the rear, interior half. When the White section became full, the bus driver instructed Parks to surrender her seat to a White man so that he would not have to stand; this prompted her refusal and arrest, triggering the Montgomery boycott. All the MIA wanted was for Whites to adhere to the racist rules they themselves had created, which, in the South, had been accepted by most blacks. Such a compromise, however, was unacceptable to Rev. Fred Shuttlesworth.

That same evening, Thursday night, December 1st, 1955, Mrs. Jo Ann Robinson, an African American educator and activist, stayed up mimeographing thousands of flyers calling for an all-out boycott of the Montgomery bus system on Monday, December 5th. The leaflets were distributed the next day (Friday) at an emergency meeting of Baptist and AME Zionist clergy. During the meeting, ministers were asked to stress to their congregations on Sunday the need to participate in the boycott. The flyer read as follows:

*"Another woman has been arrested and thrown in jail because she refused to get up out of her seat on the bus, for a white person to sit down. It is the second time since the Claudette Colvin case that a Negro woman has been arrested for the same thing. This has to be stopped. Negroes have rights too, for if Negroes did not ride the buses, they could not operate. Three-fourths of the riders are Negro, yet we are arrested, or have to stand over empty seats. If we do not do something to stop these arrests, they will continue. The next time it may be you, or your daughter, or mother. This woman's case will come up on Monday. We are, therefore, asking every Negro to stay off the buses Monday in protest of the arrest and trial. Don't ride the buses to work, to town, to school, or anywhere on Monday. You can afford to stay out of school for one day if you have no other way to go except by bus. You can also afford to stay out of town for one day. If you work, take a cab, or walk. But please, children and grown-ups, don't ride the bus at all on Monday. Please stay off all buses Monday."*[69]

The Montgomery bus boycott campaign would ultimately last over a year and introduce Rev. Dr. Martin Luther King Jr. to the nation. The campaign ended with a federal

---

[69] Carson, Clayborne / "The Autobiography of Martin Luther King" 1998 "The Letters from Birmingham Jail" / Warner Books, Inc.

ruling on December 20, 1956, which ultimately led to the Supreme Court decision that segregation of any kind on Montgomery buses or any bus was unconstitutional.

Although it ultimately achieved its objective, the MIA's request for compromise angered and frustrated Fred Shuttlesworth, who did not believe that true equality and desegregation could be achieved through such a passive approach. From his viewpoint, no less than a *demand* for full desegregation and equality was called for to wipe out Jim Crow laws. To be certain, Shuttlesworth took a hard line on these issues, but then again, Shuttlesworth lived in Birmingham, the most volatile city in America, and to effect change there, Blacks would require more than just passive leadership. They would need a battlefield general.

## "Bombingham," Alabama

Birmingham was the largest city in Alabama, and under its Governor, George Wallace, and police commissioner, Eugene "Bull" Conner, its large, politically, socially, and economically marginalized African American population was subjected to a unique brand of hatred, violence, racism, and segregation, as seen only in the deepest, darkest regions of America's South. The Rev. Dr. Martin Luther King Jr. would refer to Birmingham, Alabama, as "the most thoroughly segregated city in the United States..." Between 1936 and 1950, there were an estimated 35 to 40 reported bombings there, earning the city the moniker: "Bombingham".

Rev. Shuttlesworth had been elected membership chairman for the Alabama chapter of the N.A.A.C.P.; however, following the Montgomery Bus Boycott, the NAACP was effectively banned in Birmingham. In response, Shuttlesworth founded the **Alabama Christian Movement for Human Rights**. This move made him public enemy number one among White Birmingham segregationists, many of whom, if not most, were affiliated with the local Ku Klux Klan.

Birmingham was a known breeding ground for the nefarious Ku Klux Klan, whose powerful Southern presence was now being threatened by the Civil Rights movement and its leaders – leaders like Rev. Dr. King and Rev. Shuttlesworth. Many Birmingham police officers were openly KKK members and were known to proudly patrol the streets in full Klan attire, striking terror into the hearts and minds of Black residents. Those officers who were not Klan members dared not stand against the Klan's hateful, terrorist will, lest they and their families become targets of the KKK's deadly cocktail of violent retribution.

The Montgomery bus boycott inspired Fred Shuttlesworth to challenge segregation on Birmingham's buses. He had no plans, however, to boycott Birmingham's buses. Instead, he publicly demanded that Birmingham's city commissioners rescind their Jim Crow bus laws outright in light of the Supreme Court ruling in Montgomery. He then announced that he would personally ride Birmingham buses in the designated White-only section, regardless of whether the city commissioners agreed to his demands. Shuttlesworth's well-publicized "ride" was scheduled for December 26th, 1956, the day after Christmas.

At 9:15 pm on December 25th, 1956, the night before Shuttlesworth's campaign of civil disobedience would begin, a bomb made of 16 sticks of dynamite exploded beneath Shuttlesworth's bedroom, completely destroying the Bethel Street Baptist Church parsonage—his home. Shuttlesworth was in bed at the time but somehow emerged from the rubble unharmed. Later, he told reporters that before the bombing, he "would not have boarded an airplane for a million dollars," but immediately after the explosion, realizing his life had been spared, he felt no fear and has been afraid of nothing since. Shuttlesworth later recalled that "Klansman Police" were the first to respond to the crime scene, one of whom said to him, "Reverend, if I were you, I'd get out of town as fast as I could." To which Shuttlesworth replied, "You're not me, officer, now you go back and tell your Klan brothers that if God could get me through this, then I'm here for the duration."

The bombing was clearly intended to kill Shuttlesworth and his family, but by the grace of God, they all survived. Ironically, in addition to fueling his fearlessness, his survival galvanized the movement and led Shuttlesworth to feel that God had called him to this mission. It also helped build a large following of supporters for Rev. Shuttlesworth and his causes—people who believed his life had been spared for such a purpose.

## Helping Hands

Following the bombing of Shuttlesworth's home, 15 local pastors and their congregations joined together in spiritual, financial, and physical support of his mission to desegregate Birmingham. The ministers decided on Monday night to hold meetings at their respective churches to discuss "movement affairs" and disseminate important information. These meetings always began with prayer and song and often developed into emotion-filled worship. In fact, it was sometimes difficult to know exactly where the movement meeting began and where the worship meeting ended.

In addition to ministers and deacons, lay members of these Black churches made essential contributions to the movement's Monday night meetings. The men of the church, for example, would collect and safeguard offerings, lead the devotional prayer, and serve as bodyguards for Rev. Shuttlesworth and his family. Some of these men were off-duty police officers and WWII veterans who, in some cases, carried guns and were well-trained in defense, surveillance, and combat.

The women of the African American church, however, were true, unsung heroines of the Montgomery and Birmingham movements, serving in countless and invaluable ways. Like Louise, some of these women were highly gifted in music and composed inspirational songs for the movement. Singers, choir directors, and organists also helped inspire and motivate bus boycotters through song. Others organized food preparation, child care, cleaning committees, choirs, and prayer groups for various events. These dedicated servants would meet at their respective churches, homes, or meeting places to sing, pray, work, and help plan and prepare for the week's movement-related activities. They were also crucial in disseminating important, up-to-the-minute information to the local African American populace.

Many songs sung at these meetings combined Gospel music with freedom songs of the day, as the message of the Gospels and that of freedom were, theologically speaking, one and the same. African American churchgoers fervently believed the biblical truth that only God had the power to overcome the evil and hate in the hearts of Southern Whites. They also believed the scriptural truth that only God could replenish them with the spiritual faith needed to maintain their strength and resolve during these difficult times.

*"Do not be overcome by evil, but overcome evil with good."*

*-Romans 12:21*

Rev. Shuttlesworth would need to empower, engage, and dispatch these faithful foot-soldiers to achieve any measure of desegregation in Birmingham. This would prove far more difficult and dangerous than in Montgomery, where the KKK was far more vicious. His public defiance of "Bull' Conner would frequently remind him and his family to look to God for strength and patience.

In 1956, Shuttlesworth helps establish the **Southern Christian Leadership Conference (SCLC)**, of which Dr. Martin Luther King was also a founder.[70]

**September 2, 1957.** Dr. King delivers a speech at the 25th Anniversary of the Highlander Folk School in Monteagle, Tennessee. Rev. Shuttlesworth is also in attendance. While there, he meets Myles Horton, Pete Seeger, and Guy Carawan.

Left to right, Dr. King, Pete Seeger, unknown, Rosa Parks, Rev. Ralph Abernathy, 1957, Highlander Folk School

---

[70] Abbe A. Debolt, James S. Baugess; Encyclopedia of the Sixties: A Decade of Culture and Counterculture; ABC-CLIO, Dec 31, 2011; p. 599

Pictured L to R: Ella Baker, Rev. Fred Shuttlesworth, Unknown, James Bevel, Guy Carawan, Unknown, 1957 25th anniversary. Courtesy Highlander Research and Education Center

## Highlander Folk School

Established in 1932 by Myles Horton in the hills of Monteagle, Tennessee, the Highlander Folk School was led by Horton and his wife, Zilphia. The school hosted interracial workshops on social justice and leadership training for labor movements and Civil Rights activism. Rosa Parks, Ralph Abernathy, Rev. Dr. King Jr., Rev. Shuttlesworth, Andrew Young, and Stokely Carmichael each visited the school. Rosa Parks spent six weeks at Highlander in 1955, four months before her Montgomery bus protest.

On **September 17, 1957,** Rev. Fred Shuttlesworth and his wife, Ruby, were stabbed and beaten with baseball bats and chains by members of the Ku Klux Klan while attempting to enroll their two daughters in an all-White public high school. No police came to their aid. One of the assailants, Bobby Cherry, later helped carry out the **16th Street Baptist Church bombing**, in which 4 innocent African American girls were murdered during

Sunday school. Together, King and Shuttlesworth would face many tribulations of racism, hatred, violence, and injustice.

# Revelations

Sometime between 1957 and 1960, Louise and her family join the **Revelation Missionary Baptist Church** in the West End area of Cincinnati.

**September 1959** - Charges of Communist activity, illegal alcohol consumption, and sexual impropriety are brought against Highlander Folk School. A judge threatens to shut the school down. Rev. Dr. Martin Luther King Jr. denies a request to testify on Highlander's behalf but signs a petition affirming the school's right to exist for educational purposes without intimidation. [71]

**February 16, 1960** – The Highlander Folk School's administration building is padlocked, and its charter is revoked. [72]

**June 1960** – Rev. Fred Shuttlesworth attends a meeting at Highlander Folk School. While there, he shares popular Gospel songs with Guy Carawan, Pete Seeger, and others.[73]

**In July 1960**, Louise establishes her own record label, **Shropshire Records,** and releases a 45-rpm recording of her composition, "Trying My Best to Get Home to See Jesus," performed by Truzella McClain and the "Revelation Baptist Church Choir." The song becomes a local hit.

Revelation Missionary Baptist Church, circa 1925

---

[71] Martin Luther King Papers Project / Stanford University. / "23 September 1959 From Anne Braden Louisville, Ky."
[72] "Charter Is Lost by Mixed School," *New York Times*, 17 February 1960; see also *Highlander Folk School et al. v. Tennessee Ex Rel. Sloan, District Attorney General*, 368 U.S. 840 [1961
[73] October 2011 Interview with Fred Shuttlesworth Jr. / Cincinnati Ohio

45 rpm Recording of Louise Shropshire's, "Trying My Best to Get Home to see Jesus."

Later that year, Rev. Shuttlesworth delivers a sermon at the Zion Baptist Church in Cincinnati commemorating the anniversary of its pastor, **Rev. L. Venchael Booth**. Most Black Cincinnatians know of the bombing of Rev. Shuttlesworth's Alabama home and church. After the service, Rev. Booth approaches Shuttlesworth and mentions that Revelation Baptist Church, a large Cincinnati congregation of nearly 1,000 "upwardly mobile" African Americans, is in need of a pastor like him, whose reputation matches the church's. Shuttlesworth thanks Rev. Booth for the information but respectfully declines to pursue it.

Not accepting "no" for an answer, Rev. Booth later mentions Shuttlesworth's impressive sermon to the Revelation Baptist Church "Pulpit Committee," of which Louise Shropshire is a member. Thrilled at the prospect of such a committed and celebrated pastor, Louise and other committee members immediately began efforts to secure Rev. Shuttlesworth for their church. Eventually, Shuttlesworth agreed to deliver several sermons at Revelation as a "guest preacher." Following his first few sermons, the pulpit committee enthusiastically decided to appoint Shuttlesworth as their pastor. Shuttlesworth, however, respectfully declined the Revelation offer, asserting his loyalty to Birmingham and his current congregation, the Bethel Baptist Church.

In 1961, Louise and her choir perform at the National Convention of Choirs and Choruses. Rev. Fred Shuttlesworth attends. During the convention, Louise, representing the Revelation Baptist Church, makes a spiritual appeal to Shuttlesworth to accept the pastorate at Revelation. In a candid, unofficial negotiation, Louise appeals to Shuttlesworth's family values, noting that the position would include a spacious parsonage, salary, and health insurance for his family. To Louise's great satisfaction, Shuttlesworth agrees to begin official negotiations with Revelation. Shuttlesworth's wife, Ruby, would unwittingly contribute greatly to his decision. She had weathered more than her share of bombings, beatings, and near-death experiences in Birmingham and also saw Cincinnati as a place where her children, bearing the name Shuttlesworth, could receive better education and employment opportunities than they would in Alabama.

During negotiations with the Revelation Baptist Church, Shuttlesworth agrees to serve as Pastor. However, he does so on the condition that he be permitted to return to Birmingham to continue his desegregation efforts whenever he deems it necessary. Rev. Shuttlesworth also requests permission to preach at Revelation every other Sunday to maintain a leadership presence at Bethel Baptist Church while Bethel Baptist Church secures his replacement. The Revelation Baptist Church pulpit committee agrees to his requests. With all terms mutually agreed upon, Rev. Fred Shuttlesworth accepts the position of Pastor at the Revelation Baptist Church and relocates his family to Cincinnati.

In September of 1961, Louise establishes "Mrs. Shropshire's Bargain Center".

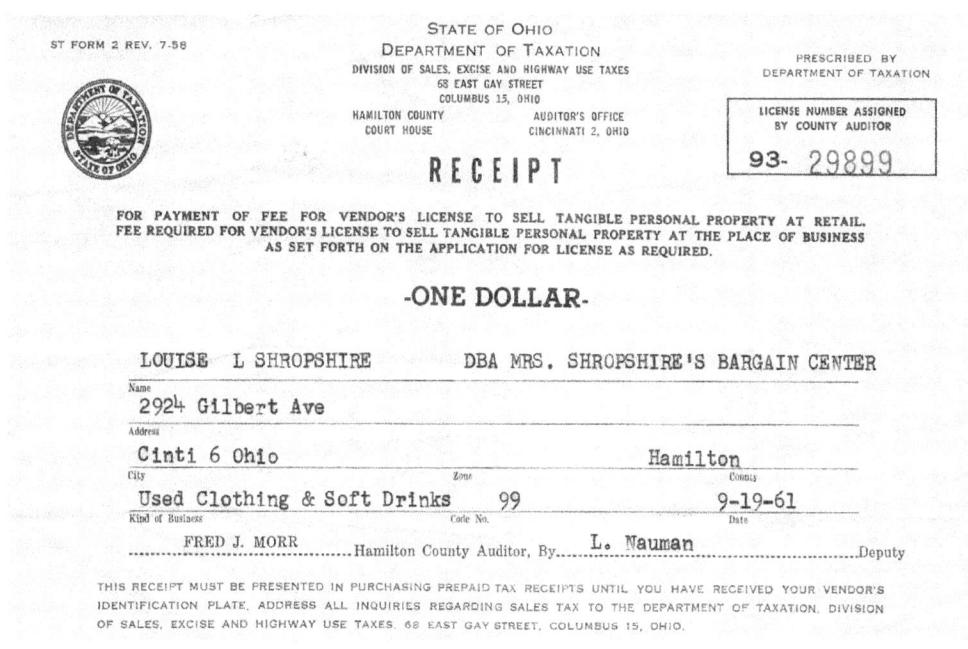

Courtesy Louise Shropshire Foundation

# A New Home

March 1962 – Rev. Fred Shuttlesworth, the new pastor of the Revelation Baptist Church, has arrived, and the national spotlight is on Cincinnati. Louise, having been introduced to Rev. Dr. Martin Luther King by Rev. Shuttlesworth, organizes and chairs a high-profile testimonial banquet in honor of Shuttlesworth's new role as pastor of the Revelation Baptist Church. Dr. King is the featured speaker, and proceeds from the event help post bail bonds for protesters being arrested in Birmingham. The event is photographed and featured in the local newspaper, and handbills are distributed to the church congregation.

Courtesy, Cleveland Call and Post

-Fundraising Banquet for Fred Shuttlesworth, March 23, 1962; Netherland Hilton Hotel, Cincinnati, OH. Dr. King is at the podium, Louise Shropshire chairs the event and is pictured in a white dress, third from right, Fred Shuttlesworth- far Left.
Courtesy Louise Shropshire Foundation

## The Birmingham Campaign

Since moving to Cincinnati, Rev. Shuttlesworth has remained highly active in Birmingham's desegregation efforts, ever vigilant in fulfilling his promises to the city's disenfranchised Black residents. Birmingham's city leaders and merchants, however, have not yielded to his demands for equal employment and the desegregation of restrooms, lunch counters, and fitting rooms at downtown department stores. That is, until Shuttlesworth threatens to call in Dr. King to help with his Birmingham campaign. Terrified of the national attention Dr. King will surely bring to Birmingham, the City's White leaders ask for an unprecedented meeting with Rev. Shuttlesworth. During the meeting, however, they essentially ask for a compromise to keep the Dr. King media frenzy away from their city. That was the wrong thing to ask. There would be no such concession from Rev. Shuttlesworth, who had the influence to arrange a boycott without agreeing to a compromise. As far as Blacks in Birmingham were concerned, Bull Conner or no Bull Conner, Shuttlesworth still held the marbles.

In 1963, at the invitation of Rev. Thomas Dorsey, Fred Shuttlesworth speaks on civil rights at the NCGCC convention in Pittsburgh, Pennsylvania. Louise directs the Mass Choir in songs of praise.[74]

**On April 3, 1963**, the full force of Rev. Fred Shuttlesworth, Dr. Martin Luther King Jr., the SCLC, and the national media arrived in Birmingham. Their strategy was to launch a massive campaign to desegregate the area's local merchants during the Easter holiday—Birmingham's second-busiest shopping season. The campaign began with a series of mass church meetings, during which Dr. King emphasized the power of nonviolent protest and solicited volunteers for various campaign activities. These meetings were followed by marches on city hall, lunch-counter sit-ins, and the boycott of Birmingham's downtown merchants. By April 10th, however, the city had obtained an injunction against the protests and civil disobedience. After submitting to Rev. Shuttlesworth's passionate arguments, however, campaign leaders agreed to defy the court order. King declared: *"We cannot in all good conscience obey such an injunction which is an unjust, undemocratic, and unconstitutional misuse of the legal process."*

Complications arose, however, as civil disobedience intensified, resulting in more arrests, each requiring additional bail. A fund had been established for this purpose, but given the campaign's size, it was now nearly depleted. This was a problem. With limited bail money available, movement leaders could not guarantee that protesters would be released promptly. Dr. King knew that raising funds would be necessary, which meant leaving Birmingham. He was concerned, however, that leaving town could be misinterpreted by protesters as a sign of fear, damaging his credibility. At the risk of running out of bail funds, Dr. King chose to stay with the protesters and risk incarceration, stating, *"I don't know what will happen; I don't know where the money will come from. But I have to make a faith act."*

Rev. Shuttlesworth calls Louise, who, with her husband, Robert, hosts a series of fundraisers in their home for Cincinnati's affluent, African American middle-class and upwardly mobile Civil Rights Movement supporters. On April 12th, 1963, Good Friday, Dr. King is arrested in Birmingham for violating the city's injunction against protests. He is held in solitary confinement. During this time, King pens his famous "Letter from Birmingham Jail". Bail has been posted, and Dr. King is released on April 20th. The Shropshires and many others are valued allies in raising funds to free jailed Civil Rights protesters; however, it becomes increasingly difficult to recruit volunteers willing to be jailed and risk losing their jobs.

To sustain the Birmingham campaign, SCLC organizer James Bevel proposes involving high school students in protests and demonstrations. On May 2nd, 1963, over 6,000 African American schoolchildren demonstrate against school segregation... nearly 1,000 are arrested. When hundreds more gather the next day, "Bull" Connor directs local police and fire departments to use force to end the demonstrations. Connor's tactic backfires, however, as images of children being attacked by police dogs, pelted with high-

---

[74] Source: National Convention of Gospel Choirs and Choruses (NCGCC)

pressure fire hoses, and beaten by Birmingham police officers appear in newspapers and on television across America. Shuttlesworth himself is slammed into a wall by a high-pressure fire hose and knocked unconscious. He is hospitalized for several days.

During Shuttlesworth's hospitalization, Dr. King is contacted by President John F. Kennedy and Justice Department officials, who urge him to call off the Birmingham demonstrations. On May 9th, after Rev. Shuttlesworth is discharged from the hospital, and per the advice of Andrew Young, Dr. King meets with Shuttlesworth to "inform" him that, in his absence, an arrangement with the President has been made to announce at a press conference the termination of the hard-fought Birmingham campaign. King informs Shuttlesworth that the city's merchants had not budged an inch in negotiations and that the Birmingham jails were now filled to capacity with demonstrators. The President's brother, Robert Kennedy, is standing by to issue a joint press announcement.

Stunned by these developments, a livid but controlled Shuttlesworth then spoke these carefully measured words:

*"We're not calling it off, Martin; the people in Birmingham trust me, and I've never disappointed them. They understand that I speak the truth. Your sun has been high, and you're Mr. Big now, but you'll be Mr. Nothing if you call this off. I'm going back home to bed and will wait to see what you do. If you do call it off, with what strength I have, I will go to church and into the streets, and your name will be mud."*

With that, Shuttlesworth turned and left. The King/Kennedy press conference scheduled for that day was canceled. The following day, Dr. King, Rev. Shuttlesworth, and Rev. Abernathy publicly announced that White merchants had acquiesced to the SCLC's demands and would be given 90 days to desegregate their places of business. Those in jail were released on bond after the United Steelworkers Union, United Auto Workers Union, National Maritime Union, and the American Federation of Labor and Congress of Industrial Organizations (AFL-CIO) raised $237,000 in bail—the 2012 equivalent of $1,800,000. Birmingham's White racists, however, were highly displeased with these developments and knew just how to show it.

Birmingham Press Conference announcing the success of the 1963 Campaign, L to R - Rev. Dr. Martin Luther King Jr., Rev. Fred Shuttlesworth, and Rev. Ralph Abernathy

On May 11th, 1963, a bomb destroyed the Gaston Motel, where Dr. King and leaders of the SCLC had been staying. King had left just a few hours earlier. The Gaston Motel was owned by Arthur George Gaston, a local African American businessman. That same evening, Dr. King's brother, A.D. King, had his Birmingham home bombed and destroyed. Although A.D. King's wife and five children were home and terrified, they were unharmed. Outraged, local African Americans began rioting, and 3,000 Alabama State Troopers moved into Birmingham. Martial law was declared.

છ

# Chapter 14

# Song of the South

**Racism:** "a belief that race is the primary determinant of human traits and capacities, and that racial differences produce an inherent superiority of a particular race."
*(Source: Merriam-Webster)*

It's 1960, and John F. Kennedy has been elected the 35th president of the United States. Promising to enact Civil Rights legislation, he receives seventy percent of the African American vote. Although Kennedy's election represents a step forward for African Americans, many Black residents in Southern states are not counted because of racist tactics of intimidation and violence, poll taxes, and literacy tests intended to weaken the African American vote. It's not until the ratification of the 24th Amendment on January 23, 1964, that poll taxes and literacy tests are rendered unconstitutional. [75]

In the South, there was an open and notorious conspiracy to weaken the political influence of Black Americans. Legislated and supported by Southern Whites, these racist strategies emerged during the post-Reconstruction era. These discriminatory laws and measures were designed to marginalize and disenfranchise African Americans from the legislative and political processes. The poll tax was affirmed by the Supreme Court in 1937, reflecting how little the Civil War had done to end bigotry, hatred, and discrimination in America. But how was this possible? How could the highest court in the land affirm a law designed to harm Americans purely because of their skin color? Wasn't this unconstitutional?

The US Constitution *was* written to ensure the freedoms of the "people"; however, this historic document did not include Black people in its "people" classification, thereby excluding them from entitlement to its so-called "unalienable rights" and emphasizing America's racist creed. In fact, as far as the Constitution was concerned, Black people were considered only "three-fifths" of a human being. This code became known as the **"Three-Fifths Compromise."**

### Article 1, Section 2, Paragraph 3 of the US Constitution:

*"Representatives and direct Taxes shall be apportioned among the several States which may be included within this Union, according to their respective Numbers, which shall be determined by adding to the whole Number of free Persons, including those bound to*

---

[75] Keyssar, Alexander; The Right to Vote: The Contested History of Democracy in the United States; Basic Books; 2001; p. 271

*Service for a Term of Years, and excluding Indians not taxed,* **three fifths of all other Persons."**

The Three-Fifths Compromise was a settlement reached between Northern and Southern states during the 1787 Philadelphia Convention. This agreement permitted three-fifths of the enslaved population to be counted for the purposes of the geographical distribution of the members of the United States House of Representatives.

According to the US Constitution, for every 30,000 residents in a state, that state would receive one political representative to Congress. Northern Delegates, who were opposed to slavery, wanted to count only the free Blacks of each state, so as not to give the Southern states, where the vast majority of Blacks resided, disproportionate political influence. Southern Delegates, who were supportive of slavery, however, wanted to count slaves in their actual numbers. As slaves could not vote, Southern slave owners desperately wanted the benefit of increased numerical representation in the US House of Representatives and the Electoral College, which would advance their racist political and capitalist agendas.

As a result of the compromise, every 50,000 enslaved people would now be represented by one White Southern congressional representative—compared with one representative for every 30,000 enslaved people. The final concession, counting Black people ("all other persons") as only three-fifths of their actual numbers, reduced the political influence of the slave states only in comparison with their initial demands. The Three-Fifths Compromise is credited with giving Southern pro-slavery forces disproportionate political power in the U.S. government from the establishment of the U.S. Constitution until the Civil War. [76]

Aside from the brutal horrors of slavery, African Americans had now become victims of political subjugation and economic manipulation, manifestations of pure American racism and greed. This was America's open, infected wound of injustice, which would spread throughout its entire political and ideological body.

Although in 1870 the Fifteenth Amendment to the U.S. Constitution would ostensibly grant African American *men* the right to vote, all eleven former Confederate slave states had already enacted their own poll tax laws, and as a result, nearly a century later, many Southern Blacks were still unable to exercise their constitutional rights.

The Ku Klux Klan and its bilious brotherhood also did its part to prevent Black voters from flexing their new voting muscle. With its clandestine and well-connected "good-ol'-boy" network across the South, the KKK carried out lynching, bombings, beatings, intimidation, and other detestable assaults against prospective Black voters, their supporters, and their families.[77]

---

[76] Carl Smith, Karnie C. Smith, Sr.; Frederick Douglass Republicans: The Movement to Re-Ignite America's Passion for Liberty; AuthorHouse, Apr 25, 2011; p. 19

[77] Johnson, Kimberly S.; Reforming Jim Crow: Southern Politics and State in the Age Before Brown; Oxford University Press; 2010; p. 04

Tragically, as a result of the hateful and sadistic actions by racist Whites, who continued to abuse, belittle, and deny the human and political worth of African Americans for hundreds of years, many generations of Black people would grow to maturity, psychologically conditioned to believe a lie—that their minds, feelings, opinions, ideas, and efforts had little to no true value. These sentiments were vehemently voiced by Dr. King:

*"Discrimination is a hellhound that gnaws at Negroes in every waking moment of their lives to remind them that the lie of their inferiority is accepted as truth in the society dominating them."* -Rev. Dr. Martin Luther King Jr.

Meanwhile, the very-real and very-tangible economic, political, and intellectual value of African Americans had skyrocketed like a Texas oil gusher. Like their African ancestors before them, Blacks would once again be hunted—this time for their votes, labor, music, art, athleticism, literature, thoughts, and ideas. Once captured, these precious resources would be exploited for profit and pumped directly into the bank accounts of profiteers, perpetuating the same inequities, attitudes, and arrogance that had thrived and metastasized during the height of American slavery. In the process, poor and poorly educated Blacks, unaware of their true value, would be paid in lies and cornpone, told to put on their widest "Uncle Remus" grins, sing "Zippity Do Da," and be bamboozled into turning over their most sacred and irreplaceable intellectual possessions—the very ones that could have ensured their economic and cultural independence from a hateful, repressive, biased, and discriminatory system. [78]

Masquerading as scholars and entrepreneurs, parasites such as these demonstrate a profound lack of respect, consideration, and recognition for the rights of African Americans as equals under God *or* the law. The fact that the repugnant thoughts and deeds of these men have been celebrated rather than condemned speaks to the ideological petri-dish in which they have been cultured and bred—an environment in which, like bloated maggots, they have grown fat by gorging themselves on the gaping, infected wounds of slavery—wounds inflicted by barbed laws and political bullwhips. Men such as these, with their racist, neo-colonialist belief in their superiority to Blacks, have spawned malignant attitudes of entrepreneurial entitlement to the unearned cultural and economic fruits of African American physical, cultural, and intellectual production and endeavor. It is precisely this mindset that motivated the plagiarism and unlawful exploitation of Louise Shropshire's sacred hymn.

Disturbingly, these xenophobic illusions may have been bequeathed to these Americans and others like them, in part by a man for whom they built a monument. –A man who owned upwards of 700 slaves; at least one of whom, a child of 14, he raped multiple times. –A man who, until his death, believed avidly in the inferiority of Blacks. –A man most Americans affectionately refer to as their Founding Father. –A man named Thomas Jefferson.

---

[78] Lawson, Steven F.; Black Ballots: Voting Rights in the South, 1944-1969; Lexington Books; 1976; P. 44-46

Isaias Gamboa

# The House that Jefferson Built

*"Train up a child in the way he should go,
And when he is old, he will not depart from it."* **Proverbs 22:6**

From the biblical book of Proverbs, Louise Shropshire often invoked the insight cited above to teach the long-term benefits of providing a child with a consistent, biblically based moral education. Conversely, would not this same principle apply to a child trained in the ideologies of racism, conscious or unconscious? When suckled formative, the venomous mother's milk of prejudice and discrimination seldom departs from the heart, mind, and sinew of its spawn. Could this warped ideology, handed down to men like Pete Seeger and his associates, have caused them to devalue Black sacred music and to misappropriate Louise Shropshire's intellectual property?

America's time-honored ideals and values were nurtured on the pabulum of the United States Constitution, the Bill of Rights, and the Declaration of Independence. The men who helped forge these documents are reverently referred to as America's "Founding Fathers." One of the most notable and celebrated of these men is Thomas Jefferson, the author of the Declaration of Independence and a powerful advocate of the First Amendment to the Bill of Rights. When engaging in political rhetoric, American legislators, pundits, educators, and intellectuals alike fondly refer to Jefferson as one of the most influential of America's historic figures. Few would dispute that during America's ideological infancy, Thomas Jefferson was tremendously influential in helping define and shape the country's mores, values, and ideals…as any father would for his offspring. Jefferson's lesson plans, however, for a young, slave-holding America, seemed to have been drawn from his own deeply felt belief in White supremacy. The following, authored by Jefferson, illustrates this fact.

In 1781, Thomas Jefferson authored a document espousing his somewhat unrestrained views on race in America, particularly in the state of Virginia, where he lived and owned slaves. Published in 1784, his manuscript was entitled *Notes on the State of Virginia*. The following are excerpts:

### From "Notes on the State of Virginia"

*"…The first difference which strikes us is that of [color]. Whether the black of the Negro resides in the reticular membrane between the skin and scarf-skin, or in the scarfskin itself; whether it proceeds from the colour of the blood, the colour of the bile, or from that of some other secretion, the difference is fixed in nature…And is this difference of no importance? Is it not the foundation of a greater or lesser share of beauty in the two races? …The circumstance of superior beauty is thought worthy of attention in the propagation of our horses, dogs, and other domestic animals; why not in that of man?*

*"…Besides those of colour, figure, and hair, there are other physical distinctions proving a difference of race. They have less hair on the face and body. They secrete less by*

the [kidneys], and more by the glands of the skin, which gives them a very strong and disagreeable odour. This greater degree of transpiration renders them more tolerant of heat and less so of cold than the whites. ...They seem to require less sleep. A black, after hard labour through the day, will be induced by the slightest amusements to sit up till midnight, or later, though knowing he must be out with the first dawn of the morning. They are at least as brave and more adventuresome. But this may perhaps proceed from a want of forethought, which prevents their seeing a danger till it be present. When present, they do not go through it with more coolness or steadiness than the whites...

"They are more ardent after their female, but love seems with them to be more an eager desire than a tender, delicate mixture of sentiment and sensation. Their [griefs] are transient. Those numberless afflictions, which render it doubtful whether heaven has given life to us in mercy or in wrath, are less felt, and sooner forgotten with them. In general, their existence appears to participate more of sensation than reflection. To this must be ascribed their disposition to sleep when abstracted from their diversions and unemployed in labour. An animal whose body is at rest, and who does not reflect, must be disposed to sleep, of course...

"Comparing them by their faculties of memory, reason, and imagination, it appears to me, that in memory they are equal to the whites; in reason much inferior, as I think one could scarcely be found capable of tracing and comprehending the investigations of Euclid; and that in imagination they are dull, tasteless, and anomalous. It would be unfair to follow them to Africa for this investigation. We will consider them here, on the same stage with the whites, and where the facts are not apocryphal on which a judgment is to be formed...

"It will be right to make great allowances for the difference of condition, of education, of conversation, of the sphere in which they move. Many millions of them have been brought to, and born in America. Most of them indeed have been confined to tillage, to their own homes, and their own society; yet many have been so situated that they might have availed themselves of the conversation of their masters; many have been brought up to the handicraft arts, and from that circumstance have always been associated with the whites. Some have been liberally educated, and all have lived in countries where the arts and sciences are cultivated to a considerable degree, and have had before their eyes samples of the best works from abroad.

"The Indians, with no advantages of this kind, will often carve figures on their pipes not destitute of design and merit. They will crayon out an animal, a plant, or a country, so as to prove the existence of a germ in their minds which only wants cultivation. They astonish you with strokes of the most sublime oratory, such as prove their reason and sentiment strong, their imagination glowing and elevated. But never yet could I find that a black had uttered a thought above the level of plain narration; never saw even an elementary trait of painting or sculpture.

"In music, they are more generally gifted than the whites with accurate ears for tune and time...Whether they will be equal to the composition of a more extensive run of melody, or of complicated harmony, is yet to be proved.

"Misery is often the parent of the most affecting touches in poetry. Among the blacks is misery enough, God knows, but no poetry. Love is the peculiar oestrum of the poet. Their love is ardent, but it kindles the senses only, not the imagination. Religion indeed has produced a Phyllis Wheatley, but it could not produce a poet. [79] The compositions published under her name are below the dignity of criticism.

"I advance it therefore as a suspicion only, that the blacks, whether originally a distinct race, or made distinct by time and circumstances, are inferior to the whites in the endowments both of body and mind. It is not against experience to suppose that different Species of the same genus, or varieties of the same species, may possess different qualifications. Will not a lover of natural history then, one who views the gradations in all the races of animals with the eye of philosophy, excuse an effort to keep those in the department of man as distinct as nature has formed them?

"This unfortunate difference of colour, and perhaps of faculty, is a powerful obstacle to the emancipation of these people. Many of their advocates, while they wish to vindicate the liberty of human nature, are anxious also to preserve its dignity and beauty. Some of these, embarrassed by the question 'What further is to be done with them?' join themselves in opposition with those who are actuated by sordid avarice only. Among the Romans, emancipation required but one effort. The slave, when made free, might mix with, without staining the blood of his master. But with us, a second is necessary, unknown to history. When freed, he is to be removed beyond the reach of mixture.

"For if a slave can have a country in this world, it must be any other in preference to that in which he is born to live and labour for another; in which he must lock up the faculties of his nature, contribute as far as depends on his individual [endeavors] to the evanishment of the human race, or entail his own miserable condition on the endless generations proceeding from him...

"With the morals of the people, their industry also is destroyed. For in a warm climate, no man will labour for himself who can make another labour for him. This is so true that of the proprietors of slaves, a very small proportion indeed are ever seen to labour. And can the liberties of a nation be thought secure when we have removed their only firm basis, a conviction in the minds of the people that these liberties are of the gift of God? -That they are not to be violated but with his wrath? Indeed, I tremble for my country when I reflect that God is just: that his justice cannot sleep forever: that considering numbers, nature, and natural means only, a revolution of the wheel of fortune, an exchange of situation is among possible events: that it may become probable by supernatural interference! The almighty has no attribute which can take side with us in such a contest.

"But it is impossible to be temperate and to pursue this subject through the various considerations of policy, of morals, of history—natural and civil. We must be contented to hope they will force their way into every one's mind. I think a change already perceptible, since the origin of the present revolution. The spirit of the master is abating, that of the slave rising from the dust, his condition mollifying, the way I hope preparing, under the auspices of

---

[79] Phillis Wheatley was the first African American poet and first African American woman to publish her writing. Born in Gambia, Africa; she was sold into slavery at the age of 7 or 8 and transported to North America. She was purchased by the Wheatley family of Boston, who taught her to read and write, and encouraged her poetry when they saw her talent. (Source: Robin Santos Doak; Phyllis Wheatley: Slave and Poet; Compass Point Books, Aug 1, 2006

*heaven, for a total emancipation, and that this is disposed, in the order of events, to be with the consent of the masters, rather than by their extirpation."* **~Thomas Jefferson, 1784** [80] (Source: *Notes on the State of Virginia, 1781,* from the Avalon Project at Yale Law School)

Six years earlier, Thomas Jefferson drafted the Declaration of Independence, and in 1801, he was elected the third president of the United States of America.[81]

With the aforementioned declarations being well-known to highly educated American men and women in positions of legislative influence, knowing he regarded Blacks as little more than beasts of burden, it is greatly disturbing to see how highly venerated Thomas Jefferson remains in their minds and hearts. My examination of these and other facts corroborates my belief that to facilitate the profitable practice of slavery, Jefferson consciously sought to sever America's ideological relationship of subordination to God's authority by promoting a "Separation of Church and State". His deeply-rooted, personal, ideological, and political views regarding Blacks had as much to do with his belief in White supremacy as they did with maintaining his own personal fortune and lifestyle. –A view that Jefferson would bequeath to his political and ideological descendants.

With this affirmation, Jefferson was asserting that Bible-based morality, which, among other things, advocates loving your neighbor as yourself, had no place in American capitalism, which encourages and rewards self-interest and the profit motive, whatever the means. Jefferson's tireless efforts would help ensure that the United States of America's future interests, fueled by its relentless "pursuit of happiness, wealth, luxury, and prosperity," would not be constrained by objective biblical morality.

I believe Jesus Christ said it best:

*"No one can serve two masters. Either you will hate the one and love the other, or you will be devoted to the one and despise the other. You cannot serve both God and money."* (Luke 16:13, NIV)

It is clear which *'master'* Jefferson had chosen to serve. In 1791, seven years after writing Notes on the State of Virginia, Thomas Jefferson would zealously support the First Amendment to the US Constitution, which, by his own words, created a "Wall between Church and State".[82]

***"Congress shall make no law respecting an establishment of religion, or prohibiting the free exercise thereof; or abridging the freedom of speech, or of the press; or the right of the people peaceably to assemble, and to petition the Government for a redress of grievances."*** **(First Amendment to the United States Constitution)**

---

[80] Source: 1781, *Notes on the State of Virginia* from the Avalon Project at Yale Law School; http://avalon.law.yale.edu/18th_century/jeffvir.asp
[81] Frank Freidel; The Presidents of the United States of America; DIANE Publishing, Jun 1, 1998; p. 13
[82] Daniel L. Dreisbach; Thomas Jefferson and the Wall of Separation Between Church and State; NYU Press, Sep 1, 2002

This legislation preordained that as long as the people demanded it, slavery could and would continue without legal or political interference from religious anti-slavery advocates.

Shortly after being elected President, Jefferson responded to a letter from the **Danbury Baptist Association**, which criticized his support for the Amendment, with a letter that made his political agenda and objectives clear.

*"To: Messrs. Nehemiah Dodge, Ephraim Robbins, & Stephen S. Nelson, a committee of the Danbury Baptist association in the state of Connecticut.*

*Gentlemen,*

*The affectionate sentiments of esteem and approbation which you are so good as to express towards me, on behalf of the Danbury Baptist association, give me the highest satisfaction. My duties dictate a faithful and zealous pursuit of the interests of my constituents, & in proportion as they are persuaded of my fidelity to those duties, the discharge of them becomes more and more pleasing.*

*Believing with you that religion is a matter which lies solely between Man & his God, that he owes account to none other for his faith or his worship, that the legitimate powers of government reach actions only, & not opinions, I contemplate with sovereign reverence, that act of the whole American people which declared that their legislature should "make no law respecting an establishment of religion, or prohibiting the free exercise thereof,"* **thus building a wall of separation between Church & State***.* **Adhering to this expression of the supreme will of the nation in behalf of the rights of conscience***, I shall see with sincere satisfaction the progress of those sentiments which tend to restore to man all his natural rights, convinced he has no natural right in opposition to his social duties.*

*I reciprocate your kind prayers for the protection & blessing of the common father and creator of man, and tender you for yourselves & your religious association, assurances of my high respect & esteem. ~ Thomas Jefferson" (Source: U.S. Library of Congress)*

Paradoxically, while claiming to ensure religious freedoms, the First Amendment would give birth to America's spirit of unbridled entrepreneurial endeavor by slitting its moral throat. In doing so, it would also unleash legions of gluttonous predators to prowl and feed among the lambs of Black cultural production. These beliefs would be embraced, venerated, and memorialized by Americans, ultimately shaping attitudes that led to the misappropriation of Louise Shropshire's sacred hymn.

Now that America's Godhead of objective morality had been banished from the great halls and backrooms of government, how could its body—its people—avoid moral, social, and cultural decomposition? Perhaps the Rev. Martin Luther King had the answer:

*"The church must be reminded that it is not the master or the servant of the state, but rather the conscience of the state. It must be the guide and the critic of the state, and never its tool. If the church does not recapture its prophetic zeal, it will become an irrelevant social club without moral or spiritual authority."* -Rev. Dr. Martin Luther King Jr.

We Shall Overcome: Sacred Song on the Devil's Tongue

The next time you visit the **Thomas Jefferson Memorial** in Washington, D.C., should you choose to do so, think twice about the Declaration of Independence and the First Amendment to the Constitution, and remember that you are not just looking up at a former president and so-called Founding Father, but also a slave owner, racist, and rapist.

# Action Item # 2 – Founding Fathers

1. I propose that any politician who seeks the support of American voters be asked to publicly admonish Thomas Jefferson as a slaveowner, rapist, and racist.

2. I propose that, out of respect for Black people and all people of decency, Thomas Jefferson's image on the front of the American "Nickel" and the image of his plantation, Monticello, on the obverse of the coin be permanently removed.

3.

4. I propose that Jefferson's racist actions and xenophobic views be included in the public high school curriculum as an essential part of American History studies.

*"Find out just what any people will quietly submit to, and you have the exact measure of the injustice and wrong which will be imposed on them.*
-Frederick Douglass

Isaac Granger Jefferson, one of Thomas Jefferson's enslaved people

Across a reflecting pool, the Martin Luther King Jr. National Memorial in Washington, D.C., facing the Thomas Jefferson Memorial.

Across a reflecting pool. The Thomas Jefferson National Memorial in Washington, D.C., faces the Martin Luther King National Memorial.

# Chapter 15

# Great White Hunters

*"Nobody knows exactly who wrote the original. The original was faster...it was the best-selling record I ever had. And the song went around the world."*[83]
-**Pete Seeger** on "We Shall Overcome."

By all accounts, Pete Seeger was born on third base. Raised in an upper-middle-class home, he was the son of two highly educated, classically trained musicians and music educators. His father, Charles Seeger, was a musicologist at the University of California, Berkeley, but quit during World War I after his pacifism made him unpopular there. He and his wife later taught at Julliard.

Pete Seeger                    Charles Seeger

In 1936, Pete Seeger was admitted to Harvard on a partial scholarship, but as he became increasingly involved in radical politics and folk music, his grades faltered, and he lost the scholarship. He dropped out of college in 1938. Earlier that year, Seeger's father introduced him to Communism.

That same year, Charles Seeger, through his friend John A. Lomax, pulled some strings and secured a job in Washington, D.C., for his son, Pete, working alongside Alan Lomax, John A. Lomax's son, at the Archives of American Folk Song of the U.S. Library of

---

[83] Shuman, Wendy / "Pete Seeger Session" Beliefnet.com 2006, 2011 / Wendy Shuman, interviewer)http://www.beliefnet.com/Entertainment/Music/2006/08/Pete-Seegers-Session.aspx?p=2

Congress. Nineteen-year-old Pete Seeger's job was to help twenty-three-year-old Alan Lomax sift through uncopyrighted "race" and "hillbilly" music and select recordings that best represented American folk music. The project was funded by the music division of the Pan American Union, of which Charles Seeger was head.

Alan Lomax, who would become Pete Seeger's lifelong friend, began his career at eighteen alongside his father, John A. Lomax, a musicologist like Charles Seeger. He worked to identify, record, and archive uncopyrighted songs sung by sharecroppers and chain-gang prisoners in Texas, Louisiana, and the Mississippi Delta. Alan Lomax, with a keen eye for others' talent, employed so-called "informants" to find "undiscovered" songs. Both John and Alan Lomax became well known as prolific "song-hunters." They achieved this in part by using something none of the illiterate Black sharecroppers, chain-gang prisoners, or rural Baptist congregations had ever seen: a magnetic tape recorder.

## The Recording Expeditions

Alan Lomax recording an unidentified sharecropper's song

## We Shall Overcome: Sacred Song on the Devil's Tongue

Alan Lomax

John A. Lomax

Alan Lomax and Pete Seeger—both struggling songwriters and folk singers—were now on the U.S. Library of Congress payroll, with unlimited access to thousands of uncopyrighted songs archived there. What a goldmine! It marked the beginning of what would become a "Golden Age" of Black music misappropriation and exploitation. The flagrant theft of culturally relevant African American music proved highly advantageous for White entrepreneurs such as Seeger and the Lomaxes, granting them access to a new and lucrative world of fortune and fame.

Most of these songs, especially those with higher-quality recordings, were snatched from the very mouths of poor, naive, and illiterate Black American men, women, and children, whose songs, culture, and memories would be stolen and sold to the highest bidders, such as the Prestige, Atlantic, and Decca record companies.

Although John and Alan Lomax were praised by many affluent Whites for bringing Negro songs to their living-room hi-fis, many scholars would come to find darker forces at work in the Lomaxes' endeavors. In a published article, (White) historian and history professor **Jerrold Hirsch** wrote that Alan Lomax's autobiographical work, *Adventures of a Ballad Hunter*: *"Revealed a portrait of a fundamentally racist, paternalistic Southerner who was prepared to champion the rights of Black people as long as they posed no threat to the racial status quo..."* he went on to say: *"[Lomax] believed in the fundamental inferiority of*

Isaias Gamboa

*Black people and, though he admired their culture and hoped to see their difficult lot improved, he could not accept the idea that they deserved complete equality with Whites"*[84]

First page of Lomax's "Southern Journey" log. (Courtesy of the Alan Lomax Archive)

One of John Lomax's most notable "discoveries," blues singer and former chain-gang prisoner Huddie Ledbetter, aka "Lead Belly", in addition to revealing his songs to Lomax, was used by him as a house servant and chauffeur. On various occasions, long after he had been released from prison, Ledbetter was actually made to dress in convict clothing in order to play the role of a "dangerous", racialized folk stereotype. In anticipation

---

[84] Gillian Mitchell; The North American Folk Music Revival: Nation And Identity in the United States And Canada, 1945-1980; p. 36

of his release from prison, John Lomax promoted him to the newspapers as a savage, ruthless killer…and worse. Lomax's words:

*"Lead belly is a nigger to the core of his being. In addition, he is a killer. He tells the truth only accidentally…He is as sensual as a goat, and when he sings to me, my spine tingles and sometimes tears come…"*[85] *– John Lomax*

"Aunt Harriet" McClintock dancing for John A Lomax as she sang "Shing-Shing" at the crossroads near Sumterville Ala. Cir. 1940, Courtesy: Library of Congress, Prints & Photographs Division, Lomax Collection

---

[85] Mitchell, Gillian; The North American Folk Music Revival: Nation and Identity in the United States and Canada, 1945-1980; Ashgate Publishing; 2007; p. 35-36

Isaias Gamboa

Baptist Congregation on the Alma Plantation, False River, La. Recorded and photographed by Alan Lomax, July 1934,
Courtesy: Library of Congress, Prints & Photographs Division, Lomax Collection

We Shall Overcome: Sacred Song on the Devil's Tongue

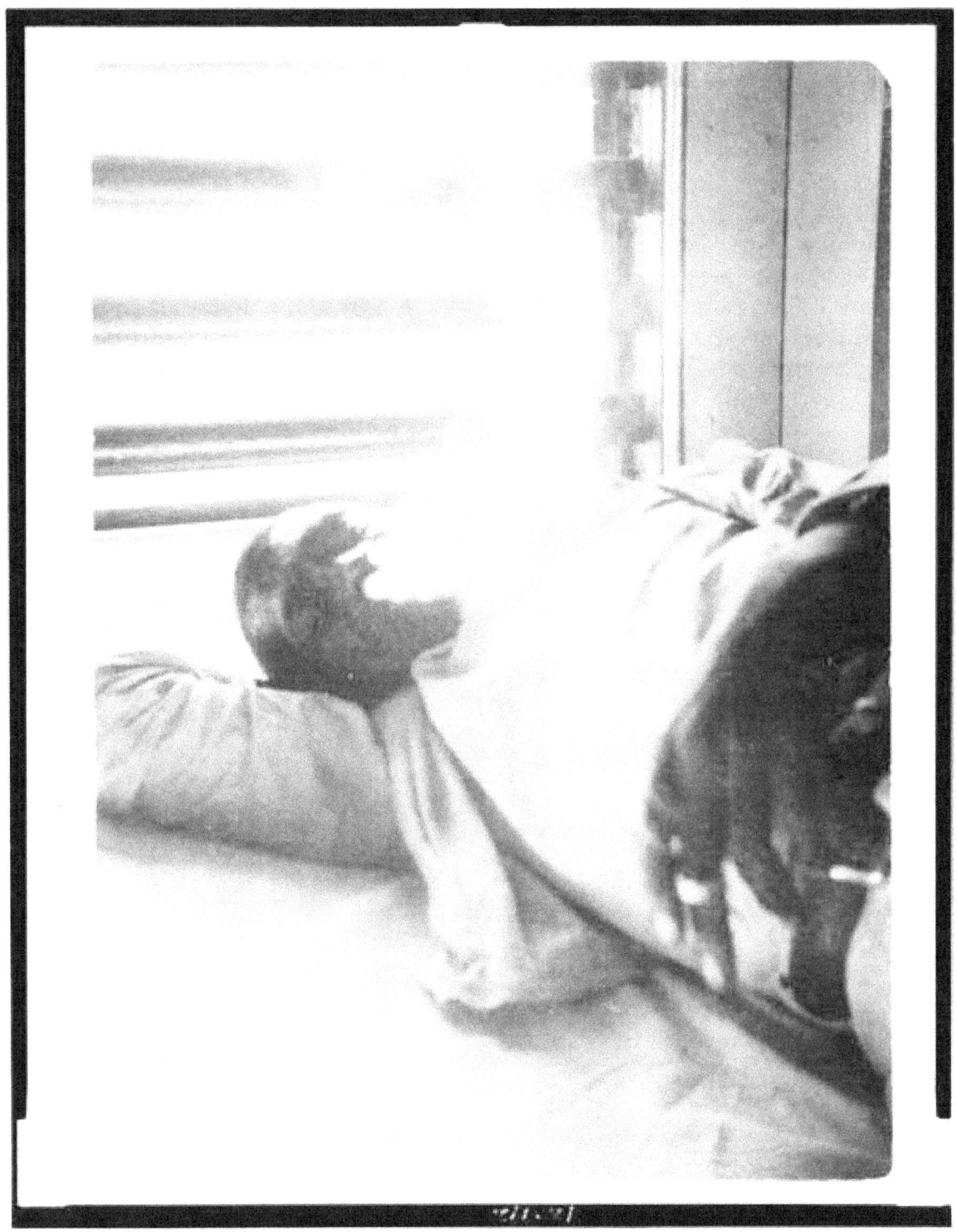

"Lightnin' Washington," an African American prisoner singing for Alan Lomax in a hospital at Darrington State Farm, Texas, Alan Lomax-Photographer, Courtesy: Library of Congress, Prints & Photographs Division, Lomax Collection

# The First Kill

In 1948, the "song hunter" John Lomax died. That same year, Pete Seeger formed a quartet called The Weavers and signed a recording contract with Decca Records. Soon afterward, Seeger and the Weavers got their first taste of success with the release of the song Good Night Irene. Good Night Irene was actually written by Huddie Ledbetter, a.k.a. "Lead Belly." However, John Lomax, claiming to have discovered both " Leadbelly " and Goodnight Irene, secured copyright ownership of the song for himself. Although an indigent Lead Belly begged and pleaded for the copyright to his death, Lomax would not relinquish or even share the song's ownership with him. Apparently, John and Alan Lomax were not satisfied with their modest Library of Congress paychecks, as by the late 1940s both had left their government posts, taking with them valuable musical treasures procured while employed there – treasures like Goodnight Irene.

Huddie Ledbetter, a.k.a. "Lead Belly" with wife; Martha Promise Ledbetter, Library of Congress, Prints & Photographs Division, Lomax Collection

On December 6, 1949, Huddie William Ledbetter died penniless in New York. His wife, Martha, traveled with his body from New York to Moringsport, Louisiana, where he was buried in the Shiloh Baptist Church Cemetery. At the time of his death, his family could not afford a grave marker. Instead, his grave was marked by a plain steel pipe sticking out of the ground. Within six months of Led Belly's death, Pete Seeger and the Weavers released their recording of Good Night Irene, which topped the music charts for 13 weeks. After years of struggling to peddle his own mediocre words and melodies, Pete Seeger had struck Black gold.

Following Lead Belly's death, more than fifty White artists would record his songs, including Frank Sinatra, Johnny Cash, Jerry Lee Lewis, and scores of others.

Although Goodnight Irene was a great commercial success for Seeger, he did not own the song's copyright and, as a result, earned only a fraction of what the Lomaxes would make. It wasn't long before Seeger was broke again. A reversal of fortune was in his future, however... thanks to an African Zulu composer named Solomon Linda and his song, *"Mbube"*—later renamed "**The Lion Sleeps Tonight**".

"The Lion Sleeps Tonight" was originally written and recorded as "**Mbube**" by Solomon Linda, a South African singer and composer of Zulu ancestry. In 1931, Linda left his homestead to find menial work in Johannesburg, as did many young African men at the time. Johannesburg had grown into a sprawling gold-mining town with an enormous demand for cheap labor. Solomon held various menial jobs while singing in a choir known as the Evening Birds, which performed at local venues and was managed by Linda's uncles. In 1939, he secured work as a record packer at the Gallo Record Company in Johannesburg.

As Linda's fate would have it, one evening a Gallo talent scout attended an Evening Birds performance and, being quite impressed, offered to let them record some of their songs at his company's recording studio. Mbube was one of those songs. In the studio, it didn't take long for Gallo executives to recognize Mbube's potential. Following that initial recording session, Solomon Linda was offered 10 shillings—the equivalent of two U.S. dollars—for the rights to Mbube. Being poor and uneducated, Linda accepted. Mbube went on to sell over 100,000 copies in Africa alone, but having sold his song to Gallo for two shillings, Solomon received no royalties.

10 years passed, and it was now 1949. As an out-of-work banjo player, Pete Seeger was struggling... living hand-to-mouth in a one-room flat with a wife and two young children. Perhaps contemplating his decision to drop out of Harvard 10 years earlier—a luxury afforded to those born with silver spoons in their mouths—Seeger, now in his 30s with less money and more mouths to feed, stood at the threshold of financial ruin. That is, until the day "the knock" came at the door—the knock that would mark Pete Seeger's reversal of fortune.

Sick in bed, Seeger could not have anticipated how his life was about to change. He dragged himself to the door to find, no other than his old Library of Congress co-worker and friend, Alan Lomax, standing there. Over the years, Lomax had become wealthy by making a deal with Decca Records to release his recordings. Recordings from his numerous government-funded *song-hunting* expeditions, deep into the heart of rural Black America, where he and his father, John, had discovered destitute and imprisoned blues geniuses like Lighnin' Washington, Muddy Waters, and Lead Belly, snatching up their soulful songs and performances in exchange for little more than cigarettes and liquor. It seemed Lomax had made the real money by saving the best songs and recordings for his own commercial gain. Well, for some reason, he was now at Seeger's door, holding a 78-rpm recording of an African hit record titled "**Mbube**," written by an African man named **Solomon Linda.**

Tired of performing for peanuts, Seeger was in desperate need of money and a proper career, and he could not have been more thrilled to see Lomax. Lomax was very excited about the recording and assured Seeger that The Weavers would be perfect to record the song. Upon hearing Linda's incredibly infectious melody soar above the scratchy 78 recording, Seeger exclaimed, "Golly, I can sing that!" He quickly produced a pen and paper and began transcribing the song note for note.

Soon after, Seeger changed the song's name from Mbube to "**Wimoweh,**" a mispronunciation of "*Uyimbube*" (Zulu for *You are a lion*, the song's original chorus) and began performing it with The Weavers. Before long, something remarkable happened... crowds started showing up at The Weavers' shows. Thanks to another Black writer's composition, Pete Seeger and his all-White folk group were back in business—rapidly transformed from washouts to wayfarers, performing on the best stages in America.

Wimoweh was a hit, and after milking it on stage for about a year, The Weavers made a new 78 single of it. The new version reached the Top Ten in Billboard magazine. This time, Seeger and The Weavers had hit the jackpot by hijacking Linda's song, while never giving him credit as the author. The Weavers were now drawing sellout crowds as the song became a huge hit.

As Seeger's fortune would have it, the printed label on Solomon Linda's original 78 recording read: "by Solomon Linda and the Evening Birds," but showed no sign that it had ever been copyrighted in the U.S. This was great news for Pete but bad news for Linda. According to Seeger and his business associates, anything not copyrighted was considered a "Wild Horse" for the purposes of appropriation, and Wild Horses in the Weaver's repertoire were usually credited to "Paul Campbell," a Seeger-manufactured pseudonym.[86]

Behind his "Paul Campbell" cover, Seeger and his cohorts became experts at commandeering "public domain" songs and reaping substantial profits. Public-domain songs were those whose copyright had expired. Appropriating songs in this way was a longstanding Tin-Pan-Alley custom, and Pete Seeger, along with his consigliere, Harold Leventhal, would become experts in this practice.

Like "If My Jesus Wills," however, Mbube wasn't in the public domain at all. To Seeger and his associates, however, it was the next best thing—an unprotected song owned by an unknown foreign music label that didn't care about protecting Solomon Linda's rights. Consequently, Linda's Zulu song would suffer the same fate as American slaves—kidnapped, renamed, and forced to labor by their White owners. Seeger maintained that Mbube was a "traditional" song, and therefore not under U.S. copyright, adding that traditional songs could not and should not be copyrighted in their original forms. In other words, he felt the song could be adapted by him without compensating or crediting its true author.

Although Seeger maintained that he thought Mbube was traditional, this was a lie, as the original recording brought to him and Alan Lomax clearly had the author's name

---

[86] Malan, Rian "Where Does The Lion Sleep Tonight" / http://www.3rdearmusic.com/forum/mbube2a.html

## We Shall Overcome: Sacred Song on the Devil's Tongue

written on its label. "The Lion Sleeps Tonight" went on to earn tens of millions of dollars, and as Pete Seeger and others grew richer, Solomon Linda received nothing. When Linda's authorship was established in the 1950s, Seeger publicly claimed to have sent him $1,000, which, by all accounts, Linda never received during his lifetime. Despite the song's popularity and widespread use, Linda died impoverished in 1962, leaving his wife, Linda... an illiterate peasant, destitute with six children to feed. Significant Zulu death rites for Linda went unperformed for years because the family was far too poor to pay. Solomon Linda was buried in a pauper's grave while Pete Seeger and his managers reaped the benefits of his cultural production. It wasn't until eighteen years later, when Linda's heirs successfully sued Disney and TRO Publishing, that a tombstone was erected at their father's gravesite.

Solomon Linda's Original "Mbube"

The Weavers aka "Paul Campbell's" "Wimoweh"

1972 Recording by Dave Newman, Note the absence of Solomon Linda's name and the presence of the phrase: *"Based on a Song by Paul Campbell."*

The mere fact that Seeger felt the need to disguise his real name speaks volumes about his true motivations. How did he sleep at night, knowing of Solomon Linda's true authorship and impoverished state, while drawing huge audiences and royalties for Linda's song, which, by his own admission, Seeger had transcribed note for note?

In a subsequent interview with Pitchfork magazine, Seeger would offer much insight into his character and, in the process, articulate an answer to this question:

> *"The good and bad are all tangled up together. American popular music is loved around the world because of its African rhythm. But that wouldn't have happened if it wasn't for slavery."*[87] – Pete Seeger

It was as if Thomas Jefferson's words had come out of Pete Seeger's mouth. Seeger's statement spoke volumes about how he viewed Black music—sacred or otherwise... Black pain was White gain. I wonder what the response would have been had Seeger said: "The Oscar®-winning movie Schindler's List is loved around the world, and we owe it all to the Nazi Holocaust!" What would the media's reaction have been? Disturbingly, the American media said and did nothing in response to Seeger's comments. Had they done so, I doubt he would have been asked to sing at Barack Obama's presidential inauguration.

Seeger's remarks revealed his insensitivity to the misery and suffering that inspired the sacred African American music he misappropriated from Louise Shropshire, Solomon Linda, and others. But were Pete Seeger's and Alan Lomax's efforts ever tru*ly* about celebrating or understanding Black culture?

Through biased copyright legislation and the financial underwriting of song-hunting expeditions, the U.S. government would ultimately reward the corrupt entrepreneurial undertakings of men like Alan Lomax and Pete Seeger. But regardless of the profits at stake, why couldn't Seeger and Lomax see that what they were doing was so very, very wrong? Was there no moral compass to guide them? Had the notion of right and wrong in America been exiled from the towers of American intellectual rhetoric? Why didn't these men understand that it was the brutal suffering, legally inflicted upon African Americans by American *Whites*, that made these powerful songs and performances OFF LIMITS to fortune hunters like them? Regardless of their monetary value, these songs represented a precious, priceless fragment of what little African Americans had salvaged from one of the cruelest periods in world history.

Following a radio interview with Seeger's avowed mentor, Alan Lomax, folk music historian and WBAI New York radio talk-show host Peter Bochan could not help but share his opinion, stating that Lomax believed: "Nothing in poor people's culture truly happened unless someone like [Lomax] documented it." Bochan would later observe that Lomax believed: "folk music needed guidance from a superior being like himself."

It is disquieting to consider that if Seeger's and Lomax's emotionally detached view of the *true* value of sacred Black music reflected the attitudes of the Northern, White, radical

---

[87] AK Press; 2004; Klein, Joshua / Pitchfork.com / 2008 / "Interviews / Pete Seeger" http://pitchfork.com/features/interviews/7543-pete-seeger

left-wing intellectual middle class, what in heaven's name did the rest of White America think and feel? What, if anything, did White America *truly* know and understand about Black culture—let alone their powerful, sacred art forms?

# Chapter 16

# Sacred Songs

*"Walk together chil'en, don't you get weary*
*Walk together chil'en, don't you get weary*
*Oh, walk together chil'en, don't you get weary*
*There's a great camp meeting in the Promised Land."*
(*"Walk Together Children"* Negro Spiritual, Unidentified Author)[88]

Negro Spirituals were the first songs Louise Shropshire would learn as a child, inspiring the sacred music she would one day compose. These deeply cathartic songs not only eased and articulated the suffering of African Americans but also conveyed the Bible's divine wisdom and moral teachings. In some cases, they served as coded messages to assist runaway slaves and deceive slave owners. These sanctified musical works were never intended to be sold and displayed like carved tribal figurines purchased by White tourists in some South African hotel gift shop. – These songs were sacred.

Since their abduction from Africa, Blacks in America had relied on the therapeutic power of song to fortify them through their trials. Because it was illegal in some states for Blacks to read or write, Negro Spirituals became the sacred scrolls of African American culture—a teaching tool by which culturally accepted values, traditions, and mores could be established, communicated, and disseminated. These songs also comforted Blacks during times of great suffering, such as the death of a beloved child or family member at the hands of a White slave owner or overseer. Like musical tears, Negro Spirituals were born of the torture, abuse, suffering, and oppression of American slavery.

Prior to the abolition of slavery in 1865, virtually all blacks who arrived in America did so shackled and chained by the neck, waist, wrists, and/or ankles. These men, women, and children were kidnapped primarily from nations and regions along the African West Coast, also known as the "Slave Coast". Many, however, were also captured from Africa's interior. Following their initial capture and prior to their long and inhumane sea voyage to the "New World", these slaves, bound and shackled, were forced to march in long caravans of up to 1,000 miles to the heavily fortified coastal slave-trading stations. Any slaves who resisted their captivity were punished and tortured, often with horrific spiked neck and waist shackles designed to shred their flesh. These caravans proved to be death marches, as half of these starved and battered people would die before ever setting foot on any slave

---

[88] Edited by Nicole Beaulieu Herder, Ronald Herder; Best-Loved Negro Spirituals: Complete Lyrics to 178 Songs of Faith; Courier Dover Publications, Jun 13, 2001; p.1

ship. It is estimated that for every African slave who arrived in America, two others had already perished.

During these torturous, often fatal caravans, these proud Africans sang chants of courage, hope, longing, and inspiration. Those who survived were separated from their families and packed together like sardines aboard floating dungeons, where they would begin their horrific "Middle Passage" voyage. Once aboard slave ships with biblically ironic names such as the "Hope," "Grace," "Amistad," "Lord," and "Jesus," slaves were sadistically bound together and forced to lie in each other's urine, feces, and blood. Along with the unbearable heat and poor nutrition, these conditions created deadly, disease-infested death chambers. Yet they still sang. They sang of courage, hope, and inspiration, even as the dead, dying, and diseased—often including small children as young as four—lay among them.

These people were forced to endure a living hell—all justified by White Europeans in the name of profit. An excerpt from Howard Zinn's *A People's History of the United States* provides firsthand accounts of these horrors:

*"They were packed aboard the slave ships, in spaces not much bigger than coffins, chained together in the dark, wet slime of the ship's bottom, choking in the stench of their own excrement...On one occasion, hearing a great noise from [below decks] where the blacks were chained together, the sailors opened the hatches and found the slaves in different stages of suffocation, many dead, some having killed others in desperate attempts to breathe. Slaves often jumped overboard to drown rather than continue their suffering. To one observer, a slave-deck was 'so covered in blood and mucus that it resembled a slaughterhouse.'"*[89]

It's estimated that fifty million African lives were lost as a result of the Atlantic slave trade. Yet perhaps those who never made it to the "New World" were the lucky ones, as the enslaved Africans who survived would soon face another inferno of hate—colonial America. Claiming its atrocities in the name of God, like the pharaohs of ancient Egypt, America would, by its merciless deeds, earn a historic place in the darkest chapters of human civilization.

---

[89] Zinn, Howard; A People's History of the Unites States; Harper Collins; 2010; p. 28-32

Conditions aboard an African Slave Ship as depicted in the exhibit at Wilberforce House Museum, Hull City, England

Like faceless beasts of burden, once captured, beaten, bound, marched, packed, and shipped to America, slaves were sold into a lifetime of bondage. Their profit-seeking slave owners and sadistic overseers would beat, rape, violate, and humiliate these men, women, and children for generations, forcing them to forget or abandon thousands of years of pride associated with their African customs, traditions, and identities. These wicked acts resulted in generations of African American slaves retaining no true cultural compass or sense of ancestral origin and distinction. Some of their oppressors, however, would pay dearly for their actions.

## A Rebel Yell / The Stono Rebellion

It began in 1739 near the Stono River in South Carolina. During this period, the majority of South Carolina's colonial population consisted of enslaved people. The Stono Rebellion was led by native Africans from the Central African kingdom of Kongo and, prior to the Revolutionary War, was the largest documented slave rebellion against slave owners in colonial America.

On Sunday, September 9, 1739, an escaped, literate, Portuguese-speaking slave named "Jemmy" organized twenty other Kongolese slaves into a band of insurgents that would eventually grow to 100 and set out for Spanish-occupied Florida. At the time, Spain was anticipating war with Great Britain and, hoping to complicate its adversary's affairs, offered freedom and land to any escaped British colonial slaves who made it to Florida.

Led by Jemmy, the escaped insurgent slaves cried out chants of inspiration and liberation to the vociferous cadence of their handmade drums… signaling their rebellion to other slaves and multiplying their numbers. During the uprising, they seized weapons, gunpowder, and ammunition from a local store, killing the two storekeepers. Like an angry fire, they raged on, burning houses and businesses. In pursuit of their objective, they killed twenty-two whites, sparing only those known to have been "kind" to their slaves. Eventually, the Stono rebels were all tracked down and killed—but ultimately, they died free.

News of this rebellion spread like wildfire throughout the South, fueling already existing fears among Whites that so-called "wild-negroes" would revolt against their captors... beating their drums, chanting, dancing, and killing. Things would never be the same for slaves as the bull-whip vengeance of White slave owners came down hard. As a result, slaves were now banned from growing their own food, assembling in groups, earning their own money, or learning to read.

As additional punishment for the uprising, Whites would declare the slave's drum forbidden and severely restrict singing, dancing, and worship. Slaves were now permitted to sing only the traditional hymns used in White church services. By the 1850s, however, slaves were composing their own original songs, drawing inspiration from the Bible and its message of freedom and salvation.

The now-forbidden drum was a particularly painful loss, as it had previously provided a fundamental musical and cultural link to the slaves' African homeland. Try as they might, however, Whites could not eradicate the slaves' powerful African spirit and rhythm. Slaves now began to use their bodies as percussive instruments—clapping their hands, stomping their feet, slapping their knees, thighs, chests, and heels to the Negro Spirituals they were now composing. In addition, as the rhythms and nuances of their African dialects had been absorbed into the English they now spoke, these elements were woven into the spiritual songs that the slaves created and sang. Like the songs they chanted during their African death-marches and those sung in the bloody bowels of slave ships, enslaved Africans would fashion their sacred musical implements to ease and document their ancestral pain, hope, and struggle, nourishing their cultural identities and survival.

Through oral communication, the tempos, rhythms, melodies, themes, and words of these sacred Black Psalms would find their agonizing way from the cruel death marches... to the infernal slave ships... to the dehumanizing auction blocks... to the sadistic cotton fields, and ultimately to the prayer-worn pews of the African American church. Here, the painful provenance of these sacred refrains would be evangelized, celebrated, and grieved. These musical masterworks were the spiritual, cultural, and intellectual property of all African Americans—historically tethered to slavery from which they were born. These hallowed songs were and still are endowed and anointed by God upon the hearts, minds, and spirits of sanctified composers, authors, musicians, and vocalists. Only the Godless would think to steal such a song for profit.

# Chapter 17

# The Folk Process

September **1959** – Federal charges of Communist activity, illegal alcohol consumption, and sexual impropriety are brought against Highlander Folk School. A judge threatens to shut the school down.[90]

**Feb. 16, 1960** – Highlander Folk School is padlocked and shut down. The school's charter is revoked. [91]

**June 1960** – Rev. Fred Shuttlesworth made yet another visit to the Highlander Folk School in Monteagle, Tennessee. While there, he met with Myles Horton, Pete Seeger, and Guy Carawan. Earlier that year, Shuttlesworth's two daughters, Pat and Ricky, along with his son, Fred Jr., had attended a six-week youth camp there.

Rev. Fred Shuttlesworth and Myles Horton, 1960 Highlander Folk School, Courtesy Fred Shuttlesworth Foundation

October 1960 – Perhaps in a desperate attempt to raise funds for Highlander Folk School, unbeknownst to Louise, Guy Carawan, Frank Hamilton, and Zilphia Horton (deceased) filed a copyright for their arrangement of We Shall Overcome. This copyright is considered a "derivative work." In 1963, Joan Baez famously sang the song at the March on Washington, and another copyright was filed to add Pete Seeger's name. A couple of

---

[90] http://www.tn.gov/tsla/history/manuscripts/findingaids/1248.pdf
[91] The Martin Luther King Papers Project / Stanford University /

## We Shall Overcome: Sacred Song on the Devil's Tongue

additional verses are added, but they are not original. The song now lists Pete Seeger, Guy Carawan, Frank Hamilton, and Zilphia Horton (wife of Highlander Folk School's founder) as "adaptors" of the song, and all four claim copyright ownership. The publishing is administered by Ludlow Music/The Richmond Organization (TRO). TRO is the same publisher that, along with Pete Seeger, also exploited Solomon Linda's "Mbube," aka "Wimoweh," aka "The Lion Sleeps Tonight."

Pete Seeger     Guy Carawan     Zilphia Horton

Myles Horton     Frank Hamilton     Harold Leventhal, Seeger's Manager

Pete Seeger claims he filed the copyright on the advice of Harold Leventhal: *"Pete, if you don't copyright this, somebody else will."*[92] This statement alone calls into question his actions and motives, as one would have expected him to say he filed the copyright because the song was, in fact, his. Seeger would become known for referring to plagiarism as "The Folk Process"—a euphemism for the practice by which some folk singers seized lyrics and/or melodies from old work songs, Negro Spirituals, and hymns, fashioned them into commercial works, and then attempted to profit from their exploitation by securing new copyrights by registering them as "derivative works." Was Seeger, in effect, operating his own musical "chop shop"? In a 1991 interview with Mike Boehm of the Los Angeles Times, folk singer Arlo Guthrie, Woody Guthrie's son, would later allude to this dishonorable practice:

> *"That sort of method used to raise howls of plagiarism until Pete Seeger came along and renamed it `the Folk Process.' Thank God for Pete."* – Arlo Guthrie

---

[92] Pete Seeger Interview with Kathy Vogel for WordPress, October 2006, https://dayafterdaydc.wordpress.com/2020/09/07/pete-seeger-discusses-woody-guthrie-martin-luther-king-and-we-shall-overcome/

The Folk Process became a device by which many unscrupulous and untalented songwriters picked pockets of songs from naïve, disadvantaged, and disenfranchised Black people. Although some claimed to have done it to preserve "American Folk-Culture," even a blind man could see it was about money. In an interview with Billboard Magazine, Pete Seeger declared, "My father, Charles, taught me that the Folk Process is tens of thousands of years old; it's a part of every field and every walk of life. Cooks rearrange old recipes for new stomachs." The problem is that, under U.S. Copyright law, the "Folk Process" may be illegal.

According to United States Copyright law, "A derivative work is a work based on or derived from one or more already existing works... Only the owner of copyright in a work has the right to prepare, or to authorize someone else to create, a new version of that work. The owner is generally the author or someone who has obtained rights from the author." In other words, without authorization from the owner of the previously registered work from which it was derived, the 1960 and 1963 copyrights of We Shall Overcome were and are unauthorized derivative works—illegal and illegitimate from the moment they were registered. It follows that, as a result of Pete Seeger, Guy Carawan, Zilphia Horton, Myles Horton, Frank Hamilton, and TRO/Ludlow Music's failure to secure Louise Shropshire's authorization to adapt "If My Jesus Wills" into "We Shall Overcome", in 1960 and 1963, they committed a federal crime by falsifying the copyright application and willfully infringing upon and commercially exploiting Shropshire's 1954 copyright.

The 1960 registration of We Shall Overcome by Guy Carawan, Frank Hamilton, and Myles Horton specifically states: **"Original registration under title I'll Overcome. Melody has been changed. Harmonization wholly original. Verses 2, 3, 4 of lead sheet attached all original."**

Setting aside the fact that verses 2-4 were not "wholly original," as recorded by the US Library of Congress in 1960, this critical document affirms that the music and accompanying lyrics to "Verse 1" of We Shall Overcome, as submitted by Ludlow Music, Inc., Guy Carawan, Frank Hamilton, and Zilphia Horton, did not belong to them and were not protected by the 1960 and 1963 copyrights.

**"We shall overcome, we shall overcome, we shall overcome someday,
O deep in my heart, I do believe, we shall overcome someday."**

# The Myth

Knowing full well they were claiming someone *else's* sacred song for themselves, wouldn't simple decency have discouraged Pete Seeger and his accomplices from securing an illegal copyright on We Shall Overcome? In an excerpt from his own book, *"Everybody Says Freedom,"* Seeger reveals the answer to this question.

> *"Thing is, I didn't know anything about protest music. After I got in and was on the bus rides, I learned how to recreate old songs with new words. I saw other people do it, and then I did it. –Natural evolution"*[93] –Pete Seeger

Perhaps in an attempt to deflect public contempt for this act, the credits listed on the sheet music for the 1963 version of *We Shall Overcome* read as follows:

> **"Inspired by African American Gospel Singing, members of the Food and Tobacco Workers Union, Charleston, SC, and the southern Civil Rights Movement."**[94]

Adding these two lines to the sheet music for "We Shall Overcome" gave the superficial impression that Seeger et al. were attributing the song to African Americans while incurring no legal or financial consequences for its misappropriation.

For the record, Pete Seeger and his publisher, The Richmond Organization, claim that Zilphia Horton, one of the copyright claimants, first heard a song called "We Will Overcome" on a union picket line in the late 1940s. According to Seeger, who was not present, it was sung slowly, very slowly, by a black woman named Lucille Simmons. Seeger claims he learned the song from Zilphia Horton in 1946 and then taught it to Guy Carawan and Frank Hamilton in 1950. Aside from statements by Seeger, his co-adapters, and his publishing company, which currently receive royalties from We Shall Overcome, no independent, unbiased sources confirm that this event ever took place.

In numerous books and interviews, before being made aware of Louise Shropshire's "If My Jesus Wills," Seeger sought to justify his claim of copyright ownership of "We Shall Overcome" by suggesting that it might have been inspired by a song entitled "I'll Overcome Someday" by Rev. Charles Albert Tindley, copyrighted in 1901. Although Tindley's hymn bears some marginal lyrical similarities to "We Shall Overcome," the structural and musical elements are radically different. Simply hearing Tindley's song is enough to settle the matter. Musicological experts agree that Tindley's hymn could not have been the inspiration for "We Shall Overcome." Any reasonable argument in favor of Tindley's hymn as the antecedent to "We Shall Overcome" would have to rely solely on Seeger's inconsistent speculations or lyrical similarity. However, because Louise Shropshire's "If My Jesus Wills" is considerably more lyrically, musically, and structurally similar to "We Shall Overcome" than Tindley's, the Tindley reasoning actually supports Louise Shropshire as the original author of "We Shall Overcome."[95]

The likely reason Seeger and his associates suggested Tindley's hymn as inspiration for "We Shall Overcome" is practical. Under copyright law, Tindley's song was in the public domain when the copyright for "We Shall Overcome" was registered in 1960 and again in 1963.[96] Had Tindley been the original author (which he wasn't) and been credited as such in the 1960 and 1963 copyrights (which he wasn't), Seeger et al and The Richmond

---

[93] Seeger, Pete and Reiser, Bob; Everybody Says Freedom; W.W. Norton and Company; p. 8, 85

[94] Glazer, Joe; Labor's Troubador; University of Illinois Press; 2002; p. xiv

[95] Dunaway, David King; How Can I Keep From Singing?: The Ballad of Pete Seeger; Random House Digital; 2008; p. 275

[96] Library of Congress/ US Copyright office; http://www.copyright.gov

Organization could have registered a new arrangement of his song with the US Copyright Office without committing fraud.

# The Facts

Louise Shropshire composed *"If My Jesus Wills"* sometime between 1932 and 1942 and copyrighted it in 1954, six years before "We Shall Overcome" was copyrighted in 1960. Compare the lyrics yourself:

**(If My Jesus Wills ©1954)**       **(We Shall Overcome ©1960 and 1960)**
I'll overcome,                                    We shall overcome,
I'll overcome,                                    We shall overcome,
I'll overcome, someday,                    We shall overcome someday,
Oh yes, If my Jesus wills, I do believe    Oh Deep in my heart, I do believe that
I'll overcome someday                       We shall overcome someday

In May 2013, in a written response to a legal challenge to their copyright of We Shall Overcome, The Richmond Organization (TRO), as represented by their attorney, Paul Licalsi, concluded that "We Will Overcome" is the precursor to 'We Shall Overcome,' which was first copyrighted in 1960.

In 2015, I discovered a 1947 recording of Zilphia Horton singing "We Will Overcome"—the very version that Pete Seeger and TRO claim was the antecedent of "We Shall Overcome." I sent this recording to two independent musicologists and asked them to transcribe it and prepare a report comparing "If My Jesus Wills" with "We Will Overcome." The results are as follows.

Easterling Transcription:

## "We Will Overcome"

## Abridged Version of the Douglass Easterling Musicological Report:

Analysis:

"Mr. Gamboa,

You have asked me to conduct a musicological comparison and analysis of the following two songs.

1. The US Copyright Office deposit copy of "If My Jesus Wills" by

Louise Shropshire, composed sometime between 1932 and 1942.

Lyrics: **"I'll overcome, I'll overcome, I'll overcome someday**

**If my Jesus wills, I do believe, I'll overcome someday,"** and,

2. A recording of the song, "I Will Overcome," as performed by Zilphia Horton

 (circa 1947).

Lyrics: **"We will overcome, we will overcome, we will overcome someday**

**Oh, down in my heart, I do believe, we will overcome someday"**

A transcription of Zilphia Horton's recording of "I Will Overcome" [above] was prepared for comparison.

After careful analysis, it seems likely and even probable that Louise Shropshire's "If My Jesus Wills" had some influence on the tune "We Will Overcome," which is believed to have been adapted into the freedom song "We Shall Overcome." The lyrics to the songs give the most obvious connection, but musical aspects of the two tunes' choruses also show strong parallels in rhythmic, melodic, harmonic, and formal characteristics.

Regarding rhythm, the most important parallel between "If My Jesus Wills" and "I Will Overcome" is the meter. Both tunes use a quadruple meter and both switch at will between duple and triple (or simple and compound) division of the beat. Both tunes also tend to show most rhythmic activity in the first half of each measure, with the second half of most measures consisting of a sustained note. However, much of that similarity is explained by the requirements of text setting. Since they have such similar texts, the rhythms are more likely to bear strong similarities of duration: "We Will Overcome" and "I'll overcome" both suggest a sustained note on the syllable "-come."

The harmonies of the two pieces (only implied in the case of "We Will Overcome" but written in Shropshire's tune) share much in terms of large-scale motion. Both choruses start on a tonic chord and, with small deviations) stay on that chord until the end of their first phrase on a dominant seventh chord. These harmonies relate to the similar form of the two tunes' choruses. Both are comprised of a single period of two four-measure phrases, the first ending on a half cadence and the last on the tonic. Furthermore, the first phrases of both tunes have similar structures. The first phrase of "We Will Overcome" takes the form of a textbook sentence structure: a melodic segment is sung ("We will overcome"), then repeated ("We will overcome") and followed by another melodic segment exactly twice as long as the original segment ("We will overcome some day"). "If My Jesus Wills" has a very similar structure, but the repetition of the first melodic segment is slightly altered, creating a near sentence structure. Still, the phrase structure of the two choruses is so similar in their harmonic, rhythmic, and lyrical content that it is very likely that one was modeled after the other.

CONCLUSION:

In listening to these two songs, the ordinary "lay" listener would likely recognize the striking and substantial lyrical, melodic, harmonic, rhythmic and formal similarities between them. Further study would likely identify additional similarities between these two works. My analysis shows that the substantial similarities between "If My Jesus Wills" and "We Will Overcome" almost surpass the possibility of coincidence. I therefore conclude that "I Will Overcome," as performed by Zilphia Horton in 1947, was not created independently of "If My Jesus Wills," composed by Louise Shropshire sometime between 1932 and 1942.

Douglas Easterling

PhD Fellow in Musicology

Department of Composition, Musicology, and Theory

University of Cincinnati College-Conservatory of Music (

end of report)

## Abridged version of the Stephen Goukas Musicological Report:

Goukas Transcription

*Analysis*:

"On the basis of my musicological analyses of "If My Jesus Wills," composed between 1932 and 1942 and copyrighted by Louise Shropshire in 1954, and of the recording of Zilphia Horton singing "We Will Overcome" from around 1947, I have found that these two songs share many substantial musical characteristics. The first, and perhaps most obvious, is the text of both songs, which I have included below."

TEXT

My analysis shows that the text setting for the two songs is identical. Both consist of short, one-measure fragments that combine to form four-measure phrases. This is emphasized through identical punctuation within the two works; this punctuation determines where the breaks, or pauses, occur in the music. Horton's 1947 performance of "I Will Overcome" documents slight adaptations to Shropshire's original text. For example, Horton sings, "We will overcome," as opposed to Shropshire's "I'll overcome," demonstrating a change in pronouns. These changes are marked below. In addition to the extraordinary textual similarities, I find that the style of declamation, as well as musical phrasing, demonstrate that "I Will Overcome," as sung by Zilphia Horton, is almost certainly derived from Shropshire's "If My Jesus Wills."

RHYTHM

Rhythmically, "If My Jesus Wills" and "I Will Overcome" are almost identical. The major difference has to do with the text change of "I'll" to "We will" and the subsequent replacement of a single note in Shropshire's version with two notes in Horton's version. This was done for purely practical purposes: Horton has two syllables, and thus needs two notes, one per syllable. There also exists a slight difference in the "o-" of "overcome"; in this case, Shropshire has an extra note. This extra note is simply an ornament, or musical decoration, to the line, "I'll overcome." Its absence from Horton's version is likely due to Horton hearing this song from the workers themselves--probably a simplified version of Shropshire's song, which lacked the decoration.

MELODY

*When one examines the melody, one finds strong differences between the songs. Zilphia Horton's version emphasizes the third and fifth scale degrees, while Shropshire's focus seems to be on the tonic and the fifth. However, musical cadences, that is, the points of rest, fall on the same harmonic material, and the formal structure of the melody in both is, as the text, identical (see Table 1).*

*This melodic difference can be explained rather easily if one considers the oral mode of transmission for songs within the African-American spiritual tradition. Within this tradition, it is not uncommon for the text of one song to have many different melodies associated with it, though each would have identical or near-identical phrase structures. This is also evident in the performance practices of this tradition; the same song, with the same text, might be performed completely differently depending on the denomination (Baptist, Adventist, Methodist, etc.), the specific church or congregation; even the same choir for different services can interpret the same piece in a completely new manner. This corresponds well to how Zilphia Horton claims she knew the song, as she says that she heard it sung by a black woman, purportedly Lucille Simmons, at a union rally.*

CONCLUSION

*Taking this all into consideration, it is almost a certainty that Zilphia Horton singing, "I Will Overcome," was in fact performing a slightly adapted version of Louise Shropshire's song, "If My Jesus Wills," which was widely popular among African American congregations from the 1930's to the 1950's. As documented by independently recorded interviews, "If My Jesus Wills" was commonly known as "I'll Overcome" for its repetitive refrain, which may have led to the erroneous title "We Will Overcome."*

*The analytical evidence is overwhelming: when Zilphia Horton sang "We Will Overcome" circa 1947, she would have had to have been familiar with some iteration of Louise Shropshire's song, "If My Jesus Wills". A comparative, holistic analysis reveals nearly identical text, rhythms, and phrasing, strongly suggest that the two songs have one source. In print (and in copyright), I conclude that this source is Louise Shropshire's "If My Jesus Wills".*

*Stephen V. Guokas, University of Cincinnati College Conservatory of Music*

*B.M.–Music Theory & Composition, M.M.–Music History*

(end of report)

As a child, I was taught that taking what did not belong to me was immoral. Was it possible that Pete Seeger and the others were not also taught this? Or did they simply not care? Could money alone have been their motivation for carrying out such reprehensible acts? And what made them think they could get away with it? As their luck and fortunes would have it, at the time Louise Shropshire, African Americans, and the nation had other things to worry about.

ଔ

# Chapter 18

# Sweet Chariots

In 1962, the Highlander Folk School, renamed the Highlander Research and Education Center, reopens its doors in Knoxville, Tennessee.

**June 11, 1963** - In a nationally televised address, President John F. Kennedy urges the nation to support Civil Rights legislation. In his speech, he guarantees equal treatment for every American, regardless of race.[97] Louise is a strong supporter of President Kennedy, having participated in campaign fundraisers on his behalf.[98]

**June 8th, 1963** – Pete Seeger performs a high-profile concert at New York's Carnegie Hall. The concert is recorded live, and an album is released titled: *Pete Seeger: We Shall Overcome-The Complete Carnegie Hall Concert*.[99]

On **July 26th, 27th, and 28th, 1963**, a sold-out crowd of 13,000, mostly White concert-goers, flocked to the Newport Folk Festival in Newport, Rhode Island. Newport—home to the sprawling estates of the super-rich—is, by no one's characterization, an ethnic melting pot. The racially homogeneous city boasts a 90.96% Caucasian population. Any African American in attendance would likely have felt like a fly in the buttermilk.

Although most consider this event nothing more than a youthful, music-filled weekend, there is more here than meets the ear. As it turns out, Pete Seeger and Alan Lomax serve on the festival's board of directors, and Seeger's powerful manager and publisher, Harold Leventhal, is a festival sponsor. In addition, the festival features a Saturday-afternoon workshop entitled "Folk Music and the Copyright Law." The workshop is taught by **Elliot Hoffman**, a high-powered, Yale-educated super-lawyer who also serves as the festival's secretary and general counsel. The festival also holds a Sunday workshop entitled "Collecting Folk Music." Peter, Paul, and Mary; Joan Baez, and Bob Dylan perform. Pete Seeger and Guy Carawan, both of whom are copyright claimants to We Shall Overcome, perform as well.

In an apparent nod to the ongoing Civil Rights Movement, a 4-person African American choir from the Deep South, known as the "Freedom Singers," is asked to close the festivities by singing the festival's most anticipated song... you guessed it; We Shall Overcome. Imagine the surprise of these four singers when Peter, Paul, and Mary, Joan

---

[97] JFK Presidential Library and Museum / http://www.jfklibrary.org/Research/Ready-Reference/JFK-Speeches/Radio-and-Television-Report-to-the-American-People-on-Civil-Rights-June-11-1963.aspx
[98] Personal Interview with Alice Jarrett McCloud; April 21, 2012, San Dimas, Ca.
[99] Stotts, Stuart and Cummings, Terrance with Seeger, Pete; We Shall Overcome; a Song that Changed the World; Houghton Mifflin Harcourt; 2010; p. 51

Baez, Bob Dylan, Pete Seeger, and actor Theodore Bikel join them to sing We Shall Overcome in the festival's grand finale. A picture is worth a thousand words.

1963 Newport Folk Festival L to R: Peter Paul and Mary, Joan Baez, Bob Dylan, Freedom Singers, Pete Seeger, Theodore Bikel (Courtesy Library of Congress)

In the festival program, Pete Seeger's manager posts an advertisement for Seeger's ten-month "21-Country World Tour," scheduled to begin immediately after the concert. The tour is likely driven by the notoriety of "We *Shall Overcome*," by far the most popular song in his repertoire.

# We Shall Overcome: Sacred Song on the Devil's Tongue

Bob Dylan and Pete Seeger/ 1963 Newport Folk Festival

While Pete Seeger was singing We Shall Overcome to sold-out crowds around the world, African Americans were fighting for their lives, simply to be treated as human beings in a country that didn't seem to want them or care.

That same year, at the suggestion of Rev. Fred Shuttlesworth, during a speaking tour leading up to the "March on Washington," Rev. Dr. Martin Luther King Jr. accepts overnight accommodations at Louise Shropshire's spacious home. He is accompanied by three FBI agents. The entire area is roped off, and for security purposes, no one is even allowed to drive down Shropshire's exclusive Mount Auburn street. Louise is very anxious, and although her home is overrun by strangers, she has known Dr. King for years and considers it a great privilege to offer him lodging.

L to R: Bob Shropshire Sr., Louise Shropshire, Rev. Dr. Martin Luther King Jr., and Rev. Fred Shuttlesworth
Shropshire Home, Cincinnati, Ohio, Courtesy Louise Shropshire Foundation

That evening, after enjoying a mouthwatering feast, Louise, her family, Dr. King, Rev. Shuttlesworth, and, of course, the FBI men retire to the parlor, where Louise sits at her well-worn piano and sings Gospel songs. This was a custom at family gatherings at the Shropshire home. Upon hearing "If My Jesus Wills," Dr. King asks Louise if he might change the words 'I'll Overcome' to 'We'll Overcome' "for the movement," as he put it. Louise responds, "I don't mind." [100]

---

[100] Interview with Louise Shropshire/ Interviewer Vasquez-Cabral, Gina / Pomona Daily Bulletin

# We Shall Overcome: Sacred Song on the Devil's Tongue

Louise Shropshire, 3rd from left, with Dr. King, Cincinnati Airport / 1963 Rev. Shuttlesworth grasping Dr. King's Left Arm. Courtesy Louise Shropshire Foundation

Courtesy Library of Congress

**August 28, 1963** – As the highlight of the March on Washington, Rev. Dr. Martin Luther King Jr. delivers his historic "I Have a Dream" speech to 300,000 attendees. Shropshire is also present.[101]

Joan Baez performing We Shall Overcome at the March on Washington (Photo: Courtesy Library of Congress)

---

[101] Personal interview with Beverly Taylor. Oct. 22, 2011, Cincinnati, OH.

As if in retaliation for the support King is receiving, at approximately 10:20 am on **Sunday, September 15th, 1963,** a witness sees a member of the Ku Klux Klan, **Robert Chambliss**, aka "Dynamite Bob," place a bomb under the steps of the **Sixteenth Street Baptist Church** in Birmingham, Alabama. Moments afterward, the bomb explodes, blasting four innocent African American girls to bits—**Denise McNair** (11), **Addie Mae Collins** (14), **Carole Robertson** (14), and **Cynthia Wesley** (14)—and injuring twenty-two other children. When the bomb detonated, the children had been attending Sunday School classes at the church in preparation for a sermon entitled "A Love That Forgives." The explosion blows a bus-sized hole in the church's rear wall and destroys all but one stained-glass window, showing Christ leading a group of little children.

Church members removing bodies from the 16th Street Baptist Church

Denise McNair (11), Addie Mae Collins (14), Carole Robertson (14), and Cynthia Wesley (14)

Robert Chambliss is arrested and charged with murder and with possessing a box of 122 sticks of dynamite without a permit. On October 8th, 1963, less than a month after the bombing, Chambliss was found not guilty of murder and received a one-hundred-dollar fine and a six-month jail sentence for possession of the dynamite. A week earlier, Alabama **Governor George Wallace** told the New York Times that what Alabama needed was a "few first-class funerals" to halt integration.

Robert Chambliss

Dr. King delivers a heartbreaking eulogy at the funerals of Carol Denise McNair, Addie Mae Collins, and Cynthia Dianne Wesley, three of the four children killed in the Sixteenth Street Baptist Church bombing. The fourth, Carole Robertson, is buried in a separate, private ceremony.[102]

**November 22nd, 1963** – President John F. Kennedy is shot and killed in Dallas, Texas. Amid much controversy, Lee Harvey Oswald is arrested and convicted of the crime. Hate is alive and well in America.

Pres. John F. Kennedy and his wife Jacqueline, John and Nellie Connally, in the presidential Limousine, moments before his assassination (photo: Library of Congress)

---

[102] Finkleman, Paul; Encyclopedia of African American History, 1896 to the Present From the Age of Segregation to the Twenty-First Century Volume 1; Oxford University Press; 2007; p. 182

Alongside a recently widowed Jacqueline Kennedy, Lyndon B. Johnson is sworn into office aboard Air Force One
Photo - Library of Congress

## Martin and Malcolm

**1964** is an important year for African Americans in the struggle for civil rights. Louise Shropshire is deeply inspired by the efforts of leaders such as Rev. Dr. Martin Luther King and **Malcolm X.**

Malcolm X, born Malcolm Little on May 19th, 1925, was the son of Earl Little, an African American Baptist preacher. His mother, Louise Little, was born in the West Indies and was of mixed race. When Malcolm was only four years old, his father, Earl—a militant "Back to Africa Movement" supporter—was found dead. He is thought to have been killed by the KKK. After her husband's murder, Malcolm's mother suffered irreparable psychological damage and, six years later, was committed to a mental institution. A ten-year-old Malcolm was then sent to live with relatives in Boston, but before long was made a ward of the court and sent to a series of foster homes. Despite his circumstances, Malcolm showed signs of superior intelligence and excelled in school. While there, he shared his dream of becoming an attorney with a White teacher, but was crushed when she advised him to become a carpenter instead.

Disillusioned, Malcolm winds up in Harlem and soon turns to crime to survive and to heroin to ease his pain. After committing an armed burglary, he serves ten years in a penitentiary. In prison, he is introduced to the Nation of Islam, a somewhat radical African American Muslim faction. Malcolm joins the Nation of Islam (NOI) and changes his name to El-Hajj Malik El-Shabazz. He now refers to his former last name, "Little," as a "Slave Name".

Upon his release from prison, he is introduced to the NOI's leader, The Honorable Elijah Muhammad, and, before long, becomes a leader within the organization. Over time, he earns a reputation as an intelligent and fearless militant whose controversial connection to the "Nation" brands him as a racist and political agitator. His courage and bitter eloquence, however, elevate him to heroic status among many disillusioned Blacks as he publicly articulates his rhetorical indictments of "White America" for its "crimes against African Americans"—a line of antagonism Dr. King would not cross.

**On March 8, 1964**, immediately after a trip to Mecca, Saudi Arabia, Malcolm X publicly declares his break with the Nation of Islam and renounces its powerful leader, Elijah Muhammad.[103]

**On March 26th, 1964**, before a Senate meeting on the Civil Rights Act, Dr. King meets Malcolm X. Together, they project solidarity to America, representing both militant and passive expressions of African American resistance to inequality, segregation, and racism. Their meeting, however, lasts only one minute, and they never cross paths again.

---

[103] Terrill, Robert E.; The Cambridge Companion to Malcolm X; Cambridge University Press; 2010; p. 102

L to R- Martin Luther King Jr., Ralph Abernathy, Malcolm X / Image Courtesy Library of Congress

Before his break with the Nation of Islam, Malcolm X was a zealous, outspoken activist, working tirelessly to secure equal rights for all African Americans. Unlike Dr. King, who preached love as the only way to overcome hatred, Malcolm believed equality must be achieved "by whatever means necessary."

Malcolm X / Image Courtesy Library of Congress

Isaias Gamboa

June 21, 1964 – At Chicago's Soldier Field, Gospel singer Mahalia Jackson performs We Shall Overcome to a crowd of 57,000 at the close of a Civil Rights rally led by Martin Luther King, Jr.

**July 2, 1964** – In the wake of JFK's assassination, the **Civil Rights Act of 1964** is signed into law.[104]

**September 13, 1964** - Louise's daughter, Darlene, is married to Richard Goins at the Shropshire home. Rev. Fred Shuttlesworth presides over the ceremony. Dr. King is in Berlin for a speaking engagement, but despite death threats, upon his return he pays his respects and signs "Best Wishes" on a keepsake napkin.[105] [106] [107]

Newlyweds, Richard A. Goins and Darlene Shropshire-Goins
Courtesy Louise Shropshire Foundation

---

[104] Riches, William Terence Martin: The Civil Rights Movement: Struggle and Resistance; Palgrave Macmillan; 2004; p. 75, 76
[105] Personal interview with Beverly Taylor. Oct. 22, 2011, Cincinnati, OH
[106] Personal Interview with Robert Anthony Goins Sr. Riverside, Ca. Oct. 6, 2010
[107] Baldwin, Lewis V., The Voice of Conscience: The Church in the Mind of Martin Luther King, Jr.; Oxford University Press; 2010; p. 340

We Shall Overcome: Sacred Song on the Devil's Tongue

Dr. King with bodyguards at Shropshire home, 1964 Courtesy, Louise Shropshire Foundation

**October 14, 1964** - Rev. Dr. Martin Luther King, Jr. is awarded the Nobel Peace Prize. In his December 10, 1964, acceptance speech, he includes the phrase *"We Shall Overcome."*[108] Following the ceremony, Dr. King returns to the Shropshire home, where he shares thoughts of dying and stories of being beaten in prison.[109] [110]

---

[108] Martin Luther King, Martin Luther King (Jr.), James Melvin Washington; A Testament of Hope: The Essential Writings and Speeches of Martin Luther King, Jr.; Harper Collins; 2001; p. 224-226

[109] Interview with Louise Shropshire, Interviewer Vasquez-Cabral, Gina, Pomona Daily Bulletin

[110] Personal Interview with Robert Goins Jr. Riverside, Ca. May. 5, 2010

Dr. Martin Luther King displaying his Nobel Prize

Later that week, Dr. King returns to the Shropshire home, and Louise invites Cincinnati's African American social elite to her Mount Auburn home for a fundraiser in recognition of Dr. King's Nobel Prize.[111] [112]

---

[111] Interview with Louise Shropshire/ Interviewer Vasquez-Cabral, Gina / Pomona Daily Bulletin
[112] Personal Interview with Robert Anthony Goins Sr. Riverside, Ca. May. 5, 2010

Louise Shropshire (seated), with family members at MLK fundraiser
Courtesy Louise Shropshire Foundation

**February 21, 1965** – Malcolm X prepares to deliver a speech at the **Audubon Ballroom** in New York's Washington Heights. He will address the **Organization of African American Unity**, a Pan-African organization he founded after his trip to Mecca. Malcolm's ambition is to reunify African Americans with their culture and "families" from the 'Motherland—the continent of Africa.

Malcolm begins his speech with the traditional Arabic greeting, "Salaam Aleichem" (peace be unto you). Those in attendance respond, "Aleichem Salaam." Suddenly, there is a commotion in the back rows of the auditorium. As everyone turns to see what is happening, Malcolm says calmly to the audience, "Cool it, brothers—don't get excited." At that moment, three men who had been seated in the front row stand up, throw open their overcoats, and discharge a firestorm of double-barreled buckshot and flesh-shredding bullets into Malcolm's face and chest. Malcolm's wife, Betty Shabazz, and his four children witness the horrifying scene. Within minutes, Malcolm is rushed to Columbia Presbyterian Medical Center but is pronounced dead at **3:30 pm on February 21, 1965**.

Malcolm X being transported to the hospital

In Harlem, a 3-day public viewing of his body is held, during which an estimated 30,000 people pay their respects. After being denied requests by larger New York sanctuaries, Malcolm X's funeral is held on **February 27, 1965**, at the Faith Temple Church of God in Christ in Harlem, New York. Although the church has a seating capacity of only 600, more than 1,000 mourners attend.

Dr. King is deeply affected by Malcolm's assassination. In a telegram to Malcolm X's wife, Betty Shabazz, Dr. King offers condolences.

*"While we did not always see eye to eye on methods to solve the race problem, I always had a deep affection for Malcolm and felt that he had a great ability to put his finger on the existence and root of the problem. He was an eloquent spokesman for his point of view, and no one can honestly doubt that Malcolm had a great concern for the problems that we face as a race."*[113] -Rev. Dr. Martin Luther King Jr.

Three men from a Nation of Islam mosque in Newark, New Jersey, were ultimately convicted of Malcolm X's killing and served prison sentences.[114]

---

[113] Martin Luther King Papers Project / Stanford University / "Telegram from Martin Luther King Jr. to Betty al Shabazz / http://mlkkpp01.stanford.edu/index.php/encyclopedia/documentsentry/telegram_from_martin_luther_king_jr_to_betty_al_shabazz/

[114] Gormley, Beatrice; Malcolm X: A Revolutionary Voice; Sterling Publishing Company, Inc.; 2010; p. 116

**March 21-25, 1965** - Rev. Dr. Martin Luther King Jr. leads a four-day protest march from Selma, Alabama, to Montgomery, Alabama, to highlight the difficulties Black voters faced in the American South. Known as the **Selma-to-Montgomery Marches**, this was the last of three marches. Pete Seeger is there, running around with paper and pencil, writing down African American songs of faith and hope as fast as he can. In Pete Seeger's own words:

*"The Songwriters and the young singers of Selma were creating one great song after another right before our eyes. One woman on the Selma march saw me trying to notate a melody and said with a smile, "Don't you know you can't write down freedom songs?"* [115]

- **First March (Bloody Sunday): March 7, 1965.**

- **Second March (Turnaround Tuesday): March 9, 1965.**

- **Third March (Final successful march): March 21–25, 1965.**

The final march spanned approximately 50 miles (80 km) over five days, crossing the **Edmund Pettus Bridge** and culminating in a rally at the Alabama State Capitol, where Dr. Martin Luther King Jr. delivered his "**How Long, Not Long**" **speech**. Five of the songs Pete Seeger "collected" and transcribed during those four days were recorded and then released later that year as "WNEW's Story of Selma" on Folkways Recordings.

ఌ

---

[115] Rosenthal, Bob; Rosenthal, Sam; "Pete Seeger: In His Own Words", Paradigm Publishers, 2012, p. 161

# Chapter 19

*"Whoever is not with me is against me, and whoever does not gather with me scatters"*
~Jesus Christ / Matthew 12:30

# The Way to the Cross

Over the next ten years, Louise Shropshire's life would take many difficult turns, as would that of most African Americans. To be certain, she would have to summon every drop of physical and spiritual strength she had to bear what was to come.

**March 15, 1965** - President Lyndon B. Johnson delivers a nationally televised speech condemning racist voter suppression tactics and supporting the Voting Rights Act of 1965. The speech responds to the violence that erupted in Alabama after the Selma police attempted to stop a peaceful protest march to Montgomery. The words President Johnson uses reflect his consideration for the struggles facing Black Americans. The following is an excerpt:

*"...the harsh fact is that in many places in this country,* **men and women are kept from voting simply because they are Negroes**. *Every device, of which human ingenuity is capable, has been used to deny this right. The Negro citizen may go to register only to be told that the day is wrong, or the hour is late, or the official in charge is absent. And if he persists and, if he manages to present himself to the registrar, he may be disqualified because he did not spell out his middle name, or because he abbreviated a word on the application. And if he manages to fill out an application, he is given a test. The registrar is the sole judge of whether he passes this test. He may be asked to recite the entire Constitution or explain the most complex provisions of state law.*

*"And even a college degree cannot be used to prove that he can read and write.* **For the fact is that the only way to pass these barriers is to show a White skin**. *Experience has clearly shown that the existing process of law cannot overcome systematic and ingenious discrimination. No law that we now have on the books, and I have helped to put three of them there, can ensure the right to vote when local officials are determined to deny it. In such a case, our duty must be clear to all of us. The Constitution says that no person shall be kept from voting because of his race or his color..."*

*"...What happened in Selma is part of a far larger movement which reaches into every section and state of America. It is the effort of American Negroes to secure for themselves the full blessings of American life. Their cause must be our cause, too. Because it is not just Negroes, but really it's all of us who must overcome the crippling legacy of bigotry and injustice.* **And we shall overcome.**

[116]

---

[116] Source: Lyndon B. Johnson Library / http://www.lbjlib.utexas.edu/johnson/archives.hom/speeches.hom/650315.asp

During President Johnson's address, he surprised many listeners by speaking the words, "...we shall overcome." These three words marked another pivotal moment in American history. But who was "*We*," and to whom did this song truly belong? After all, to American Blacks, wasn't "*We*" supposed to refer to themselves—struggling, subjugated, and disenfranchised African Americans—rather than wealthy White presidents or Harvard-educated folk singers like Pete Seeger? What did *they* have to overcome? Louise's hymn met a need by delivering a powerful dose of spiritual comfort to suffering people. Although Seeger's musically and spiritually white-washed adaptation may have soothed his empty-pocket blues, it proved little more than another "Hallmark moment" to American Blacks—an insincere sympathy card that, for the most part, remained unopened.

**1965 -** Dr. King returns several times to Louise Shropshire's home. As always, Louise serves a savory meal, often prepared by her husband, Robert, and afterward shares songs of praise and worship.[117] In addition to being a valuable ally in their Civil Rights efforts, Dr. King and Rev. Shuttlesworth each regard Louise as a close, trusted friend.

**October 1965** – Amidst discord and controversy, the Revelation Baptist Church is grappling to define its governance structure. Rev. Shuttlesworth's unyielding leadership style has drawn opponents within the congregation's leadership body. There is a split between those who want more control over church affairs, seeing Shuttlesworth as an employee of the church, and those, including Louise, who believe Shuttlesworth should have a say in all major church decisions as the congregation's very capable and divinely appointed leader. Making matters worse, some are exasperated by Shuttlesworth's many trips to Birmingham, feeling he should be spending more time in Cincinnati and in Revelation's pulpit.

Things are beginning to heat up. At one point, several dissenting members disrupt church services to protest. After ignoring repeated warnings to stop, Rev. Shuttlesworth filed disorderly conduct charges, and the court granted Shuttlesworth an injunction against the feuding members. In retaliation, the group alleges that Shuttlesworth has mismanaged church funds and assumed dictatorial authority over the church's financial affairs. They then hold a meeting with a small group of dissidents, and among themselves, they vote to remove Shuttlesworth as pastor. Soon afterward, a church audit is conducted, and Rev. Shuttlesworth is exonerated of the erroneous allegations.

In a ruling on one of the claims brought to court, Cincinnati Municipal Judge Otis R. Hess offers his commentary on the troubling circumstances:

*"It is obvious that the Revelation Baptist Church is sorely torn; from all facts and citations presented in this memorandum. It is obvious that a house divided cannot long endure; that all the warring factions must determine to immediately, peacefully adjust their difficulties, in keeping with their accepted Directory for Baptist Churches, or this church will*

---

[117] Personal Interview with Alice Jarrett McCloud; April 21, 2012; San Dimas, Ca.

*lose its Christian character. No judgment or decree of any court can cause the Holy Spirit to guide the Christian mission of any church."*[118]   -Judge Otis Hess

Reasonably upset by these events, Shuttlesworth is convinced that Cincinnati's political right wing is manipulating a few unhappy members of his congregation to discredit him. He notes that the attorney for the dissidents, Smith Tyler, actually led the failed, staunchly conservative *"Barry Goldwater for President"* campaign in 1964 and had begun attending church meetings as a representative of the dissidents. Rev. Shuttlesworth makes the following public statement:

*"I didn't come from fighting lions and tigers in the Deep South, just to bow before cats and used-to-be[sic] tigers here."*[119]

A church vote is called, and by a slim majority, the deacon's board and congregation would elect to keep Rev. Shuttlesworth as pastor. However, things would never be the same. During the ordeal, Shuttlesworth's close friend, Rev. Dr. King, sends him a telegram that provides much-needed moral support.

### Western Union Telegram / Dated Nov 4, 1965

"To: REV. FRED SHUTTLESWORTH, REVELATION BAPTIST CHURCH, 1556 JOHN STREET, CINCINNATI, OHIO.

THESE ARE THE KINDS OF TIMES THAT TRY MEN'S SOULS. KNOW THAT I AM WITH YOU IN THIS HOUR WHEN MEN SEEK TO QUESTION YOU. YOUR CONTRIBUTION TO THE LIFE AND MINISTRY OF THE CHURCH IS NOT ONLY A MATTER OF RECORD, IT IS A MATTER OF HISTORY; BUT MEN ALWAYS STONE THE PROPHETS AND PERSECUTE THOSE WHO WOULD LEAD THEM IN TRUTH. MAY GOD STRENGTHEN YOUR SPIRIT AND UPLIFT YOUR HEART THAT EVEN YOUR ACCUSERS WILL BE FORCED TO ADMIT THAT TRULY YOU ARE A MAN OF COURAGE, CONVICTION, AND INTEGRITY. YOUR BROTHER IN CHRIST, MARTIN LUTHER KING JR."[120]

---

[118] Adams, James / The Post and Times Star / Cincinnati, Oh.;  *"Rev. Shuttlesworth's Tenure Upheld by court"* / Dec. 3, 1965

[119] Manis, Andrew M./ *"A Fire You Can't Put Out: The Civil Rights Life of Birmingham's Rev. Fred Shuttlesworth"* P. 425 / 1999 / University of Alabama Press

[120] Martin Luther King Papers Project / Stanford University / "Telegram from Martin Luther King Jr. to Rev. Fred Shuttlesworth

We Shall Overcome: Sacred Song on the Devil's Tongue

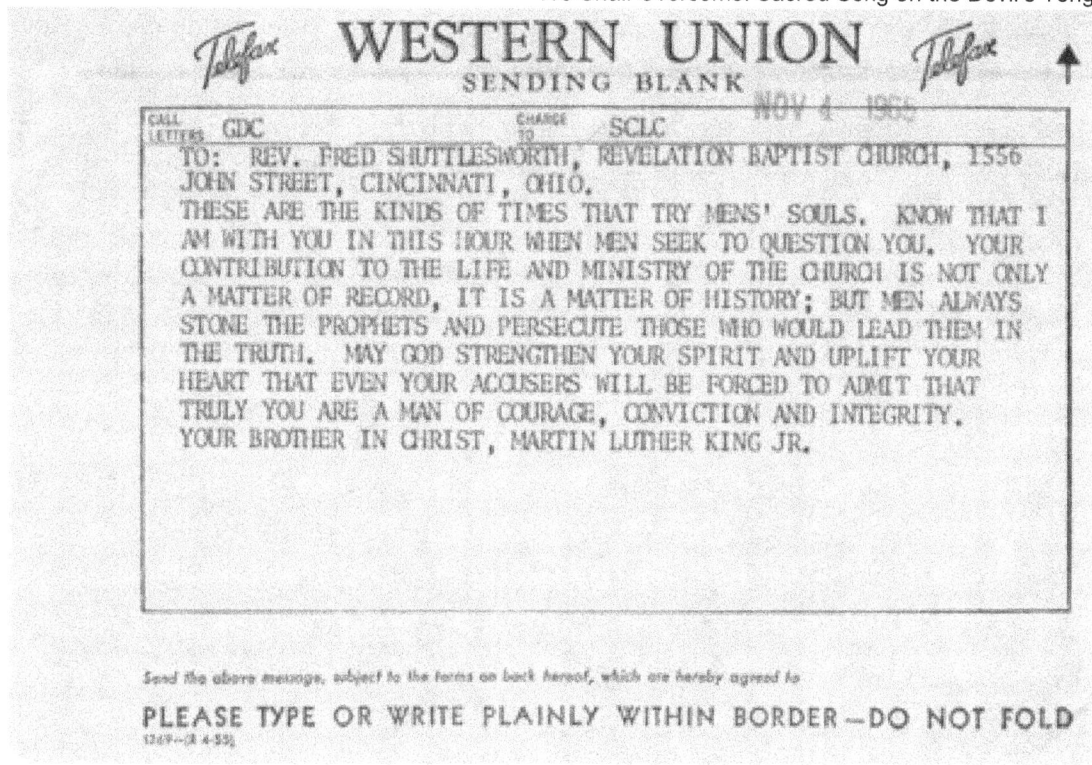

Telegram from Rev. Dr. Martin Luther King Jr. to Rev. Fred Shuttlesworth, Courtesy Martin Luther King Papers Project, Stanford University

Having been influential in persuading Rev. Shuttlesworth to come to Cincinnati, Louise is profoundly disappointed by the behavior of her fellow members...some of whom she has known for more than 20 years. Privately, she and her husband discuss the possibility of planting a new church with Shuttlesworth. Although still seeking ways to mend fences at Revelation Baptist Church, Shuttlesworth is open to the idea. At her home, Louise holds private meetings with key Revelation Baptist Church members who also stand with Rev. Shuttlesworth. Before long, a group of 150 active members is assembled. Together, they resolve to form a new church, The Greater New Light Baptist Church, which will invite Shuttlesworth to be its pastor. Louise communicates these developments to Rev. Shuttlesworth, who, after prayerful consideration, resigns as Pastor of Revelation Baptist Church.

On Sunday, January 16, 1966, 300 people gather for a worship service in the old Melrose YMCA building, located in the Walnut Hills area of Cincinnati. After an opening prayer, the "Greater New Light Baptist Church" officially votes Rev. Fred Shuttlesworth as their new pastor. In response, Shuttlesworth states: "If your motive is to serve God, I will have no objection to accepting this church..." Soon afterward, with the financial support of the Shropshires and others, the "Greater New Light Baptist Church" purchases property at 710 North Crescent Avenue in the Avondale area of Cincinnati. This street would later be named Fred Shuttlesworth Circle. Louise is appointed "Minister of Music" of the new church and is influential in bringing over additional members. By June of 1966, the congregation had grown to over 400. Although there is much to celebrate, these are bittersweet benchmarks for Louise, who has lost many longtime friends as a result of the Revelation Baptist Church's very public and contentious split.

Adding to Louise's displeasure, Big Mom, who had been suffering from multiple health problems, resolves to retire from a life of cold Ohio winters and convalesce in the warm California sun. During World War II, Louise's brother, Garland, had been stationed in San Francisco, California, where Big Mom had visited on several occasions. While there, she had fallen in love with the perennially pleasant California climate. Along with their mother, Louise's two sisters, Alice and Lara, and brother, Garland, decide to relocate to Pomona, California. It is the first time in her entire life that Louise has been without her mother and siblings.

Alice Jarrett-McCloud     Lara Jarrett-Thomas
Courtesy Louise Shropshire Foundation

Not long afterward, Louise's husband, Robert, suffers the debilitating loss of both his legs due to complications from chronic diabetes. Although he manages to get by with prosthetic legs, he suffers extended bouts of depression. Louise works hard to encourage her husband not to succumb to the emotional melancholy of his disability.

Robert Shropshire Sr. (standing, second from left) with friends in his basement, circa 1960
Courtesy Louise Shropshire Foundation

Although she tries her best to hide it, Louise is emotionally drained by this difficult chain of events. Deeply concerned about her husband's emotional state, her mother's departure from Cincinnati, and the heartbreaking disunion of her beloved Revelation Baptist Church, Louise and her husband, Robert, decide to retire to California, where Louise can be closer to Big Mom and Robert can convalesce. Louise notifies Rev. Shuttlesworth and his wife, Ruby, her good friend, of her decision. Although they are greatly saddened, the Shuttlesworths understand her reasons and offer her their blessings, support, and encouragement. Rev. Shuttlesworth even jokes that perhaps Louise will one day plant a Greater New Light Baptist Church in California. Although she will be with her family again, Louise will miss the close friendship with Rev. Shuttlesworth, his wife, Ruby, and their family.

Isaias Gamboa

**On June 17, 1966,** at **Temple Israel in Hollywood**, California, Dr. King delivered a We Shall Overcome sermon in which he explained why Blacks, albeit sometimes reluctantly, sang *We Shall Overcome*.

> *"Deep in my heart, I do believe we shall overcome. Now I join hands often with students and others behind jail bars, singing it: We shall overcome. Sometimes we've had tears in our eyes when we've joined together to sing it, but we still decided to sing it! We shall overcome."*

> *"Lord, before this victory is won, some will have to get thrown in jail some more, but we shall overcome. Don't worry about us; before the victory is won, some of us will lose jobs, but we shall overcome. Before the victory is won, even some will have to face physical death, but if physical death is the price that some must pay to free their children from a permanent psychological death, then nothing shall be more redemptive. We shall overcome.*

> *"Before the victory is won, some will be misunderstood and called bad names and dismissed as rabble-rousers and agitators, but we shall overcome. And I'll tell you why.*

> *"We shall overcome because the arc of the moral universe is long, but it bends towards justice. We shall overcome because Carlyle is right: 'No lie can live forever'. We shall overcome because William Collin Bryant is right: Truth crushed to earth will rise again. We shall overcome because James Russell Lowell is right: 'Truth forever on the scaffold, wrong forever on the throne. Yet that scaffold sways the future. And behind the dim unknown standeth God within the shadows, keeping watch above his own.'*

> *"We shall overcome because the Bible is right, 'You shall reap what you sow.' -We shall overcome. Deep in my heart, I do believe! We shall overcome. And with this faith, we will go out and adjourn the counsels of despair and bring new light into the dark chambers of pessimism, and we will be able to rise from the fatigue of despair to the buoyancy of hope. And this will be a great America! We will be the participants in making it so. And so as I leave you this evening, I say, 'Walk together chil'en, don't you get weary; there's a great camp meeting in the Promised Land'."*[121] -Rev. Dr. Martin Luther King Jr.

Unexpectedly, to Louise's delight, her husband, Robert, purchases a lovely home for them in Pomona, California. Robert pays for the property in cash, and to Louise's greater delight, the house is on the same block as her beloved Big Mom and brother Garland's homes. Almost immediately, the Shropshires begin shipping their furniture, clothing, and personal effects to California in preparation for their arrival.

Tragically, just weeks before their move, her beloved husband, Robert Shropshire Sr., suffers a massive heart attack and dies. The date is November 7th, 1966. Louise is inconsolable. Robert, or "Funny," as she called him, was not only her husband and best friend but also tended to all of the family's financial affairs. Louise makes arrangements for her late husband to be buried at Union Baptist Cemetery, Cincinnati's oldest Black Baptist

---

[121] Recording of Speech given at Temple Israel, Hollywood, Ca. ; Donated to PBS by Ms. Ruth Nussbaum, Wife of Rabbi Max Nussbaum; Courtesy of the King Center

cemetery. In addition to the memorial service, the funeral, repast, and all other posthumous rituals and responsibilities, Louise must now move to California… a widow.

Robert "Bob" Shropshire's Headstone / Union Baptist Cemetery

    For 50 years, her husband, Robert, owned and operated Bob Shropshire Bail Bonds. A few years before his death, the business name was changed to Bob Shropshire and Son Bail Bonds, as his oldest son, Robert Jr., had learned the trade and was working alongside his father. With limited education and little knowledge of her husband's business affairs, Louise leaves her oldest son, Robert Jr., in charge of the family business.

Robert "Bob" Shropshire Sr., courtesy of Louise Shropshire Foundation

## Sowing Winter Wheat

**December 1966** – Shortly after her arrival in California, Louise joins the Mount Zion Baptist Church but doesn't feel quite at home there, as its worship style is less exuberant than what she was accustomed to in Cincinnati. With support from the family business, Louise continues to provide financial support to the Greater New Light Baptist Church in Cincinnati. Before long, she and Rev. Shuttlesworth begin discussing the possibility of establishing a Greater New Light Baptist Church in Pomona.

**On April 13, 1967,** Louise Shropshire is ordained at the Church of God in Cincinnati, Ohio, by Bishop J. Draft. She returns to Pomona, California, and is thereafter known as Rev. Mother Louise Shropshire.

**March 1967** - Louise's younger sister, Alice, introduces her to Rev. E.C. Johnson, who asks for her help organizing a "prayer-band"—a ministry prayer group dedicated to intercessory prayer and composed of members who pray continuously for those who request it. Louise agrees and offers her own home for the first meetings. Before long, to accommodate additional members, they decide to rent a one-room house at 222 S. Parcels St.

Rented "Prayer-Band" House / 222 S. Parcel St., Pomona, Ca, Courtesy Louise Shropshire Foundation

Still growing, they soon relocate to a storefront in a nearby business district. At their first meeting there, Louise proposes forming a church called "Greater New Life Baptist Church". Its charter members include Rev. Mother Louise Shropshire, Ollie Jarrett (Big Mom), Alice McCloud (sister), Thelma Jarrett (sister-in-law), Lara Johnson (sister), and Garland Jarrett (brother), among others. The storefront is next to a drug paraphernalia store and an adult bookstore.[122] Louise would ultimately contribute much of her personal funds to help secure a Church sanctuary.[123]

---

[122] Personal Interview with Robert Anthony Goins Sr.; Riverside, Ca. May. 5, 2010
[123] Personal Interview with Alice Jarrett McCloud; Feb. 22, 2012; San Dimas, Ca.

Expanded Store-front location / Courtesy Louise Shropshire Foundation

**April 3rd, 1968** – Rev. Dr. Martin Luther King Jr. delivers his "I See the Promised Land" sermon at the Bishop Charles Mason Temple in Memphis, Tennessee, where he describes the power of "We Shall Overcome." [124]

*"We aren't going to let any mace stop us. We are masters in our nonviolent movement in disarming police forces; they don't know what to do. I've seen them so often. I remember in Birmingham, Alabama, when we were in that majestic struggle, there we would move out of the 16th Street Baptist Church day after day; by the hundreds, we would move out. And Bull Connor would tell them to send the dogs forth, and they did come; but we just went before the dogs singing, "Ain't gonna let nobody turn me round." Bull Connor next would say, "Turn the fire hoses on." And as I said to you the other night, Bull Connor didn't know history. We knew a kind of physics that somehow didn't relate to the transphysics that we knew about. And that was the fact that there was a certain kind of fire that no water could put out. And we went before the fire hoses; we had known water. If we were Baptist or some other*

---

[124] Finkelman, Paul; Encyclopedia of African American History, 1896 to the Present From the Age of Segregation to the Twenty-First Century, Volume 1; Oxford University Press; 2001; p. 105

*denomination, we had been immersed. If we were Methodist, and some others, we had been sprinkled, but we knew water.*

*"That couldn't stop us. And we just went on before the dogs, and we would look at them; and we'd go on before the water hoses, and we would look at it, and we'd just go on singing. "Over my head, I see freedom in the air." And then we would be thrown in the paddy wagons, and sometimes we were stacked in there like sardines in a can. And they would throw us in, and old Bull would say, "Take them off," and they did; and we would just go in the paddy wagon singing,* **"We shall Overcome."** *And every now and then we'd get thrown in jail, and we'd see the jailers looking through the windows being moved by our prayers, and being moved by our words and our songs. And there was a power there which Bull Connor couldn't adjust to; and so we ended up transforming Bull into a steer, and we won our struggle in Birmingham."*

Memphis. **The following day, April 4, 1968, Rev. Dr. Martin Luther King Jr. is assassinated** by James Earl Ray at the Lorraine Motel in Memphis, Tennessee.

James Earl Ray

**On April 9, 1963**, in fulfillment of Rev. Dr. King's prior, prophetic request, the beloved gospel song "Take My Hand, Precious Lord" –King's favorite hymn- is sung powerfully and mournfully at his funeral at Ebenezer Baptist Church in Atlanta by gospel singer Mahalia Jackson, Rev. Thomas A. Dorsey's protégé.

Mahalia Jackson singing "Take My Hand, Precious Lord" at Rev. Dr. Martin Luther King's private memorial service

We Shall Overcome: Sacred Song on the Devil's Tongue

The King family at Rev. Dr. King's funeral procession, Photo Courtesy Library of Congress

Murners view Dr. King's Open casket, Photo Courtesy Library of Congress

The loss of Dr. King is a deeply agonizing one for African Americans and lovers of peace around the world. For Louise, as a friend of his, it is also a deeply personal loss. Perhaps in an effort to ease her pain, she composes a handwritten letter and a deeply personal prayer, which she mails to President Lyndon B. Johnson. No grammatical corrections have been applied to her text.

"Louise Shropshire, 1853 Garland St. Pomona, California 91766

### April 7, 1968

"Mr. President,

"I'm just a widow still trying to find my place in life. Serving my fellow man. As you are doing. I can't say big words, but I can say God save America. I want you to know I know you are a great president. Inclosed [sic] is a program; A tribute to Dr. Martin L. King. It is not much, but with not much education, the best I can do. It is sincere. [sic] -Mrs. Louise Shropshire

Louise is also inspired to dedicate her Gospel musical-drama, **"The Way to the Cross,"** to his memory. Composed years earlier for her church in Cincinnati, the musical is performed on Easter Sunday, April 14th, 1968, at the Greater New Light Baptist Church in Pomona, 10 days after the assassination.[125]

*"THE WAY TO THE CROSS", DEDICATED TO THE LATE DR. MARTIN LUTHER KING JR.*

*By Mrs. L. Shropshire, a friend of his.*

*Presented by: Mt. Zion Senior Choir, Rev. Paschal Banks, Pastor, April 7, 1968*

*"We come tonight hearts heavy of the assassination of our Civil Rights leader, Dr. Martin Luther King, who truly was a dedicated prophet of God in serving his fellow man. By preaching non-violence, living non-violence, going to prison for non-violence, being beaten, stabbed, and now, death for non-violence, we pray this prayer. [sic]*

A MEMORIAL FOR

DR. MARTIN LUTHER KING JR.

"Assist us mercifully with thy help, O Lord God of our salvation, that all mankind should follow the example of great humility of thy Son Jesus Christ. Who art always ready to pour down upon us the abundance of mercy. O thou who art love, and Who sees all the suffering, injustice and misery which reign in this world. Have pity, we implore thee; look mercifully upon the poor, the oppressed, and all who are heavy laden with error, labor, and sorrow. Fill our hearts with deep compassion for those who suffer, and hasten the coming of thy kingdom of justice and truth. God our father, author of all good, and never far from any of thy children. We draw near to thee, that we may receive of thy spirit, the bonds and love

---

[125] Personal Interview with Alice Jarrett McCloud; April 21, 2012; San Dimas, Ca.

*and ties of friendship be made stronger for our fellow man. As Dr. Martin Luther King would say, 'Dear God, forgiver of sin, healer of sorrow, vanquisher of death, draw us onto thyself, who art our salvation and our conquering hope. Make us citizens of thy kingdom, men of invincible goodwill – builders of a world where righteousness shall reign, and the law of love shall triumph over hate and strife. Increase as true devotion unto our fellow man. For as for me [sic], I've fought a good fight. Dear Lord, please forgive them, for they know not what they do. Oh Precious Lord, take my hand and lead me through, for today, I shall be with thee in paradise.'* [sic][126]

Cast of "The Way to the Cross" Rev. Mother Louise Shropshire pictured standing far right.
Courtesy, Louise Shropshire Foundation

---

[126] Source: Lyndon B. Johnson Library Archives

**On June 2, 1968**, **Robert Francis Kennedy,** affectionately known to Americans as "Bobby," wins the California and South Dakota Democratic primaries and is poised to challenge Richard Nixon for the White House in November. Before a crowd of 500 supporters at the **Ambassador Hotel in Los Angeles**, California, Kennedy delivers an inspirational victory speech. Afterwards, he is led through the hotel kitchen, where a twenty-four-year-old **Sirhan Bishara Sirhan** lies in wait. As Bobby Kennedy stops to shake hands with a kitchen worker, Sirhan appears and fires several shots at him in rapid succession. Kennedy is hit four times. Although Sirhan's gun holds only 8 rounds, forensic experts assert that 13 shots were fired. Bobby Kennedy succumbed to his injuries in the hospital the following day.[127]

Robert F. Kennedy campaign button

Louise prays for the spiritual discernment to understand these five years of slayings—JFK–1963, Malcolm X-1965, MLK–1968, RFK-1968—and worries about the dark veil of hatred draped over America's face. Rather than succumb to melancholy, she finds peace knowing that Dr. King and the Kennedy brothers are now with the Lord. Knowing Dr.

---

[127] Tom Jackman, "The Bobby Kennedy Assassination Tape: Were 13 Shots Fired or Only 8?," *Washington Post*, June 6, 2018, https://www.washingtonpost.com/news/true-crime/wp/2018/06/06/the-bobby-kennedy-assassination-tape-were-13-shots-fired-or-only-8/.

King personally helps her come to terms with her own life and purpose. For solace and reassurance, she continues to read her Bible daily and, like Dr. King, clings to her faith in Jesus Christ's teachings.

With the assassinations of both Dr. King and Bobby Kennedy in the same year, African Americans appear to lose hope and faith in a just America. As a result, African Americans turn out in low numbers for the presidential election that November.[128] On November 5th, 1968, the Republican candidate, Richard Milhous Nixon, is elected the 37th president of the United States. -A choice Americans would come to regret.

Richard M. Nixon, Courtesy: Library of Congress

---

[128] US Census Bureau; Voter Turnout Rates among Black Voters, by Age, in U.S. Presidential Elections from 1964 to 2020; Statista; November 30, 2021; https://www.statista.com/statistics/1096577/voter-turnout-black-voters-presidential-elections-historical/

**August 15-18, 1969** – An estimated 400,000 concert-goers attend the Woodstock Festival, a three-day rock concert held in Woodstock, New York, from August 15th to August 18th. Joan Baez closes the first day of the festival with a historic performance of "We Shall Overcome." The crowd of nearly half a million people is ninety-five percent White.

Aerial view of the 1969 Woodstock Concert, Image courtesy of the U.S. Library of Congress

**April 1972** – Pete Seeger is featured in Rolling Stone Magazine.

**1975** – Louise's grandson, Robert Anthony Goins Sr., moves from Cincinnati to live with her.

Young Robert Anthony Goins Sr.

Isaias Gamboa

**November 1978** - Pete Seeger writes a letter in an attempt to justify his reasons for claiming illegitimate copyright ownership of a song he didn't write—the famous Cuban folk song, "Guantanamera". The following is an excerpt from his letter. No corrections have been made:

*"In 1971, I was welcomed warmly to Havana by Joseito. (a well-known Cuban songwriter). Three years earlier (maybe 4) I wrote the Cuban society of composers explaining why my name was listed as one of the authors of Guantanamera, and that I did not intend to keep one penny of any royalties for the song. Perhaps something has happened since then to make for a misunderstanding...Keep in mind that when a white singer sings an Afro-American song, he/she is stealing...*

*"...But here is what I said: ...Because of US policy to Cuba, Harold Leventhal suggested to me that unless someone else copyrighted the song, it would become "public domain" and no money would ever reach Cuba, or Hector or Joseito, so I agreed on the understanding that all royalties would go into an escrow until they could all be sent to Cuba. My name on the Copyright (along with Hector's and Joseito's) was simply to facilitate this. I did not want my name in it, but I was told that unless it was, the copyright could not be controlled, and no money—or credit—would ever get to Cuba. I think Joseito should get major credit for the song...I wish my name were not connected with it. All I did was change one note."* [129]     --Pete Seeger

"Guantanamera"

"We Shall Overcome", (translated as "Nosotros Venceremos")

---

[129] Seeger, Pete, Rosenthal, Rob; Rosenthal, Sam; Pete Seeger: In His Own Words / 2012 Paradigm Publishers, London

Although before his death, Louise's husband, Robert, had bequeathed to her a mortgage-free home, over the years Louise is forced to take out loans against her Pomona residence to pay her bills. Despite her circumstances, she continues sending money to the Greater New Light Baptist Church in Cincinnati and, before long, achieves her goal of seeing the mortgage on the Greater New Life Baptist Church (GNLBC) in Pomona paid off. On June 24, 1979, the church holds a mortgage-burning ceremony.

1979 GNLBC Mortgage-Burning Ceremony, Rev. Mother Louise Shropshire, pictured Far left.
Courtesy Louise Shropshire Foundation

GREATER NEW LIGHT BAPTIST CHURCH
(THE CHURCH WHERE EVERYBODY IS SOMEBODY)

MORTGAGE BURNING PROGRAM

SUNDAY, JUNE 24, 1979
3:30 P.M.

THEME: "BY FAITH - WE'VE COME THIS FAR"

REV. NEWBURN PHILLIPS, PASTOR
REV. MILLARD R. SMITH, ASS'T. PASTOR
REV. LOUISE SHROPSHIRE, MINISTER OF MUSIC
DEA. GARLAND JARRETT, CHRMN. DEACON BOARD

1734 ARROYO AVENUE
POMONA, CALIF.
PHONE: 714-623-7616

Courtesy, Louise Shropshire Foundation

On **August 15, 1983**, Louise's beloved mother, Ollie "Big-Mom" Johnson-Jarrett, takes her last breath and is called to be with the Lord.

Mrs. Ollie Johnson-Jarrett *"Big Mom"*, Courtesy Louise Shropshire Foundation

**1984** – Louise's grandson, Robert A. Goins, is nearly killed in a violent auto accident. He is not expected to live. Louise and her prayer group, which she refers to as "the Saints," hold a fourteen-hour prayer vigil at the hospital, where Robert is hanging on for his life. He survives the near-death ordeal.

Over the next fourteen years at the Greater New Light Baptist Church in Pomona, Louise serves as president of the Senior Mission, president of the Board of Directors, Minister of Music, Sunday-school teacher, choir director, and pianist for the Children's

Angelic Choir. When it came to the church, there was little her hands did not touch. She even helps clean the sanctuary after services and plant flowers on the church grounds. Her fellow church members know her for performing her church duties in sickness or in health.

Rev. Mother Louise Shropshire speaking at the Greater New Light Baptist Church, Pomona, Ca., Courtesy Louise Shropshire Foundation

Louise, now in her late 70s, struggles to make ends meet yet never stops helping others in greater need. During the 1980s and early 1990s, she takes in fourteen foster children.

**1993** – Louise takes custody of her four great-grandchildren to prevent *their* separation and loss in the foster-care system. Soon afterward, she loses the fight to keep her Pomona residence and is forced to relinquish the home her beloved husband had purchased for her. With four grandchildren in tow, she is relocated to a one-bedroom senior citizens apartment. Shortly afterward, she is transferred to a small rented house in Pomona, where she continues to care for her great-grandchildren. She is grateful to God for this home, as it has a yard where the children can play.

  Although Louise appears untiring to many, those closest to her notice her physical energy diminishing.[130]

---

[130] Personal Interview with Alice Jarrett McCloud; April 21, 2012; San Dimas, Ca.

# Chapter 20

# We Believe

In 1991, Rev. Mother Louise Shropshire delivers a powerful spiritual sermon titled "We Believe" to the congregation of the Greater New Light Baptist Church in Pomona, CA.

### "WE BELIEVE"

#### A. Sermon by Louise Shropshire, 1991

God is love, and every time we express love in some way to somebody, God is using us. As Christians, our dynamics are as:

We believe that Jesus Christ is the ultimate source of authority, and every area of life is to be subject to his leadership.

We believe the bible as an inspired revelation of God's will and way, made full and complete in the life and teachings of Christ, in our authoritative rule of faith and practice.

We believe the Holy Spirit is God, actively revealing Himself and His will to man.

We believe every individual is created in the image of God and therefore merits respect and consideration as a person of infinite dignity and worth.

We believe each person is competent under God to make his own moral and religious decisions and is responsible to God in all matters, moral and religious duties.

We believe every person is free under God in all matters and consequences and has the right to embrace or reject religion, and to witness to his religious beliefs, always with proper regard for the rights of other persons.

We believe salvation from sin is the free gift from God through Jesus Christ, conditioned only upon trust and commitment to Christ our Lord.

We believe the Christian is a Citizen of two worlds: the kingdom of God and the state and should be obedient to the law of the land as well as the higher laws of God.

We believe that the church, in its spiritual sense, is a fellowship of persons redeemed by Christ and made one in the family of God. In its local sense, it is a fellowship of baptized believers, voluntarily banded together for worship, nurture, and service.

We believe membership in the church is a privilege and properly extended only to regenerated persons who voluntarily accept baptism and commit themselves to faithful discipleship in the body of Christ.

We believe baptism and the Lord's Supper—the two ordinances of the church, symbolic of redemption and service—involve spiritual talents and personal Christian experience.

We believe worship involves an experience of communion with the living and holy God and calls for an emphasis on reverence and ordinance on confession and humility and an awareness of the holiness and majesty and grace of the purpose of God.

We believe every Christian is under obligation to minister or to serve with complete self-giving, but God calls many persons in a unique way, to dedicate their lives to a full-time church-related ministry.

We believe Christian stewardship receives the whole light by a sacred trust from God and requires the responsible use of light, time and talent with substance in the service of God. The call of the Master to proclaim the Gospel—the good news, in a universal call, is a call that must be answered by every individual that is spiritual and that bears the name, Christian.

Let us consider the great and best thing that will make life happen:

The greatest thing is wisdom. The greatest need is common sense. The greatest sin is fear. The best day is today. The greatest dissent is giving up. The greatest deceiver is the one who deceives him or herself. The best teacher is the one who wants you to learn: The greatest talk is with God. The greatest thing, bar none, in all the world, is Love.

God's people are a regenerated people. God's people are a called-out people. God's people are chosen people. God's people are a professing people. God's people are a suffering people. God's people are a praying people. God's people are a sanctified people. God's people are holy people. God's people are blessed people.

For God so loved the world, he gave his only begotten son, that whosoever believes in him shall not perish, but have everlasting life. Jesus said: "Behold, I stand at the door, and knock. If any man opens the door, I will come into him, and he with me. As I sit down with my Father on His throne." We must remember that God gives us the wisdom. God is greater than you or I. God is the husband of man. God is the builder. God is a man of war. God is a giant. God is our refuge. God is a consuming fire. God is a rock. God is a judge. God is a hiding place. God is a shelter in a time of storms. God is a full God. God is my redeemer.

We want to thank the Virgin Mary for the birth of Jesus Christ—The Rose of Sharon—The Lily of the Valley. Bright and morning star; we rejoice in praising his name today.

Jesus is our Lord and Savior, who hung on the cross. Imagine with me if you will, some of the things that ran across the mind of Mary, mother of Jesus.

She said: "My son Jesus never done no wrong. My son, Jesus, went about healing the sick—my son, Jesus, who made the lame to walk, my son, Jesus, who raised Lazarus from the dead. My son, Jesus—they tell me that they whipped Him up the hill, and there they placed thorns on His head. They tell me that they pierced Him in his side and the blood came streaming. Jesus said: 'Father, oh father, forgive them for they know not what they do. Glory, I am that I am. I am Mary's baby, born in Bethlehem, wrapped in swaddling cloth, laid in a manger, proclaimed Savior of the world. I am the same Jesus that heard Paul and Silas in Jail. I'm the same Jesus who walked the water and calmed the raging sea.'"

Must Jesus bear the cross alone and all the world go free? No, there is a cross for everyone, and there's a cross for me. I came, I came to Jesus. I was unloved. I was wounded, I was sad. I found in him a resting place, and he has made me glad. I know prayer changes things. Sin had left a crimson stain, and He washed it white as snow.

If you want to be a witness for Christ—If you want to be a messenger for Christ, tell the world of a dying savior…tell them that he loves them…tell them that he'll make a way out of no way.

I am persuaded by the blessed Bible.—By daily reading, meditation, and communion with my Lord and Savior, Jesus Christ, to live an upright, Christian life.—To the teaching of my fellow man.—To dedicate my talent and give of my time, influence, and means, through teaching and spreading the Christian religion at home and abroad.—To win souls through personal service for Christ.—To encourage and help in the enlistment of young people and Christian work, and make my home a center of light and love.—Shall we pray?[131]

**On Thanksgiving Day, November 26th, 1993**, Rev. Mother Louise Shropshire passed away. Although she would die financially insolvent, her great faith—expressed through her many selfless acts of service, love, and compassion—is remembered by all who knew her. Her grandson, Robert Goins, is at her bedside as she speaks her last words: *"One day, somebody's gon' do something with all my music."*

ॐ

---

[131] Louise Shropshire, sermon delivered at Greater New Light Baptist Church, Pomona, California, 1991, transcribed by Isaias Gamboa from audio recording.

# Chapter 21

# Unarmed Truth

*"Truth alone will endure; all the rest will be swept away before the tide of time. I must continue to bear testimony to truth even if I am forsaken by all. Mine may today be a voice in the wilderness, but it will be heard when all other voices are silenced, if it is the voice of Truth."*
-Mahatma Gandhi

When I first set out to explore the true origins of We Shall Overcome and whether Louise Shropshire had anything to do with it, I could not have anticipated the many revelations, obstacles, breakthroughs, and challenges I would encounter on the way to uncovering the who, what, when, where, and how of this remarkable story. However, one vital question still remained—why? Why would Pete Seeger and his music publisher, the Richmond Organization, misappropriate "We Shall Overcome"? Seeger claimed his manager, Harold Leventhal, put him up to it to protect it from someone else copyrighting or misusing it, but later changed his story, asserting that it was Vanguard Records president Pete Kameron. Even if either of these assertions were true, that still wouldn't justify why Seeger agreed to it and then signed his name to a fraudulent copyright registration. As a songwriter, why couldn't he have just written his own song instead of claiming authorship of one that didn't belong to him? I traveled all over the U.S. trying to solve and document this mystery. Although I did my level best to give the benefit of the doubt, the answer was always right in front of me the whole time. They did it for the money and recognition that came with claiming authorship of We Shall Overcome, the most influential protest anthem ever written—fame and fortune, along with the prestige, influence, privileges, and honors that came with it.

**1993**—Pete Seeger receives a Grammy© Lifetime Achievement Award.

**June 1994—Pete Seeger writes a handwritten letter** to Larry Richmond, VP of his music publisher, The Richmond Organization (TRO), **requesting that his name be removed from the copyright of "We Shall Overcome"** and "Guantanamera," another song he copyrighted and is thought to have authored. In the letter, Seeger confesses that he did not author either song.

**June 1994**—TRO VP Larry Richmond sends an inter-office memo to TRO President Howie Richmond, affirming Seeger's desire to have his name removed from We Shall Overcome and suggesting deceiving Seeger by telling him they would comply, **in the hope that he would forget.**[132]

---

[132] Pete Seeger to Larry Richmond, handwritten letter, June 2010, The Richmond Organization/Ludlow Music, Inc. internal correspondence, admitting improper copyright claims for numerous songs including "Wimoweh," "Guantanamera," and "We Shall Overcome"; admitted exhibit in *We Shall Overcome Foundation et al. v. The Richmond Organization, Inc.*, No. 16-cv-2725 (S.D.N.Y.).

**December 4, 1994**—Pete Seeger is awarded the **Kennedy Center Honors** for his lifetime contributions to American culture through music and activism. At the same ceremony, he also receives the National Medal of Arts from President Bill Clinton—the highest honor bestowed by the U.S. government on artists and arts patrons.

**January 17, 1996**—Pete Seeger is inducted into the **Rock and Roll Hall of Fame**.

The American music industry has thrived for more than a century, not by hoping that its multitudes of songwriters will lay a few golden eggs, but by generously rewarding those willing to do whatever it takes to produce a hit record. People with few scruples, a lust for fortune and fame, and little regard for ethics. Each year, stolen songs—music and lyrics—are reworked and sold for billions of dollars in profits. Perhaps this is because in the US, capitalism is virtually a religion in the minds and hearts of those not anchored to any sense of objective morality—those for whom nothing—except money—is considered sacred.

Everyone knows that banks store large amounts of cash; however, relatively few people decide to rob them. For someone with an objective moral sense, doing so would simply be wrong. For those without such a sense, and with a powerful network of accomplices to help pull off the crime and avoid prosecution, the favorable odds of getting away with it would be the primary concern. For nearly 60 years, Pete Seeger, Guy Carawan, Frank Hamilton, Myles Horton, and The Richmond Organization reaped all the benefits and *none* of the consequences of misappropriating "We Shall Overcome" and many other songs.

Rather than sanctioning those who stole this music, the US music industry not only allowed it but also effectively encouraged it by making it virtually impossible to defend a copyright against a deep-pocketed publishing company like the Richmond Organization and its powerful allied organizations, such as the National Music Publishers Association (NMPA). The NMPA is the most influential music-publishing lobby in the world, cofounded by Maurice Richmond, the father of Howie Richmond and grandfather of Larry Richmond. The NMPA aggressively lobbies Congress to adopt its recommendations on copyright law. The NMPA's Chairman Emeritus, Irwin Z. Robinson, is also the "Vice President of Industry Affairs" for the Richmond Organization.

Not unlike Thomas Jefferson's endorsement of racism and slavery, which relied on the large-scale, systemic kidnapping, torture, and enslavement of men, women, and children to support his blue-blooded lifestyle, America and its wealthy White patriarchs have, for over a century, sanctioned, proliferated, and rewarded the exploitation of Black music at the unscrupulous expense of its most habitually abused citizens.

# The Folk Mafia

"The Folk Mafia" at the 1963 Newport Folk Festival. (left to right) JAC HOLZMAN; President of Electra Records; Theodore Bikel, co-founder of Newport Folk Festival; PETE and TOSHI SEEGER; Pete Seeger's manager, HAROLD LEVENTHAL; former Weaver, FRED HELLERMAN; and MAYNARD SOLOMON, President of Vanguard Records(1965). Photograph by David Gahr

On October 4th, 2005, Pete Seeger's manager, Harold Leventhal—a legendary manager, producer, publisher, concert promoter, and music-industry power broker—died. For months afterward, tributes and accolades highlighting his achievements in the music industry poured in from music's great ivory towers. Leventhal was hailed as a folk music legend and, by many insiders, considered The Godfather of American folk music—the crowned head and puppet master who reigned over what could have been dubbed "The Folk Mafia".

It was well understood that for sixty years, Harold Leventhal held the power of yes and no in the folk music industry. Leventhal was credited with managing the careers of folk music icons such as Pete Seeger, Bob Dylan, Woody Guthrie, The Weavers, Joan Baez, Peter, Paul and Mary, the Mama's and the Papas, Johnny Cash, Harry Belafonte, Neil Young, and others. In addition, he produced and promoted some of the biggest concert events and tours in the folk music world and accumulated more honors and awards than he could count. Very few in the business were known to have spoken an unkind word about him, and those who did… well, like I said… he was The Godfather.

Harold Leventhal

By his own account, Harold Leventhal, born in 1919, began his music career as a song peddler—promoting the songs of Irving Berlin on New York's infamous "Tin Pan Alley," a district that housed many of the most important music-publishing companies. This detail, underscored by Leventhal himself, was significant enough to be highlighted in virtually every biographical account of his life, including his New York Times obituary. I found this fact important, given Tin Pan Alley's history of Black degradation and exploitation, and also because it is a little-known fact that America's beloved composer, Irving Berlin, was widely rumored to have misappropriated musical ideas from African American songwriters, and had a well-established reputation for his racist beliefs.

> *"For by your words you will be acquitted, and by your words you will be condemned."* ~**Jesus Christ, Matthew 12:37**

# The Pete Seeger Interviews

In 2006, Pete Seeger shared his thoughts with an organization called **beliefnet.com.** In his outspoken interview with Wendy Schuman, Seeger unknowingly sings a few verses from Louise Shropshire's "If My Jesus Wills," aka "I'll Overcome," the song he asserts was the "original" from which *We Shall Overcome* was adapted:

The transcript below was taken from that interview:

**WS: *"Do you have a favorite spiritual song or music?"***

**PS**: *"…I was deeply, deeply changed by the Civil Rights movement.* **I'd always liked what they called Negro spirituals, and I sang 'em for the fun of it,** *"Swing Low Sweet Chariot," or "Didn't My Lord Deliver Daniel," or "Joshua Fought the Battle of Jericho.*

*"I've often felt that some of these songs may have gotten European melodies, but all of them have African treatment. For example, it might have been a slave looking through the window at a dance in the big white house, and the fiddler is playing "The Irish Washerwoman" on the fiddle [sings tune]. Out in the cotton fields the next day, the slave is in the field is singing "Rock-a my soul in the bosom of Abraham, rock-a my soul in the bosom of Abraham." Obviously, just a slowed-down different rhythm, but it was basically "The Irish Washerwoman" tune.*

*"However, other tunes are African. Allan Lomax taught me some work songs sung by black prisoners in Southern chain gangs, and I heard on a tape recording, when they invented tape, around 1950, a professor came back from West Africa with the exact same tune for a song which I'd learned with English words. The song I knew [sings], 'He's long John, he's long John, he's long gone, he's long gone, like a turkey through the corn, like a turkey through the corn, with his long clothes on, with his long clothes on. He's long John, long gone.' And so on. And that exact same melody was being sung with African words. So there's a lot more African in American music than most Americans realize."*

**WS: *"What's the origin of 'We Shall Overcome,' the hymn of the Civil Rights movement, which you popularized?"***

**PS: "Nobody knows exactly who wrote the original. The original was faster.** [Sings] *"I'll Be Alright, I'll Be Alright, I'll Be Alright….deep in my heart I do not weep, I'll Overcome someday." Or "deep in my heart* **I do believe**.*"  And other verses are* **"I'll wear the crown**, *I'll wear the crown," and "I'll be like Him, I'll be like Him" or* **"I'll overcome, I'll overcome**.

*"In 1909, some coalminers were on strike and one of them writes a letter in the United Mine Workers Journal of February 1909, "We started every meeting with a prayer and singing that good old song, 'We Will Overcome'." So it could have been in the late 19th century, sometime, that some union people put union words to the gospel song. It was in 1946 that*

Lucille Simmons, a tobacco worker, liked to sing it very slowly. "We'll overcome…" It's called long-meter style. And basses and other voices have time to feel out all sorts of harmonies, so you get a group of people who can harmonize, and you just get extraordinarily complex harmonies.[sic]

"Two friends of mine, Frank Hamilton and Guy Carawan, started singing, 'We Shall Overcome' in this way, and they liked it so much that Guy taught it to some 70 young people in 1960, at a workshop called 'Songs in the Movement." It was the hit song of the weekend. I was there, in Tennessee, at the Highlander Folk School.

"In Raleigh, North Carolina, was [sic] the founding convention of SNCC, and somebody shouted, 'Guy, teach us all 'We Shall Overcome'! Within a month, this song was all across the South, Texas to Florida to Virginia; this was not a song, **it was the song.** Three years later, I got the audience singing it at Carnegie Hall; it was my best-selling record I ever had. And the song went around the world."[133]

## Excerpt from page 33 of Pete Seeger's 1993 autobiography entitled "Where Have All the Flowers Gone"

**Pete Seeger:**
"In 1963, I recorded [We Shall Overcome] at a Carnegie Hall Concert. Within a few years, it was known worldwide. In 1994, in a small village near Calcutta, India, a man and his daughter sang it to me in Bengali.

"My manager and publisher, Harold Leventhal, said, 'Pete, if you don't copyright this song, some Hollywood character will…So Guy, Frank, and I allowed our names to be used, but we set up the We Shall Overcome Fund, chaired by Dr. Bernice Johnson Reagon. All royalties from any recording of the song go to this nonprofit fund, which distributes the funds for "For Black Music in the South."

*Excerpt from Pete Seeger's* **February 2007** *Interview with journalist Jeffrey Rogers of* **Acoustic Guitar Magazine**

**Seeger** "'"It was my late manager, Harold Leventhal—a very wonderful guy, a close friend—who said, 'Pete, you know if you don't copyright this, some character out in Hollywood will copyright it, and next thing you know they'll have a version where it says, "Come on, baby, you and me will overcome tonight." If we want to keep it from being mistreated, you've got to copyright it.' " **I said, 'I didn't write the song. I just arranged the guitar arrangement.' 'That's good enough,' he said.** So Frank, Guy, and also Zilphia Horton, our names are on the copyright. Four white people. At that time, we didn't know the name of Lucille Simmons, who had sung it [when Horton learned it from striking tobacco workers]. We put down that all royalties go to the We Shall Overcome Fund. Bernice Reagon of Sweet Honey in the Rock is the chairman of

---

[133] Shuman, Wendy; Beliefnet.com "The Pete Seeger Interview" (2006)
http://www.beliefnet.com/Entertainment/Music/2006/08/Pete-Seegers-Session.aspx

*that fund, and she and others get together every year down in Tennessee and give out several thousand dollars for black music in the South. [Royalties] come in from all over the world. You know it's sung in every part of India in the local language."*

# The Guy Carawan Interview

Excerpt from the 2010 book "Singing-Out": An Oral History of America's Folk Music Revival: **Guy Carawan**, on the origins of "We Shall Overcome":

*"[Frank Hamilton, Pete Seeger, and my] names were on the copyright at that time; so we took the money and put it in a fund. I was the only one working down there for about five years, spreading that song out in California. He'd heard it from Zilphia Horton, who had worked in the South and in the labor movement and died in 1954. She learned that song from black people."*

"The old words were: **'**I'll overcome someday,

I'll be all right

I'll wear the cross,

**I'll wear the crown**

I'll be like Him,

**I'll sing my song someday."**[134]


**Louise Shropshire's additional verses:**

*"Gonna sing a new song, someday",*

*"Gonna get my crown, someday…"*

In addition, Shropshire's "If My Jesus Wills" contains the words: "…**I do believe…**", which **do not** appear in the Rev. Charles Albert Tindley hymn, nor in any other known, copyrighted hymn alleged to be an antecedent of "We Shall Overcome".

---

[134] Dunaway, David King, Beer, Molly; "Singing Out: An Oral History of America's Folk Music Revivals" (2010) Oxford University Press / p. 142

Providing his honest perspective on this type of misappropriation, in a 1962 article for Western Folklore magazine, Pete Seeger's father, musicologist **Charles Seeger,** wrote:

*"Perhaps the Russians have done the right thing, after all, in abolishing copyright. It is well known that conscious and unconscious appropriation, borrowing, adapting, plagiarizing, and plain stealing are variously, and always have been, part and parcel of the process of artistic creation. The attempt to make sense out of copyright reaches its limit in folk song. For here is the illustration par excellence of the law of Plagiarism.* ***The folk song is, by definition and, as far as we can tell, by reality, entirely a product of Plagiarism.****"*[135]

☙

---

[135] Seeger, Charles; "Who Owns Folklore? –A Rejoinder" /"*Western Folklore"* Vol. 21, No. 2 (Apr., 1962), pp. 93-101 / Western Folklore Society / http://www.jstor.org/discover/10.2307/779765?uid=3739560&uid=2129&uid=2&uid=70&uid=4&uid=3739256&sid=21100768791081

# Chapter 22
# The Great Song Robbery

On July 19th, 2002, self-described "Song-Hunter" and musicologist Alan Lomax died. He left behind extraordinary evidence of decades of Black music misappropriation. In 2004, the Library of Congress secured a partial collection of songs that Alan Lomax and his father, John Lomax, had appropriated from poor and illiterate African Americans during the 1930s, 1940s, and 1950s. The collection was so vast that it had to be housed in several rooms of the library archives and included over 5,000 hours of sound recordings, 400,000 feet of motion picture film, 2,450 videotapes, and much more. Most of these songs were procured in the 1930s and 1940s while Alan Lomax was on the payroll of the U.S. Government, working for the U.S. Library of Congress. If this material had been deposited by Lomax with the Library of Congress over fifty years ago, why were these songs, films, and videos allowed to remain in his possession for sixty years? What is certain is that Lomax was allowed to reap huge commercial profits from these and other African American intellectual properties.

As of 2012, Alan Lomax had more than fifty-six albums listed for commercial sale, all of which contained music appropriated from the poor and illiterate. These recordings include titles such as:

**"Prison Songs Vol.2: Don'tcha Hear Poor Mother Calling?"**

**"Deep River of Song: Mississippi Saints and Sinners"**

**"Deep River of Song: South Carolina: Got the Keys to the Kingdom"**

**"Southern Music, Sacred and Sinful"**

**"Sheep, Sheep, Don'cha Know the Road?"**[136]

The facts show that Louise Shropshire's song was copyrighted six years before Seeger et al's 1960 and 1963 copyrighted versions. In my continuing effort to wrap my head around why they would do something like this, something occurred to me. As Pete Seeger and Harold Leventhal were strongly influenced by communism, this may explain their lack of moral integrity regarding We Shall Overcome. In fact, the Rev. Dr. Martin Luther King Jr. may have preached about it.

**September 30th, 1962** – At the **Ebenezer Baptist** Church in Atlanta, Ga., Rev. Dr. Martin Luther King Jr. delivers a sermon entitled **"Can a Christian be a Communist?"** His powerful words offer his answer to this question from a Christian perspective and may very well help explain the actions of Pete Seeger and the other claimants of We Shall Overcome. Below is an excerpt from Dr. King's sermon:

---

[136] Source: Amazon.com

*"Now, let us begin by answering the question which our sermon topic raises: Can a Christian be a communist? I answer that question with an emphatic—no. These two philosophies are diametrically opposed. The basic philosophy of Christianity is unalterably opposed to the basic philosophy of communism, and all the dialectics of the logician cannot make them lie down together. They are contrary philosophies."*

*"How, then, is communism irreconcilable with Christianity? In the first place, it leaves out God and Jesus Christ. Communism is avowedly [secularist] and materialist...no Christian can be a communist because communism leaves out God...."*

*"A second reason that we can't accept communism is that its methods are opposed to Christianity. Since for the communists, there is no divine government or no absolute moral order, there are no fixed, immutable principles. -So force, violence, murder, and lying are all justifiable means to bring about the millennial end..."*[137]

-Rev. Dr. Martin Luther King Jr.

Dr. King's oration on Christianity versus Communism was an epiphany that shed divine light on the actions of Pete Seeger and the other copyright claimants. But what about the law?

# Crime and Punishment

*"A nation's greatness is measured by how it treats its weakest members."*
-Mahatma Gandhi.

The laws of this country have far too often proven cruel and unjust. If history is indeed the best teacher, we cannot afford to forget that. Having little to do with morality, these laws at times seem to exist not to defend the truth or inequity, but, as Thomas Jefferson put it, "to serve the supreme will of the nation"-whatever that *will* may be. Perhaps in most cases, that will indeed bend toward justice, resulting in legislation that is fair and compassionate. However, in other cases, such as slavery and Jim Crow laws, America's legislative quill has been guided by evil, devilish forces. As innocuous as it may seem, US Copyright Law can fall into either of these categories, but in the case of African American Music, I believe the latter is the case.

In a 1917 article published by The Harvard Crimson, an anonymous author wrote:

*"**I like your Christ, but not your Christianity**." In these words of **Mahatma Gandhi**, Dr. J.H. Holmes summed up the Indian leader's view of Christianity in a recent interview with a CRIMSON reporter. Dr. Holmes, professor of Philosophy at Swarthmore College and a member of the Society of Friends, has just completed a tour around the world, during which he spent some time in India. He had several opportunities of conversing with*

---

[137] King Jr., Martin Luther; Sermon Delivered Sep. 30, 1962 at Ebenezer Baptist Church / Atlanta, Ga. / The Martin Luther King Jr. Papers Project / http://mlkkpp01.stanford.edu/index.php/encyclopedia/documentsentry/can_a_christian_be_a_communist_30_sept_1962

Gandhi. He was present at the meeting of the All-Indian Congress and had the honor of being the only westerner ever allowed to speak from their platform.

*Continuing in Gandhi's words, Dr. Holmes said, 'I believe in the teachings of Christ, but you, on the other side of the world, do not. I read the Bible faithfully and see little in Christendom that those who profess faith pretend to see.'*

*"The Christians above all others are seeking after wealth. Their aim is to be rich at the expense of their neighbors. They come among aliens to exploit them for their own good and cheat them to do so. Their prosperity is far more essential to them than the life, liberty, and happiness of others…The Christians are the most warlike people."*

As a follower of the teachings of Jesus Christ, I believe people should bear the responsibility of ensuring that our laws—should they lean to one side or another—do so in favor of the poor and defenseless—"the least of God's children". This aim, however, seems to conflict with the objectives of many of America's citizens, who, instead of seeking to help the poor and needy, faithfully worship and serve the principles and tenets of Capitalism.

From the same 1962 article referenced earlier, Pete Seeger's father, **Charles Seeger,** wrote the following regarding U.S. copyright laws and folk music:

*"The problem must be viewed in two distinct aspects—the legal and the ethical. They are inextricably intertwined. Justice is a factor of both. Of course, any law should meet the requirements of ethics, and ethics should be incorporated into law. But we all know that these ideals are often not realized in practical life. Certainly, there is general agreement that the United States copyright law falls short for realizing them. This is particularly evident in the application of this part of the national legal code to American folk song and to folklore in general. The result is that we are left with legal practices that are unethical and with ethical beliefs for which there is no legal support. Like many other laws, both American and European,* **the copyright law has been designed to encourage the acquisition and retention of property under rules favoring the more enterprising citizens."**[138]

Once again, Charles Seeger and his son, Pete, appeared to hold widely opposing principles.

We cannot continue to allow profiteers such as Pete Seeger, Guy Carawan, Frank Hamilton, Myles Horton, Harold Leventhal, and TRO to exploit people like Louise Shropshire. As people of faith, we must do our best to stand for what is morally right and trust in God to do the rest. As a result of the separation of God and country, the notion of right and wrong in America has been reduced to the outer fringes of political rhetoric. Those of us who believe in a *righteous* God know that He is always on the side of justice and truth,

---

[138] Seeger, Charles; "Who Owns Folklore? –A Rejoinder" /"*Western Folklore"* Vol. 21, No. 2 (Apr., 1962), pp. 93-101 / Western Folklore Society /
http://www.jstor.org/discover/10.2307/779765?uid=3739560&uid=2129&uid=2&uid=70&uid=4&uid=3739256&sid=21100768791081

and that a just nation will not tolerate laws designed to take from the poor and give to the rich.

Pete Seeger and his longtime friend, Alan Lomax—both well-v*ersed* in the intricacies of US copyright law—strip-mined African American music for their own financial gain. The laws they relied on to carry out their dirty work must be reformed. Like Jim Crow poll taxes and literacy tests, US copyright laws have enabled the victimization of countless African Americans, who, at the very least, should have been informed of their property rights, both verbally and in writing, by someone other than the Song-Hunters. Something must be done to correct this injustice and ensure it cannot happen again.

Alan Lomax recording Texas Chain-Gang Prisoners, Alan Lomax-photographer
Courtesy Library of Congress

The trunk of John A. Lomax's Ford Sedan in 1933, equipped with the latest state-of-the-art, Live-Recording equipment, including a 300-pound aluminum phonograph-disc recorder, all financed by the US Government.
Photo: Library of Congress

## *Action Item # 3* - Copyright Reform

Before allowing any third party to claim copyright ownership of a song not written, in whole or in part, by them, I propose amending U.S. copyright laws to require a signed written release from the initial performer of the composition. This agreement would include a simple explanation of the value and potential for exploitation of the musical and literary intellectual property rights being secured. As an additional safeguard, this release should also be read aloud by a neutral third party, such as a notary, to prevent the exploitation of poorly educated song-holders.

Lastly, I propose that all copyright ownership of songs recorded and "collected" by John and/or Alan Lomax while employed by the US Government be placed in the public domain or, alternatively, transferred back to the persons or the heirs of those persons who originally performed the so-called field recordings.

**In 2006,** Bruce Springsteen releases a full-length album titled; "We Shall Overcome: The Pete Seeger Sessions". The recording features the song "We Shall Overcome" and sells more than 500,000 copies in its first 30 days of release.[139] **In 2007,** Springsteen was awarded a Grammy® in the Best Traditional Folk Album category.

**In 2008,** Pete Seeger's supporters launched a campaign to have him awarded a Nobel® Prize.[140]

**In January of 2009, Pete Seeger and Bruce Springsteen sing for President Barack Obama's Presidential Inauguration.**[141]

**On February 10, 2010,** Joan Baez performed " We Shall Overcome at the White House in front of President Barack Obama and his family, who all sang along.[142]

☙

---

[139] Source: Recording Industry Association of America, Gold and Platinum Searchable Database / http://www.riaa.com/goldandplatinumdata.php?content_selector=gold-platinum-searchable-database

[140] Source: Dryer, Peter; Huffington Post; 5-3-2012; Happy Birthday Pete Seeger

[141] Washington Post; The Inauguration of Barack Obama; Triumph books; 2009; p. 60

[142] Wolffe, Richard; Revival: The Struggle for Survival Inside the Obama White House; Random House Digital, Inc. 2011; p. 48

# Chapter 23

## Uncaged

*"...But a bird that stalks down his narrow cage
can seldom see through his bars of rage,
His wings are clipped, and his feet are tied
so he opens his throat to sing..."*
**-Maya Angelou**

For 250 years, African Americans have opened their throats and sung a song of suffering, injustice, and inequality—a song long imprisoned in a cage of betrayal. But the caged bird of truth must now be released. African Americans singing We Shall Overcome in the sixties did not achieve what most African Americans or their ancestors had longed for—freedom, dignity, and equality. Freedom to live as equals, free from racial discrimination, segregation, prejudice, or abuse. These rights must be demanded, not wished for. African Americans have not yet overcome.

With the powerful spiritual references removed from Louise Shropshire's hymn, Pete Seeger's secularized "We Shall Overcome" may have served as the soundtrack of the Civil Rights Movement and indeed sustained many struggles in many countries across the globe, but as far as American Blacks are concerned, the folk adaptation of Shropshire's song made a promise it could not fulfill. Despite its popularity, without submission to God's will in its narrative, "We Shall Overcome" was rendered little more than a placebo for American Blacks—as helpful to their everyday struggles as the theme song from the mid-seventies popular comedic TV sitcom "Good Times," depicting a stereotypical underprivileged African American family with "coon-ish" characters living in an urban ghetto setting. Ironically, though not surprisingly, the theme song from "Good Times" was composed by three very wealthy Caucasian songwriters: Dave Grusin, Alan Bergman, and Marilyn Bergman. I suppose a Black songwriter would have been deemed inappropriate to help perpetuate this stereotype.

### Theme from "Good Times"

*"Good Times, any time you meet a payment.*

*Good Times, any time you need a friend.*

*Good Times, any time you're out from under.*

*Not getting hassled, not getting hustled.*

*Keepin' your head above water,*

*Making a wave when you can.*

*We Shall Overcome: Sacred Song on the Devil's Tongue*

*Temporary layoffs, good times.*

*Easy credit rip-offs, good times.*

*Scratchin' and surviving, good times.*

*Hangin' in a chow line, good times.*

*Ain't we lucky we got 'em-*

*Good Times."*


Louise Shropshire composed "If My Jesus Wills" in reverence for the sacred words of the Lord's Prayer, "...Thy will be done..." She understood that her African American brothers and sisters needed more than musical snake oil to endure and overcome hatred, bigotry, and injustice. The following verses from scripture illustrate this point.

*"Dear friends, do not be surprised at the fiery ordeal that has come on you to test you, as though something strange were happening to you. But rejoice inasmuch as you participate in the sufferings of Christ, so that you may be overjoyed when his glory is revealed. If you are insulted because of the name of Christ, you are blessed, for the Spirit of glory and of God rests on you. If you suffer, it should not be as a murderer or thief or any other kind of criminal, or even as a meddler. However, if you suffer as a Christian, do not be ashamed, but praise God that you bear that name. For it is time for judgment to begin with God's household; and if it begins with us, what will the outcome be for those who do not obey the gospel of God? And, "If it is hard for the righteous to be saved, what will become of the ungodly and the sinner?" So then, those who suffer according to God's will should commit themselves to their faithful Creator and continue to do good." (1 Peter 4: 12-19, NIV)*

Although Louise and the Rev. Dr. Martin Luther King Jr. shared a bond of friendship, it was not forged by their similar tastes in music or their love of good food—but by their shared love for the selfless teachings of Jesus Christ and their total submission to His will.

**In his final sermon**, delivered on **April 3rd, 1968**, Dr. King's sanctified words echoed a hallowed Christian principle. The following is an excerpt from his spirit-filled "*Mountaintop*" sermon.

*"Well, I don't know what will happen now. We've got some difficult days ahead. But it doesn't matter with me now, because I've been to the mountaintop. And I don't mind. Like anybody, I would like to live a long life. Longevity has its place. But I'm not concerned about that now.* **I just want to do God's will***. And He's allowed me to go up to the mountain. And I've looked over. And I've seen the Promised Land. I may not get there with you. But I want you to know tonight that we, as a people, will get to the Promised Land. And I'm happy tonight. I'm not worried about anything. I'm not fearing any man. Mine eyes have seen the glory of the coming of the Lord."*[143] **-Rev. Dr. Martin Luther King Jr.**

---

[143] Bruns, Robert; Martin Luther King Jr.: A Biography; Greenwood Publishing Group; 2006; p. 143.

For followers of Christ, such as Dr. King and Rev. Mother Louise Shropshire, seeing the "Promised Land" meant trusting in what God promised, in *His* time and according to *His* will. The secular adaptation from "If My Jesus Wills" to "We Shall Overcome" remained sanctified in the minds and hearts of African Americans by God's divine will.

The divine power and influence of "We Shall Overcome" helped strengthen and galvanize good people worldwide in various righteous causes. Although the empathy and/or sympathy of others can be deeply comforting, suffering remains a deeply personal experience. It is also often a hallmark of true followers of the teachings of Jesus Christ, who characteristically make deep and loving sacrifices by denying themselves physically and economically to help those most in need. This is another reason Louise's "If My Jesus Wills" (aka "*I'll* Overcome Someday") was so spiritually relevant.

While in church, one person may have been suffering the loss of his job due to a bus boycott or a racist employer, while another in the pew next to him or her could be in pain from the death of a child killed by a KKK bomb. "If My Jesus Wills" provided the spiritual comfort and healing they needed to carry on. Singing "We Shall Overcome" may have helped much of America open its eyes to the brutality of racism in its own backyard, but the truth is that America always knew racism existed. America knew it then, and knows it now. Singing "We Shall Overcome" alone cannot eradicate hate, violence, bigotry, segregation, or discrimination. Nonviolent action is needed.

Although the U.S. spends seventeen billion dollars a year probing outer space in an attempt to "touch the face of God," it has yet to come down to earth to claim responsibility and atone for the atrocities, iniquities, and crimes it has committed. The U.S. has built its foundation on the keloid-scarred backs of enslaved Black men, women, and children, and should be held accountable for its deeds and the repercussions of those unconscionable acts, just as it holds others accountable for wrongs committed against it or its citizens.

The United States of America, like a majestic cedar with beautiful branches overshadowing the forest, has towered on high, its top above the thick foliage. The waters have nourished it, deep springs have made it grow tall; their springs have flowed all around its base and sent their channels to all the trees of the field. So it towered higher than all the trees of the field; its boughs have increased, and its branches have grown long, spreading because of abundant waters. All the birds of the sky have nested in its boughs, all the animals of the wild have given birth under its branches; all the great nations have lived in its shade. It is majestic in beauty, with its spreading boughs, for its roots go down to abundant waters.[144]

The time has come for America to admit to and atone for its iniquities against African Americans. The time has also come for the music industry to acknowledge what has been its dirty little secret for more than a century—that poor and poorly educated Black songwriters, musicians, and performers have been cheated by unscrupulous songwriters, publishing companies, music moguls, and media corporations—plunderers who have filled their bellies and carried out their immoral, contemptible trade, using copyright law to justify

---

[144] Inspired by The Holy Bible; Ezekiel 31; New International Version

their acts. In the name of their "almighty dollar," exercising academic, economic, social, and political advantages, these wolves, not unlike their slave-owning predecessors, have climbed to the summits of worldly wealth and power by misappropriating and exploiting Black labor and creative and intellectual production.

Historically speaking, the U.S., unlike countries, nations, and civilizations such as Ethiopia, China, England, Egypt, Russia, Japan, Greece, or India, is but an infant on planet Earth. Although as a nation we have achieved many industrial, technological, and scientific accomplishments, we have done so through an oppressive economic organism that nourishes, fortifies, and rewards greed and profit motives above truth, justice, and morality…placing the will of its citizens above the will of God.

Woefully, there will likely come a day when simply uttering the words Jesus Christ, Yahweh, Allah, Buddha, Waheguru, or Vishnu will bring ridicule, ruin, rage, mockery, mistreatment, hatred, and death. –A day when the "supreme will of the people" will proclaim it unlawful and hateful to proclaim or even believe that there exists such a thing as God. – A day when espousing the biblical teachings of Jesus Christ will be considered hate speech. It is during those times that followers of Jesus Christ will *need* sacred hymns like "We Shall Overcome" and "If My Jesus Wills." Although its charter was inspired by Christian virtue, somewhere along the way toward fulfilling its "pursuit of happiness and quest for wealth and power," the United States of America has chosen to serve Money instead of God and has tossed His Holy teachings of love, compassion, peace, and forgiveness overboard.

Consider this short speech, recited by President Lyndon B. Johnson immediately after President John F. Kennedy's assassination. As he stepped down from Air Force One on Nov. 22, 1963, at Andrews Air Force Base, just outside Washington, D.C., a newly sworn-in President Johnson delivered the following words to a nation still very much in shock:

***"This is a sad time for all people. We have suffered a loss that cannot be weighed. For me, it is a deep personal tragedy. I know that the world shares the sorrow that Mrs. Kennedy and her family bear. I will do my best. That is all I can do. I ask for your help and God's."***[145]

There was something significant in those 58 words—something telling.

Johnson's short statement was originally penned by Liz Carpenter, former press secretary to Johnson's wife, "Ladybird" Johnson, and now acting press secretary to the newly appointed President Johnson. Carpenter was aboard Air Force One as it transported the newly sworn-in president and the newly widowed, bloodstained Jacqueline Kennedy back to Washington, D.C. However, Carpenter's original words were slightly different. Instead of "…*I ask for your help and God's,*" Carpenter wrote: **"I ask for God's help, and yours,"** recognizing the supreme need for God's help, guidance, and support over that of the American people.

---

[145] Source: Notecard written by Liz Carpenter with modifications by LBJ; National Archives and Records Administration / Lyndon Baines Johnson Presidential Library

For reasons perhaps known only to him, amid the blood, chaos, confusion, and grief undeniably present aboard his presidential aircraft, America's new president—now considered the most powerful man in the world—felt called to undermine God's spiritual hierarchy and, with his little number-two pencil, the unelected leader of the so-called free world publicly relegated God's importance in America to second place. And as any Christian, Jew, or Muslim will attest, God always comes before man.

*Liz Carpenter's speech, with modifications inscribed in pencil by newly-sworn-in President Lyndon B. Johnson, 1968*
*Image Courtesy LBJ Library and Museum*

Prior to her death in 2010, Liz Carpenter wrote a book about speechwriting, entitled *Start with a Laugh.* In it, she shared an extraordinary revelation about that fifty-eight-word speech – a speech she ultimately became best remembered for. In her own words: *"I can't really say I wrote it;* **God was my ghostwriter.***"*[146] God, of course, inspired her *unedited* words—not the ones uttered to grieving Americas from President Johnson's lips.

Like the lyrics to *If My Jesus Wills*, Liz Carpenter's words were divinely crafted to comfort and console a grieving nation in desperate need of healing. And like Pete Seeger, Guy Carawan, Myles Horton, Frank Hamilton, and Zilphia Horton, who thought it best to remove Louise's scriptural references from We Shall Overcome, President Lyndon Baines Johnson also chose to diminish God's authority and weaken His divine message. For me, this once again brought to mind the haunting words of the newly elected Thomas Jefferson in his letter to the Danbury Baptist Association.

"*I contemplate with sovereign reverence, that act of the whole American people which declared that their legislature should* **'make no law respecting an establishment of religion**, *or prohibiting the free exercise thereof,' thus building a wall of separation between*

---

[146] Carpenter, Liz and Runnells Sondra Williamson; Start With a Laugh; Eakin Press; 2000; p. x.

*Church & State.* **Adhering to this expression of the supreme will of the nation in behalf of the rights of conscience**, *I shall see with sincere satisfaction the progress of those sentiments which tend to restore to man all his natural rights,* **convinced he has no natural right in opposition to his social duties."** [147]

Jefferson's avowal that the "will of the nation" was supreme and subject only to the "rights of conscience" made clear that fulfilling God's will would never again be his or America's primary objective. –A sentiment made manifest in President Lyndon B. Johnson's brief speech.

Tragically, because of its refusal to submit to *God's* supreme will, Americans appear fated to wander the desert of spiritual fulfillment, understanding, and enlightenment. Although the U.S., through its First Amendment rights to freedom of speech and assembly, has the capacity to address, diagnose, and cure its malignant spiritual condition, the First Amendment's Separation of Church and State has removed the moral stethoscope and scalpel from its "black bag" of remediation. Gone, along with these instruments of universal redemption, is America's sense of objective right or wrong—good or evil as it relates to slavery, and now to the treatment of its racial minorities by what—for now—is its White, ruling majority.

☙

---

[147] Hall, Timothy L.; Religion in America; Excerpt from Thomas Jefferson's 1802 *Letter to the Danbury Baptist Association*; Infobase Publishing; 2007; p, 139

# Chapter 24

# A Love Supreme

*"We also came here today to affirm that we will no longer sit idly by in agonizing deprivation and wait on others to provide our freedom. We will be sadly mistaken if we think freedom is some lavish dish that the federal government and the White man will pass out on a silver platter, while the Negro merely furnishes the appetite. Freedom is never voluntarily granted by the oppressor; it must be demanded by the oppressed."*[148]
**-Rev. Dr. Martin Luther King Jr.**

Although I am neither an attorney nor a representative of Louise Shropshire's family or heirs, in keeping with the objectives of this book, it is my belief that the Rev. Mother Louise Shropshire *and* her heirs are entitled to, but by no means limited to, the following:

1. A public acknowledgement by its current copyright claimants, The Richmond Organization, that We Shall Overcome was in fact derived from Shropshire's "If My Jesus Wills."
2. The assignment of any and all copyright interests in *We Shall Overcome* from this point forward to the public domain.
3. The complete audit and subsequent transfer of any funds held in the so-called *"We Shall Overcome Fund"* by the Highlander Research and Education Center administrators, or legal administrators and signatories of said fund, to the heirs of Louise Shropshire.
4. Louise Shropshire would henceforth be designated as the "original author" of We Shall Overcome and her heirs, entitled to all legal recourse in connection with this truth.

*"When truth is replaced by silence, the silence is a lie."*
**~Yevgeny Yevtushenko**.

Louise Shropshire was a simple, humble woman, but the white-hot beacon of light and hope that shone within her could not be restrained. Through her sacred compositions, this woman of God would deliver a two-thousand-year-old message—one of faith and hope—not in this world but in God's power of forgiveness and redemption. Anyone who knew her would testify that Louise was on fire for the Lord—a fire fueled by unconditional love, compassion, and service to her neighbor.

During her lifetime, she would never know the full extent to which her sacred song was disseminated—its sacred cry, sung in dozens of languages and across nations unknown to her. Nevertheless, her song's powerful voice would reach the ears of God and reflect back upon a troubled world as long, warm, loving beams of courage and hope. Her

---

[148] King Jr., Martin Luther and Carson, Clayborne; The Autobiography of Martin Luther King Jr.; Hachette Digital, Inc.; Nov. 1, 1998, Ch. 18

story must not perish. Her deeply meaningful and transcendent hymn, "If My Jesus Wills," was intended to ease the centuries of suffering inflicted by Whites in America upon Blacks in America.

In 1960 and 1963, The Richmond Organization, Pete Seeger, and his accomplices copyrighted an unauthorized derivative of "If My Jesus Wills," titled "We Shall Overcome." They went on to collect a fortune by performing and licensing it all over the world. It's been more than half a century since they changed Louise's words, "I'll overcome" to *"We shall Overcome"* and "If my Jesus wills" to "Deep in My Heart." What do African Americans have to show for it?

-To borrow from Dr. King:

*"Fifty-two years later, the Negro is still not free. Fifty-two years later, the Negro is still crippled by the chains of segregation and discrimination. Fifty-two years later, the Negro still lives on a lonely island of poverty in an ocean of material prosperity. One hundred years later, the Negro is still languishing in the corners of American society—an exile in his own land. Once again, America has defaulted on its promissory note to African Americans and ignored its sacred obligation to blacks. Instead, it has passed another bad check, which has been returned marked 'Insufficient Funds.'*[149]

Although Dr. King would refer to We Shall Overcome as "the battle hymn of our movement," perhaps for African Americans, Seeger's adaptation was, in fact, more of a lullaby—a cradle song to hush their midnight screams of racism and injustice—leading them to believe that "deep in their hearts," it was all just a bad dream. Perhaps White America was tired of seeing so much Black on their black-and-white TV sets and needed Pete Seeger to adjust the contrast. Perhaps what this country *really* wanted was to return to its regularly scheduled programming.

If My Jesus Wills was a sacred song of vision, hope, and faith in a higher, heavenly place. It was about submitting to *God's* will and authority, regardless of the outcome, in return for fearlessness, forgiveness, fulfillment, peace, and eternal life.

**"O let us all from bondage flee,**
**Let my people go,**
**And let us all *in Christ* be free,**
**Let my people go."**

(From the Negro Spiritual, *Go Down Moses / Author unknown*)

---

[149] Disparate passages borrowed from Rev. Dr. Martin Luther King Jr.'s "I Have a Dream" speech; August 28, 1963 at the Lincoln Memorial in Washington, D.C.

As Louise Shropshire's name is secured in its rightful place in history, her memory, spirit, and Christian love for her fellow man will live on in her words and music, and in the song that the Library of Congress has called "The most powerful song of the 20th Century"—a song conceived in humility, nourished by the hopes and dreams of the suffering and the unnamed, and born in the servant hearts and sacred pews of the African American Church—a song kidnapped from its cradle in the dark of night—secularized and gentrified, yet whose spirit has toppled governments across the globe and watched over the greatest Civil Rights movement in American history.

Although Louise Shropshire would die poor and unrecognized, she is indeed bound for the Promised Land, and *her* sacred song—like the infant Moses, drawn from the Nile and raised by Pharaoh—must now return to its chosen people.

On August 13, 2012, in connection with the documentary film "Claim the Sky: We Shall Overcome," produced and directed by me, Louise Shropshire's grandson, Robert A. Goins Shropshire, accompanied by a camera crew, flew to Pete Seeger's hilltop home in Beacon, New York, walked to the front door, and presented him with the sheet music for If My Jesus Wills—evidence of his grandmother's original authorship of We Shall Overcome. Before noticing the camera, Seeger's first response upon seeing the music was, "This is wonderful." A 90-minute interview with Seeger followed. After being shown additional lyrical, musical, and photographic evidence of Shropshire's authorship, Seeger finally said, "I think her name should be in the story." Excerpts from the Seeger interview appear in the film.

Ultimately, New York-based The Richmond Organization, aka TRO ESSEX, holds the rights to We Shall Overcome. However, the heirs of Louise Shropshire are seeking legal assistance to permanently change this. The quest for truth, justice, reform, and atonement must continue.

*"For whatever is born of God, overcomes the world. And this is the victory that has overcome the world—our faith. Who is he who overcomes the world, but he who believes that Jesus is the Son of God?"*

1 John 5:4-5

# Copyright Status Update (2026)

Since the original publication of this book, the legal status of "We Shall Overcome " has undergone a monumental shift. After years of research and documentation tracing the song's origins to Louise Shropshire's gospel hymn "If My Jesus Wills," the We Shall Overcome Foundation filed a federal class-action lawsuit in 2016, challenging the 1960 and 1963 copyright claims held by Pete Seeger, The Richmond Organization (TRO), and Ludlow Music for We Shall Overcome. In 2018, in the Southern District of New York, Judge Denise Cote ordered that "We Shall Overcome" be dedicated to the public domain. This ruling not only restored public access to the anthem but also represented a powerful act of cultural justice — affirming that a sacred freedom song born in the Black church could not be owned, silenced, or sold. We Shall Overcome is legally and forever free.

A summary of the evidence, and images of the exhibits presented to the court, including the Pete Seeger Letter requesting that TRO remove his name from the copyright; the TRO internal memo affirming Seeger's request and suggesting lying to him about granting it; and the full list of 50+ songs that Pete Seeger misappropriated, can be found in the 2024 book **"SO HELP ME, GOD: Pete Seeger Stole We Shall Overcome,"** by Isaias Gamboa—available on Amazon.com. Production on Gamboa's documentary, **"CLAIM THE SKY: We Shall Overcome,"** was completed in 2024 and is scheduled for release in 2026.

**Rev. Mother Louise Shropshire**

## The End

# About the Author

*"All labor that uplifts humanity has dignity and importance and should be undertaken with painstaking excellence."*
~Rev. Dr. Martin Luther King Jr.

Isaias Gamboa

Isaias Gamboa was born in San José, Costa Rica, to parents of Spanish and Afro-Caribbean ancestry, with Jewish heritage through his maternal Jamaican grandmother, Louise Teitelbaum. His mother, a Baptist from the Caribbean coastal city of Puerto Limón, and his father, a Catholic from the provincial city of San Ramón, immigrated to the United States in 1965 and settled in South Central Los Angeles. Throughout his youth, Isaias navigated the complexities of growing up in a predominantly African American neighborhood while being raised in a Costa Rican, Spanish-speaking, mixed-race household.

Music became the lens through which Isaias discovered his identity. Beginning piano lessons at age five, he was recognized as a prodigy by eight and soon taught himself to sing, compose, and play six instruments. During high school, he performed in gospel choirs and the All-City Honor Choir, demonstrating his compositional prowess by scoring his school's annual musical theatre production in just two days.

At seventeen, Isaias was discovered by music producer Leon Sylvers III, who mentored him for twelve years in the intricacies of music production and the industry. He signed his first recording contract with Arista Records as a member of the band Real to Reel, spending five years under the direction of music mogul Clive Davis.

In the 1980s, Isaias was introduced to pop icon Michael Jackson, who had just completed his Off the Wall album. Invited to Jackson's Encino home recording studio, Isaias produced music for Jackson's newly formed publishing company, ATV Music. In the early 1990s, he signed with Polydor Records as a member of the singing group Double Action Theatre before pursuing his passion as an independent songwriter and producer.

During a recording session at Studio 55 in Los Angeles, legendary producer Richard Perry employed Isaias as his Associate Producer for projects with The Pointer Sisters and The Temptations. Through The Temptations sessions, Isaias formed a close friendship with founder Otis Williams, contributing production and songwriting to six Temptations albums, one of which earned a Grammy® Award.

Throughout his career, Isaias has composed over 200 songs and provided his talents as songwriter, arranger, musician, and producer for artists including Tupac Shakur, The Temptations, Gladys Knight, and Bamboleo. In 2010, he formed his independent music label, Plum Recordings, and released a critically acclaimed solo album, Don't Lie to Me.

Beyond music, Isaias is a devoted husband and father of five children, three now adults. He has coached youth sports and served as head coach for the American club affiliate of FC Barcelona.

In 2000, while on a humanitarian trip to Colombia, Isaias was ambushed and held at gunpoint by four heavily armed men who demanded he exit his taxi. To his own surprise, he refused to comply and was released unharmed within minutes—an experience that revealed to him that he did not fear death.

Feeling his life had been spared for a spiritual purpose, Isaias embarked on a quest for enlightenment, reading the Holy Bible from Genesis to Revelation. Two years later, he was ordained a Christian minister. He remains active in humanitarian and ministerial work, having traveled to nine Latin American countries in this pursuit.

In his own words: "By any definition, I am no political, historical, or religious scholar. I am, however, a child of the King and a devout student of the Holy Bible. Whatever gifts I may possess are God-given and have been called to action for the creation of this book…in submission to His will."

Contact

www.WeShallOvercomeFoundation.org

# Bibliography

1. Alexander, Michelle; The New Jim Crow: Mass Incarceration in the Age of Colorblindness; The New Press, Jan 5, 2010; p. 195.

An Oral History of the Civil Rights Movement from the 1950s Through The 1980s; Random House Digital, Inc.; 2001.

2. Baldwin, Lewis V.; The Voice of Conscience: The Church in the Mind of Martin Luther King, Jr.; Oxford University Press; 2010.
3. Bankston, Leon and Carl Leon; Racial and Ethnic Relations in America: Ethnic entrepreneurship; Salem Press; 2000.
4. Beaulieu Herder, Nicole –Editor and Ronald Herder; Best-Loved Negro Spirituals: Complete Lyrics to 178 Songs of Faith; Courier Dover Publications, Jun 13, 2001.
5. Bergreen, Lawrence; "As Thousands Cheer; The Life of Irving Berlin" (2001).
6. Bernstein, Richard R.; Thomas Jefferson; Oxford University Press; 2005.
7. Black, Conrad; Franklin Delano Roosevelt: Champion Of Freedom; PublicAffairs, Mar 16, 2005 – 1280.
8. Blaine, Gerald with McCubbin, Lisa and Hill, Clint; The Kennedy Detail: JFK's Secret Service Agents Break Their Silence; Simon and Schuster, 2011.
9. Blocker, Jack S. and David M. Fahey, Ian R. Tyrrell; Alcohol and Temperance in Modern History: An International …, Volume 1; ABC-CLIO, 2003.
10. Bodroghkozy, Aniko; Equal Time: Television and the Civil Rights Movement; University of Illinois Press, Feb 15, 2012.
11. Bogdanov, Vladimir and Woodstra, Chris; All Music Guide: The Definitive Guide to Popular Music; Hal Leonard Corporation; 2001.
12. Bogle, Donald; **Toms, Coons, Mulattoes, Mammies, and Bucks:** An Interpretive History of Blacks in American Films; Continuum International Publishing Group; 2001.
13. Brinkley, Douglass; Wheels for the world: Henry Ford, his company, and a century of progress; 1903–2003; Viking, 2003, p.475 / My forty years with Ford, Charles E. Sorensen, David Lanier Lewis, Samuel T. Williamson, Wayne State University Press.
14. Bruns, Robert; Martin Luther King Jr.: A Biography; Greenwood Publishing Group; 2006.
15. Buhle, Mari Jo and Paul Buhle; The American Radical; Quotation from Andrew Young on We Shall Overcome; Psychology Press, Jan 11, 1994.
16. Burgan, Michael; Shima: Birth of the Nuclear Age; Marshall Cavendish, Sep 1, 2009; p. 12, 13, 16.
17. Callan; Jim; America in the 1930's; Infobase Publishing, Aug 1, 2005.
18. Carbado, Devon W.; Black Men on Race, Gender, and Sexuality: A Critical Reader; Quoting Author James Baldwin; p. 240; New York University Press; 1999.
19. Carpenter, Liz and Runnells Sondra Williamson; Start With a Laugh; Eakin Press; 2000.
20. Carson, Clayborne / "The Autobiography of Martin Luther King" 1998 "The Letters From Birmingham Jail" / Warner Books, Inc.
21. Cockburn, Alexander and St Clair, Jeffrey; Serpents in the Garden; Liaison's with Culture and Sex.
22. Cohen, Ronald D.; A History of Folk Music Festivals in the United States Scarecrow Press, Nov 30, 2008.
23. Cook, William A.; King of the Bootleggers: a Biography of George Remus; McFarland; 2008.
24. Crowe, Charles Robert; The age of Civil War and Reconstruction, 1830-1900: a book of interpretive essays; Dorsey Press, 1975.

Isaias Gamboa

25. Davies, Carole Boyce; Encyclopedia of the African Diaspora, and Culture, Volume 1; ABC-CLIO; 2008.

26. Davis, David Brion and Steven Mintz; The Boisterous Sea of Liberty: A Documentary History of America from Discovery Through the Civil War; Oxford University Press, Jan 13, 2000.

27. Debolt, Abbe A. and James S. Baugess; Encyclopedia of the Sixties: A Decade of Culture and Counterculture; ABC-CLIO, Dec 31, 2011.

28. DeCaro Jr., Louis, A.; Malcolm and the Cross: The Nation of Islam, Malcolm X, and Christianity; NYU Press; 2000.

29. Dreisbach, Daniel L.; Thomas Jefferson and the Wall of Separation Between Church and State; NYU Press, Sep 1, 2002.

30. Dubois, W.E.B. / The Negro American Family (The Atlanta University publications series).

31. Dunaway, David King and Beer, Molly; Singing Out: An Oral History of America's Folk Music Revivals; Oxford University Press.

32. DuRocher, Kristina; Raising Racists: The Socialization of White Children in the Jim Crow South; University of Kentucky Press.

33. Einstein, Albert; The Einstein Reader; Citadel Press, Jun 1, 2006; The Negro Question.

34. English, Tim; Sounds Like Teen Spirit: Stolen Melodies, Ripped-Off Riffs, and the Secret History of Rock and Roll; iUniverse, Oct 12, 2007.

35. Eyerman, Ron and Jamison, Andrew; Music and Social Movements: Mobilizing Traditions in the Twentieth Century; Cambridge University Press; 1998.

36. Fea, John; Was America Founded as a Christian Nation?: A Historical Introduction; Westminster John Knox Press, Feb 16, 2011.

37. Federal Bureau of Investigation; Robert F. Kennedy Assassination: The FBI Files; Filiquarian Publishing, LLC; 2007.

38. Ferguson, Robert A.; The American Enlightenment, 1750-1820; Harvard University Press, 1994.

39. Finkelman, Paul, editor; Encyclopedia of African American History, 1619-1895: From the ..., Colonial Period to the Age of Frederick Douglass, Volume 2; Oxford University Press, 2006.

40. Fleming, Maria; Southern Poverty Law Center; A Place at the Table: Struggles for Equality in America; Oxford University Press.

41. Ford, Henry; Crowther, Samuel; My Life and Work; Doubleday, Page and Company; 1922.

42. Ford, Lacy K.; Deliver Us from Evil: The Slavery Question in the Old South; Oxford University Press, Sep 3, 2009.

43. Frank Freidel; The Presidents of the United States of America; DIANE Publishing, Jun 1, 1998.

44. Franklin, Donna L.; Ensuring Inequality: The Structural Transformation of the African American Family; Oxford University Press, May 1, 1997.

45. Franz, Kathleen and Smulyan, Susan: Major Problems in Popular American Culture: Cengage Learning; 2011.

46. Freedman, Russell; Freedom Walkers: The Story of the Montgomery Bus Boycott; Holiday House; 2006.

47. Furia, Philip and Lasser, Michael L.; America's Songs: The Stories Behind The Songs Of Broadway, Hollywood, And Tin Pan Alley; CRC Press; 2006.

48. Gangrade, K.D.; Moral Lessons From Gandhi S Autobiography And Other Essays; Concept Publishing Company; Jan 1, 2004.

49. Garrow, David J.; Montgomery Bus Boycott; (Brooklyn; Carlson Publishing, 1989).

50. Gellately, Robert; Lenin, Stalin, and Hitler: The Age of Social Catastrophe; Random House Digital, Inc., Nov 11, 2009.

51. Giffin, William Wayne; Can Americans And the Color Line in Ohio, 1915-1930; Ohio State University Press, Nov 22, 2005.

52. Gitlin, Martin; The Prohibition Era; ABDO, Sep 1, 2010.
53. Glazer, Joe; Labor's Troubador; University of Illinois Press; 2002.
54. Goldberg, Isaac; Gershwin, George; Tin Pan Alley a Chronicle of the American Popular Music Racket; The John Day Company, Kessinger Publishing; 1930, 2005.
55. Goodman, Rebecca and Barrett J. Brunsman; This Day In Ohio History; Emmis Books, Mar 1, 2005.
56. Gormley, Beatrice; Malcolm X: A Revolutionary Voice; Sterling Publishing Company, Inc.; 2010.
57. Gottheimer; Josh; Ripples Of Hope: Great American Civil Rights Speeches; Basic Civitas Books, Aug 4, 2004.
58. Grey, Thomas R. / Confessions of Nat turner; The Leader of the late insurrection in Southhampton, Va. / Kessinger Publishing.
59. Haggard, Dixie Ray; African Americans in the Nineteenth Century: People and Perspectives; African Americans in the Nineteenth Century: People and Perspectives; ABC-CLIO, Mar 11, 2010.
60. Hall, Timothy L.; Religion in America; Excerpt from Thomas Jefferson's 1802 *Letter to the Danbury Baptist Association*; Infobase Publishing; 2007.
61. Hannings, Bud; Every Day of the Civil War; A Chronological Encyclopedia; p. 525,526; McFarland; 2010.
62. Hare, Kenneth M.; They Walked to Freedom 1955-1956: The Story of the Montgomery Bus Boycott; Sports Publishing LLC, Nov 1, 2005.
63. Harrell, David Edwin and Gaustad, Edwin S.; Unto A Good Land: A History Of The American People; Wm. B. Eerdmans Publishing; Sep 15, 2005.
64. Harris, Michael W.; *The Rise of Gospel Blues: The Music of Thomas Andrew Dorsey in the Urban Church* Oxford University Press, 1992.
65. Hasan, Heather; Wikipedia, 3.5 Million Articles & Counting:Using and Assessing the People's Encyclopedia; The Rosen Publishing Group, Dec 15, 2011.
66. Haugen, Brenda; Winston Churchill: British Soldier, Writer, Statesman; Compass Point Books, May 30, 2006.
67. Hazen, Walter; American Black History; p.42; The Great Migration; Lorenz Educational Press; 2004.
68. Hemmings, Annette B.; Coming of Age in U.S. Hugh Schools: Economic, Kinship, Religious, and Political Crosscurrents; Psychology Press, Feb 23, 2004.
69. Henderson, Bill; Simple Gifts: Great Hymns: One Man's Search for Grace; Simon and Schuster; 2006.
70. Horton, Oliver James; Horton, Lois E.; Slavery and the Making of America; p.214-217; Oxford University Press; 2005.
71. Humez, Jean McMahon; Harriet Tubman; The Life and the Life Stories / p.12, 13, 14, 136, / University of Wisconsin Press / 2003.
72. James, Etta and David Ritz; Rage to Survive: The Etta James Story; Da Capo Press, Jun 5, 2003.
73. Jensen, Robert; The Heart of Whiteness: Confronting Race, Racism, and White Privilege; City Lights Books, Sep 1, 2005.
74. Jerome, Fred and Taylor, Rodger; Einstein on Race And Racism; Rutgers University Press; Jul 25, 2006.
75. Johanson, Donald C. and Kate Wong; Lucy's Legacy: The Quest for Human Origins; Random House Digital, Inc., Jun 1, 2010.
76. Johnson, Kimberly S.; Reforming Jim Crow: Southern Politics and State in the Age Before Brown; Oxford University Press; 2010.
77. Johnson, Leanor Boulin and Staples, Robert; Black Families At The Crossroads: Challenges and Prospects; John Wiley & Sons, 2005.
78. Kahn, Roger; Into My Own: Macmillan; 2006.
79. Kallen, Stuart A.; The Civil War and Reconstruction.

Isaias Gamboa

80. Keyssar, Alexander; The Right to Vote: The Contested History of Democracy in the United States; Basic Books; 2001.
81. King Jr., Martin Luther and Carson, Clayborne; The Autobiography of Martin Luther King Jr.; Hatchette Digital, Inc.; 1998.
82. King Jr., Martin Luther and John Bellm; I Have a Dream; Harper Collins; 1985.
83. King Jr., Martin Luther with Jackson, Jesse; Why We Can't Wait; Penguin; 2000.
84. King, Martin Luther; Martin Luther King (Jr.), James Melvin Washington; A Testament of Hope: The Essential Writings and Speeches of Martin Luther King, Jr.; Harper Collins.
85. Kirszner, Laurie G. and Mandell, Stephen R.; Patterns for College Writing: A Rhetorical Reader and Guide; Macmillan.
86. Kofi Lomotey; Encyclopedia of African American Education, Volume 1; SAGE, Sep 15, 2009.
87. LaFraniere, Sharon; "In the Jungle, the Unjust Jungle, a Small Victory"; March 22, 2006; New York Times.
88. Laird, Tracey E. W.; Louisiana Hayride: Radio and Roots Music Along the Red River; p. 34-36; Oxford University Press; 2005.
89. Lane Sr., Ambrose I.; For Whites Only? How and Why America Became a Racist Nation; AuthorHouse, Nov 5, 2008.
90. Lawson, Kate Clifford; Bound for the Promised Land: Harriet Tubman, Portrait of an American Hero / Random House Digital, Inc, 2004.
91. Lawson, Steven F.; Black Ballots: Voting Rights in the South, 1944-1969; Lexington Books; 1976.
92. LeBor, Adam and Roger Boyes; Seduced by Hitler: The Choices of a Nation and the Ethics of Survival; Sourcebooks, Inc., Feb 1, 2004.
93. Lee, Debbie; Slavery and the Romantic Imagination / University of Pennsylvania Press / p. 197 / 2004
94. Lesher, Stephan; George Wallace, American Populist; DeCapo Press; 1995; p. 247.
95. Liebergen, Patrick M.; Singer's Library of Song; Medium Voice; p.143; Alfred Music Publishing.
96. Lincoln, C. Eric; Mamiya, Lawrence H.; The Black Church in the African American Experience; 1990; Duke University Press.
97. Lindop, Edmund and Margaret J. Goldstein; America In The 1920s; Twenty-First Century Books, Sep 1, 2009.
98. Lomax, Alan and Cohen, Ronald D.; Alan Lomax: Selected Writings, 1934-1937; Psychology Press; 2003.
99. Longenecker White, Marjorie-Editor and Andrew Michael Manis; Birmingham Revolutionaries: The Reverend Fred Shuttlesworth and the Alabama Christian Movement for Human Rights.
100. Mac Adams, Lewis; Rebirth of the Cool: Beat, Bebop, and the American Avant Garde; Simon and Schuster.
101. Magee, Jeffrey; Irving Berlin's American Musical Theater; Oxford University Press; 2012.
102. Malan, Rian; In The Jungle; Rolling Stone Magazine; May 24, 2000.
103. Manis, Andrew M. (1999) *A Fire You Can't Put Out: The Civil Rights Life of Birmingham's Reverend Fred Shuttlesworth.* Tuscaloosa: University of Alabama Press.
104. Marini, Stephen A.; Sacred Song in America: Religion, Music, and Public Culture; University of Illinois Press, Jun 9, 2003.
105. McCann, Joseph T.; Terrorism on American Soil: A Concise History of Plots and Perpetrators from the Famous to the Forgotten; Sentient Publication; 2006.
106. McCarty, Mary / Cincinnati Magazine / 1987; "Maurice Cracken and the Original Activists" "The Freedom Fighters" "Fred Shuttlesworth".
107. McGowan, James A.; Kashatus, William, C. / Harriet Tubman; A Biography / ABC-CLIO / 2007.

108. McWhorter, Diane; **Carry Me Home:** Birmingham, Alabama--The Climactic Battle of the Civil Rights Revolution.

109. McWilliams, Bill; Sunday in Hell: Pearl Harbor Minute by Minute; E-reads/E-rights, Nov 3, 2011.

110. Meyers, Helen; Ethnomusicology: Historical and Regional Studies; W. W. Norton & Company; 1993.

111. Mikell, Gwendolyn; African Feminism: The Politics of Survival in Sub-Saharan Africa; University of Pennsylvania Press, 1997.

112. Mitchell, Gillian; The North American Folk Music Revival: Nation And Identity in the United States And Canada, 1945-1980.

113. Mitchell, Gillian; The North American Folk Music Revival: Nation and Identity in the United States and Canada, 1945-1980; Ashgate Publishing; 2007.

114. Monson, Ingrid; The African Diaspora: A Musical Perspective; Psychology Press, Jun 9, 2003.

115. Morris, Jeff; Morris, Michael A.; Haunted Cincinnati and Southwest Ohio; Arcadia Publishing; 2009.

116. Muhammad, Bilal, R.; The African American Odyssey; Author House; Author House Publishing; 2007.

117. Murphy, Sean D.; United States Practice in International Law: 1999-2001; Cambridge University Press, 2002.

118. Nicholis, David; American Experimental Music 1890-1940; Cambridge University Press; 1991.

119. Ortiz, Paul; Emancipation Betrayed: The Hidden History of Black Organizing and White Violence in Florida from Reconstruction to the Bloody Election of 1920; University of California Press; 2006.

120. Pauley, Garth E.; The Modern Presidency & Civil Rights: Rhetoric on Race from Roosevelt to Nixon; Texas A&M University Press; 2001.

121. Perone, James E.; Music of the Counterculture Era; Greenwood Publishing Group; 2004.

122. Price, Emmett G. III with Kernodle, Tammy L. and Maxile, Jr. Horace J.; Encyclopedia of African American Music Volume 3; ABC-CLIO; 2010.

123. Price, Emmett G., Editor and III, Tammy L. Kernodle, Horace J. Maxile, Jr.; Encyclopedia of African American Music, Volume 3; C-CLIO, Dec 17, 2010.

124. Raymond, Henry Jarvis and Francis Bicknell Carpenter, Abraham Lincoln; Lincoln, his life and time; Thompson & Thomas, 1891.

125. Riches, William Terence Martin: The Civil Rights Movement: Struggle and Resistance; Palgrave Macmillan; 2004.

126. Rodriguez, Junius P.; Slavery in the United States; A Social, Political and Historical Encyclopedia Volume 2.

127. Sandler, Martin W; Driving Around the USA: Automobiles in American Life; Oxford University Press, 2003.

128. Sears, Alan and Craig Osten; The ACLU Vs America: Exposing the Agenda to Redefine Moral Values; B&H Publishing Group, Sep 1, 2005.

129. Sears, Benjamin; The Irving Berlin Reader; Oxford University Press; 2012.

130. Seeger, Charles; "Who Owns Folklore? –A Rejoinder" /"*Western Folklore"* Vol. 21, No. 2 (Apr., 1962).

131. Seeger, Pete / "Where Have All The Flowers Gone"1993; W.W. Norton and Co.

132. Seeger, Pete and Reiser, Bob; Everybody Says Freedom; W.W. Norton and Company.

133. Smith, Carl and Karnie C. Smith, Sr.; Frederick Douglass Republicans: The Movement to Re-Ignite America's Passion for Liberty; AuthorHouse, Apr 25, 2011.

134. Smith, Mark Michael; Stono: Documenting And Interpreting a Southern Slave Revolt; University of Carolina Press; 2005.

135. Smith, Stephen W.; The Transformation of a Man's Heart: Reflections on the Masculine Journey; InterVarsity Press; 2006.

136. Sondhaus, Lawrence; World War One: The Global Revolution; Cambridge University Press, Mar 31, 2011.

137. Sotiropoulos, Karen, "Staging Race: Black Cultural Politics before the Harlem Renaissance, 1893-1915" / (2000)/ City University of New York.

138. Stotts, Stuart and Cummings, Terrance with Seeger, Pete; We Shall Overcome; a Song that Changed the World; Houghton Mifflin Harcourt; 2010.

139. Strong, Bryan and Christine DeVault, Theodore F. Cohen; The Marriage and Family Experience: Intimate Relationships in a Changing Society; Cengage Learning, Feb 19, 2010.

140. Sutton, Bettye. "1930-1939."; *American Cultural History*; Lone Star College-Kingwood Library; 1999. Web. 7 Feb. 2011.

141. Szwed, John; Alan Lomax: The Man Who Recorded the World; Penguin; 2010.

142. Taylor; Henry Louis; Race and the City: Work, Community, and Protest in Cincinnati, 1820-1970; University of Illinois Press, Oct 1, 1993.

143. Terrill, Robert E.; The Cambridge Companion to Malcolm X; Cambridge University Press; 2010.

144. Terrill, Robert; Malcolm X: Inventing Radical Judgment; MSU Press; 2004.

145. Thompson, Jerry D.; Civil War to the Bloody End; The Life and Times of General Samuel P. Heintzelman; Texas A&M University Press; 2006.

146. Vile, John R.; A Companion to the United States Constitution and its Amendments; ABL-CIO; 2010.

147. Von Schmidt, Eric; Rooney, Jim /"Baby, let me follow you down: the illustrated story of the Cambridge Folk Years" 1994 / University of Massachusetts Press.

148. Warshauer, Matthew; Civil War: Slavery, Sacrifice, and Survival; Wesleyan University Press; Apr 4, 2011.

149. Washington Post; The Inauguration of Barack Obama; Triumph books; 2009.

150. Weir, Robert E.; Class in America, Q-Z; Greenwood Publishing Group.

151. Weissman, Dick; Which Side Are You On?: An Inside History of the Folk Music Revival in America; p. 65; Continuum International Publishing Group; 2006.

152. Whitfield, Stephen; Death in the Delta: The Story of Emmett Till; JHU Press; 1991.

153. Wilkerson, Isabel; The Warmth of Other Suns: the Epic Story of America's Great Migration; Random House Digital, Inc.; 2010.

154. Wilmeth, Don B. with Bigsby, C. W. E.; The Cambridge History of American Theatre, Volume 2; Cambridge University Press; 1999.

155. Wimbush, Vincent L. and Rodman, Rosamond C.: African Americans and the Bible: Sacred Texts and Social Textures; Continuum International Publishing Group; 2001.

156. Winkler, Alan M.; "To Everything There is a Season": Pete Seeger and the Power of Song; Oxford University Press; 2009.

157. Wolffe, Richard; Revival: The Struggle for Survival Inside the Obama White House; Random House Digital, Inc. 2011.

158. Yancey, George A.; Who Is White?: Latinos, Asians, and the New Black/Nonblack Divide; Lynne Rienner Publishers, 2003.

159. Zinn, Howard; A People's History of the United States; Harper Collins; 2010.

Zweigenhaft, Richard L. and Domhoff, G.William; The New CEOs: Women, African American, Latino, and Asian American Leaders of Fortune 500 Companies; Rowman & Littlefield, Jun 23, 2011.

# Index

1. Abernathy, Ralph; 147, 159, 209.
2. Baez, Joan; 178, 200, 204, 241, 245, 255, 276, 285.
3. Booth, L. Venchael; 149.
4. Bush, George W; 36.
5. Capone, Al; 89, 90, 91.
6. Carawan, Guy; 27, 146, 147, 194, 195, 196, 197, 200.
7. Carpenter; Liz; 282, 283.
8. Chambliss, Robert; 205, 206.
9. Christ, Jesus; 5, 13, 34, 54, 64, 168, 234, 240, 249, 251, 252, 271, 272, 279, 280, 281.
10. Churchill, Winston; 31, 253.
11. Cincinnati; 11, 70, 71, 75, 76, 77, 79, 80, 83, 87, 89, 90, 91, 92, 97, 116, 119, 126, 18, 148, 149, 150, 153, 155, 156, 157, 203, 215, 219, 220, 221, 222, 224, 226, 228, 229, 239, 243, 296, 297, 300.
12. Connor, Bull; 135, 156.
13. Coon Songs; 113, 136, 256, 259, 264.
14. Copyright; 2, 4, 24, 25, 27, 28, 29, 113, 120, 122, 124, 126, 128, 146, 176, 177, 182, 183, 184, 185, 187, 194, 195, 196, 197, 200, 245, 254, 265, 268, 271, 272, 273, 275, 281, 285, 286.
15. Costa Rica; 7, 14, 289.
16. Crow, Jim; 33, 35, 42, 97, 140, 141, 142, 272, 292, 293, 295.
17. Declaration of Independence; 40, 164, 167, 170, 254.
18. Dorsey, Thomas A; 15, 21, 97, 99, 10, 101, 14, 115, 123, 128, 130, 230.
19. Douglass, Fredrick; 65, 171, 293, 297.
20. Dubois, W.E.B; 47, 48, 293.
21. Dylan, Bob; 178, 201, 285.
22. Elijah Muhammad; 209, 211.
23. First Amendment; 164, 168, 169, 170.
24. Garvey, Marcus; 79.
25. Goins, Robert A.; 5, 11, 24, 212, 243, 246, 252.
26. Goodnight Irene; 18, 183.
27. Gospel Music; 21, 100, 102, 113, 114, 128, 145, 239.
28. Greater New Light Baptist Church; 11, 19, 222, 225, 228, 229, 239, 243, 247, 29.
29. Green, Vetter; 131.
30. Guthrie, Arlo; 195.
31. Hamilton, Frank; 27, 194, 195, 196, 267, 268.
32. Harkin, Tom; 33, 35.
33. Highlander Folk School; 146, 147, 194, 267.
34. Hiroshima; 98, 131.
35. Hitler, Adolph; 13, 96, 97.
36. Horton, Myles; 27, 146, 147, 194, 195, 283.
37. Horton, Zilphia; 27, 194, 195, 196, 268, 283.

38. If My Jesus Wills; 2, 52, 97, 117, 124, 197, 198, 202, 219, 266, 268, 273, 279, 280, 281, 283, 285, 286, 27, 288.
39. Jackson, Mahalia; 21, 98, 114, 120, 230, 231.
40. Jackson, Michael; 290.
41. Jarrett, James "Pig Meat"; 78, 81, 83, 88, 92, 102.
42. Jefferson, Thomas; 163, 164, 167, 170, 171, 172, 173, 187, 254, 283, 292, 293, 294.
43. Johnson, Lyndon B; 208, 218, 233, 281, 282, 283.
44. Kennedy, Jacqueline; 207, 208, 282.
45. Kennedy, Robert F; 158.
46. Kenney, John F; 151, 157, 160, 199, 207, 281.
47. King Jr., Martin Luther; 1, 2, 3, 34, 51, 126, 127, 133, 139, 142, 146, 152, 153, 156, 159, 162, 170, 172, 173, 204, 2074, 209, 214, 221, 226, 230, 231, 233, 234, 271, 279, 280, 285, 289, 292, 295.
48. Ku Klux Klan (KKK); 63, 142, 146, 148, 150, 162, 205, 211.
49. Lead Belly; 178, 182, 183, 184.
50. Leventhal, Harold; 18, 194, 195, 200, 254, 255, 256, 265.
51. Lincoln, Abraham; 60, 63, 296.
52. Lomax, Alan; 113, 176, 177, 178, 180, 181, 182, 182, 184, 187, 270, 273, 274, 275, 295, 297, 299.
53. Lomax, John A; 178, 182.
54. Longevity Entertainment; 16.
55. Mbube; 183, 184, 185, 186.
56. Montgomery Bus Boycott: 126, 139, 141, 142.
57. Muhammad, Elijah; 209, 211.
58. N.A.A.C.P.; 139, 142.
59. Nagasaki; 98.
60. National Convention of Gospel Choirs and Choruses; (N.C.G.C.C.): 97, 98, 115, 121, 124, 131, 150, 157.
61. Nation of Islam; 209, 211, 293,
62. Negro Spiritual; 4, 54, 72, 189, 190, 193, 195, 266, 287, 292.
63. New Prospect Baptist Church; 80, 117, 120, 128.
64. Obama, Barack; xiii, 6, 7, 12, 13, 16, 33, 35, 38, 187, 276, 297.
65. Oswald, Lee Harvey.
66. Parks, Rosa; 139, 147.
67. Perry, Richard; xi, 290.
68. Plagiarism; 28, 163, 195, 268.
69. Poll Taxes; 160, 161, 273.
70. Puttin on the Ritz; 256, 257, 264.
71. Ray, James Earl; 230.
72. Reagan, Ronald; 36.
73. Remus, George; 89, 90, 91, 292.
74. Revelation Missionary Baptist Church; 83, 92, 148, 149, 150, 153, 219, 220, 221, 222.
75. Seeger, Charles; 175, 176, 268, 269, 27.
76. Seeger, Pete; 110 Entries

77. Shabazz, Betty; 216, 217.
78. Shropshire Sr., Robert Bob; 82, 87, 89, 91, 202, 224, 226, 227, 248.
79. Shuttlesworth, Fred; 111, 115, 130, 131, 132, 133, 135, 136, 141, 142, 144, 147, 18, 149, 150, 153, 155, 156, 159, 194, 201, 202, 212, 221, 222, 228, 295, 296.
80. Sirhan Sirhan; 240.
81. Slavery; xiii, 12, 13, 31, 32, 33, 34, 35, 36, 37, 40, 41, 42, 43, 47, 48, 49, 50, 51, 54, 56, 59, 60, 61, 63, 65, 102, 134, 161, 162, 163, 167, 169, 187, 190, 193, 254, 256, 260, 272, 26, 293, 294, 295, 296, 297.
82. Smith, Bessie; 92, 114.
83. Springsteen, Bruce; 276, 285.
84. Stono Rebellion; 9, 192.
85. Sylvers III, Leon; 289.
86. Take My Hand Precious Lord; 21, 22, 103, 104, 105, 107, 112, 230, 231, 234, 252.
87. The Lion Sleeps Tonight; 120, 183, 184.
88. The Temptations; 290.
89. Till, Emmett; 138, 139.
90. Tubman, Harriet; 7, 58, 295, 296.
91. Turner, Nat; 7, 55, 56, 57, 58, 294.
92. We Shall Overcome; 125 entries throughout book.
93. Wikipedia; 26, 27.
94. Wimoweh; 120, 183, 184, 185, 186.
95. Malcolm X; 209, 210, 211, 25, 216, 217, 293, 294, 297.
96. Young, Andrew; 147, 158.
97. Zilphia Horton; 27, 194, 195, 196, 268, 283.

# NOTES

Isaias Gamboa

We Shall Overcome: Sacred Song on the Devil's Tongue

www.ingramcontent.com/pod-product-compliance
Lightning Source LLC
Chambersburg PA
CBHW080727230426
43665CB00020B/2647